Praise for *Cri*

"This book is chock-full of ideas that will help any nurse in any setting. Clancy provides hints, tips, and tidbits of communication advice, using real-life clinical scenarios and experiences from her nursing practice. The use of acronyms throughout the book helps readers remember information. The most basic is CAR (C=consider, A=act, and R=ROI), a tidy process that can benefit nurses in a variety of settings. The author returns again and again to the CAR model as a means to process new information. Complete chapters on body language, emotional intelligence, and organizational culture are another plus, as are the 'scripts' that walk the reader through situations that can be a communication nightmare: asking someone to stop gossiping, checking in on perceptions, and giving difficult news."

–Cheryl Dellasega, PhD, CRNP
Professor, Penn State College of Medicine
Author, *When Nurses Hurt Nurses* and the award-winning *Toxic Nursing*

"Critical Conversations *is a treasure trove of pragmatic, action-oriented communication tools for all levels of healthcare providers, from novice to expert. Leaders, mentors, coaches, and educators can easily use the numerous mnemonic acronyms, such as CAR, to inspire and engage every member of a healthcare team.*"

–Victoria L. Rich, PhD, RN, FAAN
Associate Professor, Nurse Administration, University of Pennsylvania
ANCC Magnet Consultant

"Critical Conversations *offers valuable information and tips on how to engage in dialogue. The book is helpful and easy to read; it should be included in your reading list for self-improvement and lifelong learning. The author's presentation makes the material simple to comprehend. I recommend that you read this book and share it with others.*"

–Linda Burnes Bolton, DrPH, RN, FAAN
Vice President and Chief Nursing Officer
Cedars-Sinai Medical Center

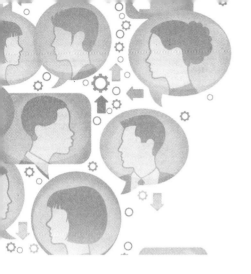

CRITICAL
CONVERSATIONS

Scripts & Techniques for Effective
Interprofessional & Patient Communication

Cheri Clancy, MSN, MS, RN, NE-BC

Sigma Theta Tau International
Honor Society of Nursing®

The Honor Society of Nursing, Sigma Theta Tau International (STTI) is a nonprofit organization whose mission is to support the learning, knowledge, and professional development of nurses committed to making a difference in health worldwide. Founded in 1922, members include practicing nurses, instructors, researchers, policymakers, entrepreneurs, and others. STTI's 494 chapters are located at 676 institutions of higher education throughout Australia, Botswana, Brazil, Canada, Colombia, Ghana, Hong Kong, Japan, Kenya, Malawi, Mexico, the Netherlands, Pakistan, Portugal, Singapore, South Africa, South Korea, Swaziland, Sweden, Taiwan, Tanzania, United Kingdom, United States, and Wales. More information about STTI can be found online at www.nursingsociety.org.

Sigma Theta Tau International
550 West North Street
Indianapolis, IN, USA 46202

To order additional books, buy in bulk, or order for corporate use, contact Nursing Knowledge International at 888.NKI.4YOU (888.654.4968/US and Canada) or +1.317.634.8171 (outside US and Canada).

To request a review copy for course adoption, email solutions@nursingknowledge.org or call 888.NKI.4YOU (888.654.4968/US and Canada) or +1.317.634.8171 (outside US and Canada).

To request author information, or for speaker or other media requests, contact Marketing, the Honor Society of Nursing, Sigma Theta Tau International at 888.634.7575 (US and Canada) or +1.317.634.8171 (outside US and Canada).

ISBN: 9781938835469
EPUB ISBN: 9781938835476
PDF ISBN: 9781938835483
MOBI ISBN: 9781938835490

Library of Congress Cataloging-in-Publication Data

Clancy, Cheri, 1972- author.
  Critical conversations : scripts & techniques for effective
interprofessional & patient communication / Cheri Clancy.
     p. ; cm.
  Includes bibliographical references.
  ISBN 978-1-938835-46-9 (alk. paper) -- ISBN 978-1-938835-47-6 (EPUB) --
ISBN 978-1-938835-48-3 (PDF) -- ISBN 978-1-938835-49-0 (MOBI)
  I. Title.
  [DNLM: 1. Communication. 2. Nurse-Patient Relations. 3.
Interprofessional Relations. WY 88]
  RT82
  610.7306'9--dc23
                    2014012899

First Printing, 2014

Publisher: Renee Wilmeth
Acquisitions Editor: Emily Hatch
Editorial Coordinator: Paula Jeffers
Cover Designer: Rebecca Batchelor
Interior Design/Page Layout: Rebecca Batchelor
Illustrator: Amy Parker Hassos

Principal Book Editor: Carla Hall
Development and Project Editor: Jennifer Lynn
Copy Editor: Charlotte Kughen
Proofreader: Barbara Bennett
Indexer: Joy Dean Lee

Dedication

This book is dedicated to:

My three beautiful children, Paige (13), Shane (10), and Colin (9). "I love you right up to the moon—and back." –Sam McBratney

My entire family, especially my Mom and Dad, for all your unconditional love, support, and laughter.

My friends for supporting me on this endeavor.

My colleagues and fellow nurses for sharing in our life-long journey of caring for others.

Acknowledgments

A special thank-you to Mary Ann Scott and Emily Hatch of Sigma Theta Tau International and Jennifer Lynn for making it happen!

Thank-you to Dr. Shelley Johnson for your contributions to Chapter 8 and your genuine friendship and mentorship over the years.

Thank-you to Dr. Marie O'Toole and my colleagues at Rutgers University, Stratford, NJ.

Thank-you to Nancy Edwards and colleagues with Mead Johnson Nutritionals.

Thank-you to the American Organization of Nurse Executives (AONE), Advance Nursing, and ASHRM for publishing my articles.

Thank-you to the leaders of Kennedy Health System for believing in my passion to improve the patient experience and welcoming me into the Kennedy Health System family.

About the Author

Cheri Clancy, MSN, MS, RN, NE-BC

Cheri Clancy is a seasoned leadership speaker and trainer, nurse educator, and board-certified ANCC nurse executive with more than 15 years of healthcare leadership experience. She holds a Bachelor of Science in Nursing (BSN), a Master of Science (MS) in Health Administration and Wellness Promotion, and a Master of Science in Nursing (MSN) in Organizational Leadership.

Clancy has been a keynote leadership speaker at numerous events and health-care seminars across the United States. She is a member of many professional organizations, including the National Honor Society of Nursing, Sigma Theta Tau International; American Nurses Association (ANA); American Organization of Nurse Executives (AONE); American Association of Ambulatory Nurses (AAAN); The Beryl Institute; National Nursing Staff Development Organization (NNSDO); and the American College of Healthcare Executives (ACHE). Clancy has received various honors and awards, including recognition from the March of Dimes in Nursing Leadership Excellence. She has also published numerous articles on various nursing leadership topics.

Clancy began her career as a clinical neonatal and pediatric nurse. Her passion for listening to the voice of the patient and family was the genesis for her progressive healthcare leadership experience.

Currently, Clancy is the assistant vice president of The Patient Experience at Kennedy Health System, a faculty member at Rutgers University's School of Nursing, and a national speaker on nursing leadership and healthcare service excellence. Some of her prevalent presentation topics include transformational nursing leadership, conflict resolution, managing and leading change, above-the-line leadership, rounding to improve the patient experience, and coaching for success.

About the Contributing Author—Chapter 8

Shelley A. Johnson, RN, EdD

Shelley A. Johnson received her baccalaureate degree from The University of Pennsylvania, School of Nursing in 1997. She received a scholarship from the National Black Nurses Association to attend The Pennsylvania State University in 1999, where she received a Master's of Science in Community Health Nursing. She completed her doctoral education at the University of Phoenix with a focus on educational leadership.

Dr. Johnson has taught in undergraduate and graduate programs for more than 15 years. She has taught for The Pennsylvania State University, Raritan Valley Community College, Rutgers University, LaSalle University, and University of Medicine and Dentistry of New Jersey.

She is currently the founding director and chair of Nursing and Health Science in the College of Sciences and Technology at The Lincoln University in Pennsylvania. Her specialties are in education, leadership, mental health, and community health. She is certified as a staff developer, a nurse executive, a nurse educator, and as a comprehensive systematic reviewer.

She has conducted presentations and workshops, published articles, and participated in research related to a variety of topics. These topics include perceptions of student bullying, health disparities, cultural diversity, advocacy, leadership, and nursing education. Research interests include nursing and educational practices, the academic environment, and leadership development.

Table of Contents

Preface

"I've learned that people will forget what you said, people will forget what you did, but people will never forget how you made them feel."

–Maya Angelou

Have you ever found yourself in the midst of a conversation and you either completely forgot what you are talking about or feel the person you are speaking to has no idea what you are talking about? How comfortable are you in those conversations that require you to coach someone (e.g., someone's poor work performance, their inappropriate dress attire, or their poor workplace behaviors)? What is your comfort level with public speaking? Does your nervousness ever highjack your train of thought—leaving you and your audience paralyzed with awkwardness?

Unfortunately, I have found myself in many of these situations, and I believe Ms. Angelou's quote perfectly sums up the way I remember how I felt during conversations that run the continuum of engaging to disengaging. I may not remember exactly what was said, but I do always remember how I felt.

My first profound experience in miscommunication was when I was 13 years of age. I was in the 8th grade and had entered my small town's annual pageant. At the time I was a shy, petite introvert, and I thought the pageant would be a great way to build confidence, self-esteem, and poise.

On the day of the pageant, I felt pretty good about my onstage turns, my outfits, and even my answer to a very easy question (I think the question was, "What do you like most about your town?"), but that all came to a brutal halt when it was time for my speech. Each contestant was charged with telling the judges and audience a little bit about herself, including her career aspirations, activities, and so on. I rehearsed and rehearsed my speech for weeks and countless hours.

As a typical 13-year-old, I felt my own speech wasn't good enough because I really didn't know what my career *aspirations* were. I wondered, what did the word *aspiration* really mean? What do the judges really want to know about me? Did they really want to know I just wanted to be a mom one day—just like my mom? I didn't think that sounded as compelling as my competitors' aspirations. Many of them wanted to be doctors, lawyers, broadcast journalists, and so on, so I asked my mom to help me craft a better, more worthwhile speech. I thought my mom was so smart, and I knew that with her help, I would have a winning speech whether they were actually my "aspirations" or not.

Prior to my big moment, I remember taking a big breath and thinking, "I'm ready!" I walked up to the microphone and confidently stated, "My name is Cheri, and I'm 13 years old." My confidence steadily fell as I saw the bright lights and the silhouettes of the audience members staring at me. I grabbed at my gown, looked up in the air, and continued, "I… I… I…" That's all I could remember!

As I reflect today on what I thought was the end of my social life, I remember looking out into the audience and "feeling" *their* uncomfortableness with my presentation. It was almost like (okay, it *was* like) the audience was embarrassed for me! I remember my loving mom calling out to me from the audience saying, "Cheri, say, 'Thank you'…. Honey, just say thank you."

Seconds felt like hours to me as the heat of the lights made me break out into a disgusting sweat, and I felt the tears roll down my face, but I really couldn't understand why. All I could think was, "This is just a bad dream. Why am I crying? This isn't real." My feet were paralyzed; I couldn't move.

I finally saw the audience members shifting in their seats, and I actually recognized someone sitting there. This was what "woke me up" from my daze. I actually felt their awkwardness. I finally spoke into the microphone, as my mom persistently encouraged me to do, and I swiftly said, "Thank you," as I ran off the stage with my head dropped down as low as I could hang it.

After I reached backstage, I fell to the ground in utter shame and disappointment. "How could this happen?" I asked myself. "How? I practiced! I guess I
am really dumb." My older sister, Tracey, was a contestant, too, and I remember
asking her, "Tracey, was I as bad as I think I was?" She said nothing, but helped
me stand back up on my feet and wiped the tears from my face with her white
gloves. Her silence was deafening. All I could think about was, "I'm starting
high school next year, and now I've made the biggest fool of myself! I'm such a
loser. I'm so dumb."

Over the course of the next 2 years, I continually asked myself, "How could I
have improved? How could I have remembered my speech? How can I influence
others to want to hear what I have to say?" Most importantly, I asked myself,
"How do I even remember what I want to say?" There had to be an easier way to
communicate when faced with pressure.

As this was one of the most overwhelming (not to mention *embarrassing*) experiences I ever endured, it was also one of the most important life lessons I experienced. I learned that the words we choose are meaningless unless we believe
in what we are saying and we organize the thoughts so that we don't forget key
talking points. We can all choose the most articulate words and form the most
articulately beautiful sentences, but if we don't have meaning or organization
in what we are saying, we are just saying words without purpose. This becomes
apparent because our body language reveals more than we think.

Two years later, I reentered the pageant. This time my mom, who was still my
number-one fan, encouraged me to craft my own speech by using my own
words so I would believe in what I said. I remembered my speech because I
took her advice, but I also applied the help of my teacher, Mr. Martin. As an
assignment in life skills, we had to apply an acronym for an upcoming test. The
acronyms helped me remember the test as well as what came next in my speech
(in case my emotions highjacked my thought process again). For example, I

used the acronym CHAIN in my speech that year. The C represented *Cheri*. So, I could remember to introduce my name, age, and school attended. The H represented *hobbies* I liked. The A reminded me to speak about the *As* I received in my classes. The I stood for what *I wanted to be when I grew up* (and I was honest this time), and the N stood for *near the end*, so I knew to wrap up my speech by saying "thank you."

In addition to developing my acronym, I also studied other contestants' poise. I saw how powerful their confidence was as they paused in between sentences. The power of pausing, making eye contact, and keeping their bodies open appeared to keep them looking remarkably confident. This was captivating to me. I thought, "What if I added these technique to my speech—to my whole stage presence? Would that help me redeem myself in front of my town, and now my high school classmates?" At age 15, social acceptance was my goal, not a title or crown.

Although winning was a great vehicle to achieving social acceptance, it wasn't the clear-cut answer as to why I had reentered the pageant. I had to prove to myself I wasn't "dumb" and that I could do better than I had the first time.

Effective communication skills doesn't come easy for all of us, and that's OK if you just work at finding the tools and resources that can help you.

During my professional career, I have still found it challenging to find the right words at the right times. Over the years, I have collected some tricks and tidbits to help me in my endless pursuit of being a polished wordsmith. Although I don't use acronyms to remember all the different types of conversations I participate in, I do reflect a lot on those I describe in this book. I hope you find some of my tips and tidbits helpful and fun. I truly believe that being cognizant of body language and emotional competence has helped me express the words I sometimes can't find when my emotions are running high.

I often think how much other people would benefit in their conversations if they knew what I have learned about acronyms, body language, emotional intelligence, and competence, as well as healthcare leadership concepts, so I consider this book my "pay it forward" to the nursing profession. After all, it is simply the right thing to do.

Whether I am attending a large conference, having a one-on-one conversation, or I'm in a small meeting at work, I see the opportunities where the techniques in this book could be of assistance to others. I believe in the big power that stems from small acts of kindness. I am honored that you are taking the time to read my thoughts, perceptions, and tips. Please, enjoy my first book; I enjoyed writing it for you.

Introduction

I am writing this book to convey two important points. The first is to bring awareness to our social differences and how this effects the outcome of our communications. The second reason is to bring some simplicity in the application of how to drive critical conversations. Life is too complicated; I prefer to learn in simple ways, such as using acronyms, rather than trying to remember everything without any aids or helpful hints.

I consider myself an "all or nothing" type of person, which means that if I find something incredibly interesting but can't apply it in some useful way, I could drop it in seconds (OK, sometimes nanoseconds). For example, I do not like when literature neither explains how I can apply the learned material nor infuses companion topics that would give a more holistic application and comprehension. For example, there are many exceptional books published on body language, emotional intelligence, and scripting techniques, but I couldn't find any that placed me in the driver's seat to actually apply the information. I wanted a book that provided all the information in one source and explained how all these topics were synergistic. Since I couldn't find a book that incorporated all these concepts, I decided to write one. And here it is.

So what's in it for you? You will learn hints, tips, and tidbits in how to apply body language, emotional intelligence, and scripting techniques to improve your communication skills with your boss, your colleagues, and your patients and their families.

As you read this book, remember, the goal is progress and practice, not perfection. Analyzing your body language and the body language of others, applying emotional competence, and using acronyms takes time, and you will need to practice these techniques often to find success. I hope to make your learning effective by developing simple processes for you to understand.

How This Book Is Organized

Driving effective conversations is like driving a car. First, we start conversations for numerous reasons such as for coaching, information seeking, or socialization, to name a few. Second, we attempt to drive the conversations in the right direction and for the right purpose. Finally, whether the conversation was successful or not, we learn from the journey of it.

Now, think about driving a car. First, we start our cars to go places. Second, we attempt to pick the right route for the right purpose. Finally, whether we were successful in arriving at the destination or not, our journey defines our success. Although there is chasm in this comparison, I wanted to simulate how you are in control of driving all aspects of conversations, even when someone tries to run you off the road.

I associated each chapter's core structure into three main steps, comparable to driving a car:

- **The Driver's Seat:** Every chapter starts by describing the overarching main idea for the chapter.

- **Your Road Map:** Midway through each chapter, I describe how you can apply the information to real-time situations.

- **The Drive Home:** Each chapter summarizes the highlighted key points.

Not only do I assimilate driving a car and driving conversations for the book's framework, but I also use CAR as an acronym, which stands for

Consideration

Action or a call to action

Return on investment (ROI)

You learn more about this concept starting in Chapter 1.

The first half of this book provides a comprehensive introduction of body language, emotional intelligence, and scripting techniques, and the second half weaves these concepts into organizational applications.

Special Features

In each chapter of this book, you'll also find these special features:

- Reflection boxes: These boxes challenge you to take a moment and consider how you can apply what you've learned.

- Tip boxes: These boxes provide quick tips that you can apply to improve the effectiveness of your conversations.

- Real World boxes: These boxes provide examples of effective communication techniques in the real world.

- Sidebars: These boxes give you important information that goes above and beyond the text in the chapter.

Goals for This Book

This book is intended to:

- Present acronyms for body language, emotional intelligence, and scripting techniques in an understandable and applicable format.

- Provide easy acronyms that will help you overcome the "deer in the headlights" reaction to difficult conversations.

- Give direction and guidance when faced with awkward or suboptimal conversations.

- Help you understand how varying personalities have varying perceptions and traits.

- Deliver ideas on how you can make a difference in your organization and in your patient's experience.

- Postulate the value of transformational leadership and healthcare.

This book is not intended to:

- Bore you

- Leave you hanging

- Speak over or under your IQ

Thank you for reading my book. I hope you find it helpful and intriguing. I wish you continued success.

> *"Common sense is not so common."*
> –Voltaire

On Finding Common Sense

Earlier in my career, I learned a valuable lesson on common sense. I was having a conversation with a group of highly esteemed healthcare leaders about strategies for achieving nursing excellence. I listened intently as these leaders shared profound stories on the trials and tribulations they faced during their journey. These leaders spoke to how the journey brought more collegiality to their organization and how it offered so many learning opportunities that they never even knew existed. Whereas some leaders' organizations achieved Magnet designation, others didn't. Those who didn't achieve this honor didn't fall short on organizational excellence; they just simply decided they weren't going to apply for the actual designation because they felt they already embodied excellence, as evidenced by outstanding (and consistent) employee and patient satisfaction scores.

What struck me during this conversation were the commonalities among all these leaders. Although their job titles, workplaces, strategies, and outcomes were different, they still emulated a similar finesse in their articulation, poise, and confidence. They embraced and embodied a transformational leadership style. Transformational leadership, introduced by James MacGregor Burns (1978), explains that leaders and followers empower each other to advance to a higher level of engagement and motivation. Transformational leaders have the unique ability to inspire followers to change expectations, perceptions, and motivations to collaboratively work toward shared goals. As a young, novice leader, I thought it was simply common sense that leaders who achieved awards would embody transformational leadership characteristics. What I learned was that the leaders who didn't have awards or designations, such as Magnet designation, were, to me, just as transformational as those who achieved such tangible awards. This was my "a-ha" moment. I realized that transformational leaders exist regardless of awards or wall plaques.

I have since learned that it's more about the actual experiences a leader endeavors and how they communicate and embrace their team that defines success. Within the journey to excellence, leadership styles are defined, and transformational leaders learn from both their wins and opportunities, as well as their team's wins and opportunities. They build teams by motivating others to share a colloborative, communicable, attainable, and sustainable vision. Transformational leaders don't necessarily need a "stamp of approval" to validate their leadership abilities. We need to put aside the checklists used for achieving awards and help leaders to place more emphasis on building teams through authentic communication and trust.

You might have heard the adage, "Ready, aim, fire." In healthcare, I consider the *ready* phase as the strategic planning of visions, goals, and objectives. In ready mode, you actually look at what the end result would optimally look like. The *aim* is the communication piece in which buy-in from teams is formed and in-novation and colloboration are united. The aim is paramount to the success of the vision, or readiness. The *fire* piece can be thought of as the actual implemen-tation of the strategic plan set forth.

Now, ready, aim, fire—This sounds like common sense in order to execute something, right? Well, not exactly. If it was so-called *common sense*, then all healthcare organizations would be flawless. The problem I often see is that leaders take a "ready-fire" approach in a hasty attempt to achieve an award of excellence or even to prepare for a regulatory compliance visit, such as from The Joint Commission.

Let's take another look at how common sense isn't so common. Have you ever worked in an organization where chaos is rampant because of poor planning? Let's use the example of a Joint Commission visit. Couple the "hurry up and get the tracers ready, workstations clean, and remove the hallway clutter" with try-ing to meet predetermined organizational benchmarks and balanced scorecards, and it's no wonder that chaos erupts. To compensate for poor planning, orga-nizations quickly place bandages over oozing wounds all over the organization and cross their fingers (and toes) they passed the JC survey. But isn't it common sense to just be prepared in the first place? Why do we not sustain regulatory readiness, knowing that we have Joint Commission visits ongoing? Organiza-tions need to concentrate on consistency, not velocity.

Bottom line: Chaos and pressures can be minimized if leaders don't jump, ignore, or forget about the key ingredient: "aim." Aim is the core to achiev-ing virtually any goal. Healthcare organizations that seek to achieve sustained excellence, not just excellence, know that taking time to aim and even re-aim is the secret to success. Now, I admit I have seen and worked in organizations that have achieved goals without mastering the aim component, but have they sustainted excellence? The answer is no. It's either vanished, fragmented, or barely hanging on (along with their employee retention rate).

It's not always about rewards, recognitions, and awards; more importantly, it's about what was learned, defined, or strengthened in the journey or process. The destination of the journey is secondary to the actual journey itself.

> Transformational leaders know that aiming one time isn't enough to reach a goal. So no matter how foolproof you think your strategy is, before you fire off any strategies, take the time to aim, re-aim, and aim some more.

The Driver's Seat: Finding Common Sense

Conceptually, common sense is centered on averages, or what a typical response would be in an aggregate setting. A lack of common sense indicates that someone or something did not act in the average, standard, normative, or typical manner. Common sense is quite subjective because there are different perceptions to what is considered "common" to various people.

For example, prior to giving a final leadership examination, I instructed my students to take an extra 10 minutes to review a short study guide that I put together for them. I explained this was quiet, independent study time. I was shocked when I witnessed one of my students putting earbuds on while reading over this important content. This exam was 40% of the final grade! Feeling annoyed, I approached this student and asked why she wasn't taking me seriously. I thought, isn't it common sense to take studying seriously—especially a final exam? The student explained to me that '80s music helps her concentrate. She received a 100% on the test and a 98% in the course. Lesson learned. My perception is not her reality.

Let's look at another example. Have you ever been involved in a conversation where everyone appears to agree with the topic at hand, yet you feel you are missing something or even blatantly disagree? I'm not talking about a small conversation during a lunch break; I'm talking about sitting in a large conference room, where everyone is nodding in acceptance to the speaker and you're in complete disagreement, looking around the room with a "Huh?" glare.

Even the "majority rule" method cannot always justify what common sense is or means. I've learned that even though the majority of what others may find common or similar doesn't always mean it's correct. We must remember that although averages can be informative, they do not provide a complete picture. To determine what is considered common sense, we must consider both the averages and variations of situations, as well as the errors that can be perceived differently.

I will bring this point down to a more granular level. Take for example a one-day postop cardiac patient. Now, we know his sternum has just been cut open and for him to move his upper body at all (with the swan catheter, chest tube, IV lines, pain, etc.) is difficult and practically impossible without help. Now, let's imagine dietary comes into the patient's room, properly identifies the patient, leaves the clear liquid diet on the table tray adjacent to the patient (with all the wrapping on the juices intact), says to him, "Enjoy," and walks out of the room. If you shared that scenario in front of all the dietary employees and asked them to identify the successes and errors made in this scenario, how many would people in that room would identify any errors? The comments I received from the dietary team's analysis of this scenario was that the dietary person made sure the table was close to the patient, the food was delivered on time, the food was correct, and the employee was cordial. According to the dietary team, they did their job well. I was the only one in the room who disagreed. Do you?

To further investigate my thoughts on how uncommon common sense can really be, I shared the same scenario with a team of nurses, and the nurses were outraged. The nurses snidely remarked to me, "If dietary had any common sense at all..." They asked how that patient could open the lids on the juices, let alone lean forward to reach for the cup or open the straw. They asked why dietary couldn't have at least opened the juice for the patient and placed a napkin over him or even tell him they would let someone know (the nurse or the aide) that the patient's food had arrived and that the patient needed assistance.

So when we talk about common sense, we need to examine the averages of how people look at things, the variations of how good care versus bad care can be perceived, and the understanding of what constitutes errors. Was this scenario a case of knowledge deficit from the dietary team in what the patient could or couldn't do, or was it a case of they'd better hurry up and deliver the food trays to all the patients so they don't receive poor service ratings? Lesson learned: Consider why people do the things they do when it doesn't appear like common sense to us. This example was remedied by educating dietary members of the limitations of the patients and explaining that they should either ask family members (if available) if they would like to assist in feeding or inform the patient that they would let the nurse or nurse's aide know the tray is there and that the patient is in need of assistance.

Recognizing Behavioral and Social Differences

When other people react to situations in a manner opposite from what you would do, it is easy to judge and make inferences. In lieu of placing judgments on others, we need to learn and understand the behavioral differences that we all have. Researchers in the fields of social and industrial psychology offer insight into four personal or social styles (Merrill & Reid, 1981; Tracom, 1991; Bolton & Bolton, 2009). This improves our communication and the quality of our relationships. A popular model used to help people better understand and communicate with various interpersonal style differences is the Social Style Model (Merrill & Reid, 1999; Tracom, 1991). This model includes four social styles:

- **Drivers—"Get It Done."** Driving style people regulate their emotions and have a tendency to communicate in an aggressive fashion. They like to take control in situations, and they move at a fast pace to get things done. Although others view them as highly efficient, they do not consider others' feelings in their decision-making nor take time to build relationships with others.

- **Amiable—"It's All About Teamwork."** Amiable style people place great precedence on building and sustaining friendships. They are complaisant and shy. Because cooperation is important to Amiable styles, they tend to get too caught up in everyone else's feelings and interactions.

- **Analytical—"Show Me The Facts."** Analytical style people like quantified content and thrive on factual data. They focus on logic, accuracy, and facts. Although they prefer to work alone, they are still cooperative and approachable. Analytics like to take their time when making decisions so that all objective information is included and correct.

- **Expressive—"Commend and Compliment."** Expressive style people are enthusiastic, attention seeking, and alluring. They work to build continuous relationships with others and like to be recognized for accomplishments. Expressive styles use metaphors and their bodies when speaking. Although others see them as artistic, they can also appear unsettled.

People with Expressive and Amiable social styles have a humanistic interaction style, whereas people with Driver and Analytical social styles are more pragmatic and performance driven. The 4 social style models can also help us to better understand and relate with the various leadership styles within an organization. People with an Expressive social style have analogous traits to that of a charismatic leader. Charismatic leaders use their enthusiasm and charm to motivate others. People with Amiable social styles resemble the traits of a laissez-faire leader because laissez-fair leaders enjoy harmony and prefer others to make decisions. People who portray a Driver social style can be aligned with autocratic leadership. Autocratic leaders relish control and often micromanage. They seldom recognize colleagues for good performance. Those with Analytical social styles are akin to bureaucratic leaders. These leaders make decisions "by the book" and prefer logic and analytics to support their decision-making. Our awareness of these styles helps us to become more effective in how we communicate and interact with others.

time to reflect

Each of us has a primary style in communicating, and although we may sometimes overlap these interaction styles, we tend to find one that is more dominant within us. Take a moment to think about what your primary and secondary interaction styles are and how that might affect your communication with others.

Taking the aBEST Approach to Effective Conversations

Conversations can be considered effective when there is no error in the message, as it relates to all participants. I have found using an acronym that infuses body language, emotional intellegence, and scripting techniques is most conducive to ensuring all pieces of communication are assessed, implemented, and evaluated. I call this the "aBEST" approach (see Figure 1.1) to having effective conversations. If you can recall this acronym from memory, you will be sure you're applying common sense in uncommon situations by being cognizant to body language, emotional intelligence, and scripting techniques—elements that are all vital to having an effective conversation.

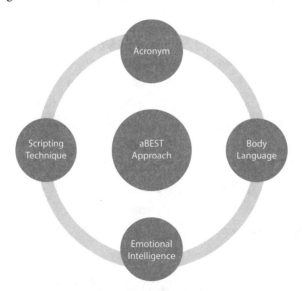

Figure 1.1   The aBest approach for effective patient and interprofessional conversations for nurses

Driving effective conversations is like driving a car. First, you start a car to go somewhere. Second, you begin with the right route and for the right purpose. Finally, whether you arrive at your destination or not, the journey is is the linchpin of your success.

Now, think about a typical conversation you may have at work. First, you start a conversation with intent. Second, your intent is what drives the conversation to the right direction and for the right purpose (hopefully). Finally, whether you found success or not in the conversation, you learn from it (remember, it's all about the journey). Although driving a car and driving conversations are not completely comparing apples to apples, this comparison simulates how you are in control of driving all aspects of conversations, even when the conversations go off course.

Although variations and deviations will naturally occur in conversations, you can limit the extent of the variation and deviation—aka confusion. For example, let's say the intent of a conversation with one of your patients is to assess pain level. The patient says it is a 2 (5 being the worst pain), yet you notice the patient has increased respirations and appears very uncomfortable. Rather than just accepting that your patient has minimal pain and saying to her, "Are you sure it's only a 2, Mrs. Davis?" try limiting the variation of "are you sure" and tell the patient what you see specifically. Explain what you see (increased respirations, limited mobility, etc.) and directly ask her to help you understand how your perception is different to what she is telling you. Now, we all know pain is subjective, but we also know patients don't take pain medications as they should due to fear of dependency, constipation, or shame—to name a few common reasons. Ask open-ended questions rather than closed questions to limit the variations and deviations in conversations. Utilizing tried-and-true cookie-cutter modalities, such as open-ended questions, as a foundation is a great technique to delivering excellent care. (We will review more techniques for open-ended questions later in this chapter.)

SOAP Documentation

Have you ever heard of SOAP documentation? If you work in healthcare, I'm confident you have. To refresh your memory, the SOAP acronym stands for

Subjective

Objective

Assessment

Plan

The SOAP acronym is another great example of a cookie-cutter process that allows for creativity and flexibility. It's a great foundation that you can customize to fit your needs. All SOAP notes do not include the same scripting type content; they only provide structure and organization for thoughts.

The process of finding common sense in communications can mirror something as simple as an acronym. Let's take a look at how the aBEST acronym breaks down, starting with *a*, which stands for *acronyms*.

Acronyms. An acronym is a type of mnemonic device that assists people in remembering an image, a sentence, or a word. An acronym is "a word formed from the first letters or groups of letters in a name or phrase. An acrostic is a series of lines from which particular letters (such as the first letters of all lines) form a word or phrase. These can be used as mnemonic devices by taking the first letters of words or names that need to be remembered and developing an acronym or acrostic." (Psych Central, 2010, para 5)

For example, Studer (2004) coined the acronym AIDET, which stands for

Acknowledge

Introduce

Duration

Explanation

Thank you

Nurses use this framework to improve their communications with patients and their families as well as with staff, members of leadership, and so on. Conversations are only as good as your ability to communicate clearly—that is, when the listener is able to thoroughly understand the intent and purpose of the conversation. AIDET is simply a framework (Studer, 2004) for driving the conversation on the right course and toward the right destination. In no way am I suggesting that *A (acknowledge)* always needs to be prescriptive, such as "Hi, Mrs. _____. It's nice to see you today." You'll have to customize the sentences relative to several variables, such as the person or situation, but using the framework, in varying situations, is helpful. Consider the following script, which you could customize for a patient coming in for preadmission testing:

Acknowledge	"Hello, Mr. Franks. Could you please sign in? We can start getting you ready for your preadmission testing."
Introduce	"My name is Laura, and I've been a registered nurse here for about 5 years."
Duration	"You will most likely be here for about an hour. We will need to ask you some questions and assess you."
Explain	"It's important we ask some questions about your health, draw some blood, and take a chest X-ray. This information will help the doctor in determining the best treatment plan for you. First, I need to ask you questions about your medical history. Next, I will take some blood. You will feel a pinch and pressure when I draw your blood, but I will let you know when I do this if you'd like to know—some people would rather not know when the pinch is coming. You can let me know either way. Finally, you will have a chest X-ray.

	This is similar to having a picture taken. You won't feel any pain. What questions do you have for me?"
Thank you	"Thank you, Mr. Franks, for trusting me with your care. We have a great team here, and I'm happy to answer any other questions you may have."

Body language. Driver (2010) explains that we continuously reveal body gestures that either match what we are saying, are completely paradoxical to what we are saying, or both. All of our nonverbal behaviors—the way we sit, the speed and tone of our voice, our proximity to others, and our eye contact send strong messages to receivers and can either help or hinder the effectiveness of our conversation and our integrity.

These messages don't stop when we stop talking, as we are still communicating in a nonverbal manner. Oftentimes, there is a vast dichotomy in the words we choose and what our bodies are actually saying. When we are challenged with this, we need to decide whether we believe the verbal or nonverbal message. Typically, the listener will choose the nonverbal gestures because they broadcast underlying feelings and intentions.

Here's a simple example: Have you ever asked someone "Are you OK?" and received the answer, "Yes, I'm fine," although the person's head and shoulders are slumped over and he doesn't make eye contact? This simple scenario describes how mixed messages may say one thing yet show another. (Chapter 2 expands more on this idea.)

The Power of Body Language

Body language is very powerful. I define it as "powerful" because even the most subtle, discreet body gestures can reveal tremendous amounts of information. Take, for instance, how different a conference call feels versus sitting in an actual room with someone. The difference we feel between these two environments is due to the vast amount of extra information we either see or don't see from body gestures. From the rise of our eyebrows to the direction of our feet, subtle body gestures can reveal a lot more than what is said. The power in body language is that we are not even cognizant we are giving more information than we may otherwise want to.

- Body language can help you understand different personalities so you don't judge others.

- Body language conveys truth, even when words do not.

- Body language enhances listening and communication skills.

- Body language allows you to hear between the words spoken to understand what is being said.

- Understanding body language helps you identify your own actions that hinder or foster success.

Source: Driver (2010).

Emotional Intelligence (EI). Goleman (2007) posited that our brain defaults to reacting and protecting us when faced with adversity. This defensiveness can arise before we can rationally think things through. For example, you have a 66-year-old diabetic patient who won't stop screaming at you (and you have no idea what you did). If you're a person with low EI, you might immediately take this situation personally and scream back at the patient in a poor attempt to stop her from screaming. If you're a person with high EI, you would look first to calm yourself down, gain your composure, and speak with a soft, normal tone of voice, such as, "I want to help you," or "I need you to speak slowly so I can better help you."

Our emotions can get the best of us unless we become aware of them and learn how to control them. We can't always change adversity, but we can change the way we react to it. Our behavior is cardinal to the way we communicate. Think about it: We hire staff based on talent, and we fire them mostly due to poor behavior. Sometimes, staff members are victims to their own emotions, especially when emotions are running high and self-preservation kicks into overdrive. This typically ends with a suboptimal outcome.

Robert, Waite, Cornwell, Morrow, and Mabern (2012) suggest that EI offers an explanation as to why some providers are better at delivering patient- and family-centered care than others. EI contributes to the provider–patient relationship as evidenced by empathy, teamwork, communication, stress management, and effective leadership (Karimi, Leggat, Donohue, Farrell, & Couper, 2013). There is also a positive correlation between EI and compassion, which positively affects nurse retention, stress adaptation, and patient clinical outcomes (Frampton, Guastello, & Lepore, 2013).

time to reflect

Identifying emotions is important for a patient's trust as well as for building collegial relationships. I recently observed a hostile interaction between a nurse and a physician. Both parties appeared to be competing for the "who was right award" regarding a patient-care issue. As the nurse was leaving the interaction, she commented that the physician always causes hostility and is insensitive.

Several hours later, I found the nurse in tears in the break room. She explained how she always feels undermined by the physician and she's never good enough. She went on to say how this physician always makes her feel dumb and irrational. As we discussed her relationship with the physician, she realized that her feelings of inadequacy pushed her into repeated conflicts with him. She attempted to prove her worth by challenging his decisions, not by considering his decisions.

After she correctly identified her emotions, she was able to make better choices in this problem-prone relationship. As she became more aware of her emotions, she was less confrontational, and her relationship with the physician improved considerably. The nurse's dominant social style was Expressive, and the doctor's style was Driver.

Think about how the styles of the physician (Driver) and the nurse (Expressive) in this example had an effect on their interactions. How might this situation have been improved if they had a better understanding of one another's style? Now, think of some challenges you've had with one particular person. Reflect on your social interaction style and the differences in the other person's interaction style. How might your social interaction style be conflicting with that person's, and what might you do differently in the future to make things work more smoothly?

ᴛʜᴇREAL WORLD | IDENTIFYING EMOTIONAL INTELLIGENCE

An adolescent female was admitted to the intensive care unit (ICU) for a self-inflicted gunshot wound to her head. She had attempted to end her life shortly after she told her mother she was a lesbian. Her mother, a very stoic and religious woman, visited her daughter in the ICU daily. During the mother's visit, she was often adversarial with the nurses and accused them for the poor changes in her daughter's condition. Her angry behavior alienated the staff and isolated the family.

One day, during an outburst, a nurse sat down next to her and empathetically said, "This isn't your fault." The mother, shocked at this statement, erupted into tears and cried desolately in the nurse's arms. This emotionally intelligent nurse had accurately determined that the mother's anger and guilt was being displaced on those who cared for her daughter. The nurse was able to connect with this suffering mother only after she could look beyond the anger and address the guilt the

Scripting techniques. Scripting is a set of messages, phrases, or sentences that you can, without much thought, weave into conversations in order to organize the flow of the conversation. Scripting and other similar techniques enable nurses to deliver thoughtful, appropriate responses or phrases in an authentic way. Nurses can develop formats for scripts and for various situations. These scripts might consist of only a single sentence, or they might reflect the wording for an entire conversation. For example, consider Script 1.1, which illustrates a conversation you might have with a colleague who isn't pulling his or her workload, or "weight." Consider also Script 1.2, which is a more one-sided conversation you might have with a "difficult" patient.

A very useful format for more comprehensive conversations is to use the TELL acronym:

Tell	Reminds us to tell the listener what has been observed or what the issue is. This also reminds us to listen, too.
Explain	Informs us to specifically explain why this is an issue or problem with what happened.
Lead	Instructs us to lead by example; demonstrate specifically what the behavior should look like.
Learn	Advises us to make sure the listener learns the consequence, should the issue or behavior not improve.

You will notice many of the scripts used throughout this book follow this format. The TELL format is discussed in more detail in Chapter 5.

With scripting it's imperative that nurses *believe* what they are saying in order to deliver the message with genuineness. Scripting also helps to deliver a consistent and comprehensive message. This is especially important in healthcare settings, where error should be zero.

Using open-ended questions is another way to incorporate scripting into conversations. An open-ended question is one that unobtrusively compels a person to volunteer more information (see Script 1.2 for examples). Did you know we talk at roughly 200–250 words per minute (wpm) but can listen at 300–500 wpm (Douglass, 1993)? We shouldn't underestimate what others hear or understand when we converse. Asking open-ended questions can ensure that what we said was actually heard. For example, the following three questions ask the same basic question, but each elicits a different response:

- Do you have any other data for me to add to the Magnet document?

- You don't have any other data to add to the Magnet document, do you?

- What data do you have to add to the Magnet document?

Script 1.1 What to say when…
a nurse colleague isn't pulling his or her weight.

Tell

To your coworker:

Jared, I just passed your patient's room, and she asked me to help her to the bathroom. I assisted her, but then she also asked me to get her water, check when her pain meds are due, and see if her test results are back. It sounds like you haven't been in to assess your patient for a while.

Explain

Your coworker is defensive:

Well, there are times your patients call on me, too. I thought we helped each other out.

Your response:

I certainly don't mind helping out, but I thought you should know this happened to me twice this week and four times last week. I appreciate all the times you help me, so I thought I should bring this to your attention because I wouldn't want you to feel any extra burden. The problem is that I am now stretched in helping your patient as well as caring for my own patient load. Can you tell me what's going on? I've never seen your patients need so much help in the past.

Your coworker is apologetic:

I'm sorry, I know. I'm just having a hard time these days.

Your response:

I appreciate all the times you help me. So can you tell me what's going on? I've never seen your patients need so much help in the past.

Lead by example

Your coworker is argumentative:

Look, we've always worked well together before. Why do you have to start trouble?

Your response:

I'm not trying to start trouble. I'm asking for you to help me by working as hard as you have in the past. Until this past month, I rarely had your patients ask me or another nurse for anything since you were always on top of their care. I used to admire how you could balance all your duties.

Your coworker is overwhelmed:

I picked up another per diem job for extra money. I'm just feeling incredibly tired.

Your response:

I'm afraid I know what you mean. Tell you what: I'll be here for you as much as I can, but I can't continue to pick up your tasks. Maybe you should speak with somebody in the employee assistance program.

Learn the consequence

Your coworker is unapologetic:

This is your problem, not mine. You're just selfish and ignorant.

Your response:

I will need to take this to our supervisor. I can't continue to pick up extra assignments like this.

Your coworker apologizes:

I'm sorry about adding more to your plate. I didn't mean to do that to you.

Your response:

I accept your apology. Let's just move forward. I'm confident you'll take the right steps to improve your work performance.

Script 1.2 What to say when…
you greet a patient and he responds negatively.

Tell

To your patient:

> Hello, Mr. Martin. How are you today?

Patient:

> Mr. Martin does not reply and appears annoyed.

Explain

To your patient:

> Mr. Martin, you appear upset. Is there something I can help you with?

Patient:

> Mr. Martin doesn't respond and looks away.

Lead by **L**example

To your patient:

> I am concerned that you are upset about something, and I want to do my best to help the situation. If you are not comfortable talking with me, who else can I ask to help us?

Patient:

> Mr. Martin shrugs his shoulders in an "I don't know" gesture.

Learn the **L**consequence

To your patient:

> I respect that you do not want to talk about what may be upsetting you, but please understand I am trying to give you the best possible care. If you can share your concerns with me, this is the only way we can help to improve the situation. What questions do you have for me?

Do you see how the first question is a closed question, requiring a simple yes/no response? The second question is a leading question; in other words, it leads the person to answer the question in a biased way. The third question is an open-ended question. This type of question takes out any bias or conclusions because it confirms or denies what was perceived and understood. Using words like *what, why,* and *how* are excellent choices to ensure your questions are open-ended.

Scripting and the Service Industry

The service industry became enamored with scripting many years ago. Think about the service you received at franchises such as Chick-fil-A or Starbucks. Almost every customer service opportunity ends with a staff member saying, "My pleasure," after being thanked by a customer. The lucrative hotel industry is yet another example. Many front desk and concierge staff follow open-ended scripts such as, "What else can I do to assist you today?" Notice they focus on open-ended questions in lieu of yes/no questions. Consider the response of asking, "Did you have a good stay with us?" where you are more likely to receive a "yes" or "no" response from the guest versus asking, "How was your stay with us?" The latter may elicit more feedback, such as the customer stating, "It was a great stay; the view was awesome," or "I've had better; I waited over an hour for room service delivery." The feedback you receive, whether positive or negative, is valuable information to identify wins and reveal opportunities.

Integrating Teach-Back Into Your Conversations

Weaving scripting and teach-back principles into conversations enables nurses to maintain a level of flexibility in dialogue. In teach-back, asking the patient to "teach back" what was said ensures information is understood. This is very effective, even for purposes regarding the Hospital Consumer Assessment of Healthcare Providers and Systems (HCAHPS) survey. As you may know, this survey is given after discharge to selected patients and asks specific questions regarding the patient's experience. Such questions evaluate the patient's perception of how effectively the nurses and doctors communicated with them, how well their pain was controlled, the quality of information presented to them at discharge, and the cleanliness and quietness in their room (HCAHPS online, n.d.). Let's look at an example HCAHPS question:

During your most recent hospital stay, how well did the nurses listen to you?

Using teach-back prompts, patients are more prone to answering the top box (the highest rating possible in that category on patient satisfaction surveys) if they recall healthcare staff stated something to the effect of, "If I heard you correctly, you said you would like [insert statement such as 'more information about the medication side effects']." This reply conveys that listening is respected and delivered.

Teach-back is also universally accepted as a best practice to overcome health illiteracy. Health illiteracy is the inability to understand basic health information and services needed to make appropriate health decisions and follow instructions for treatment (Schillinger et al., 2003). Did you know 36% of Americans are below a basic health literacy level? We need to remember that a conversation is only as good as one's ability to communicate its value and meaningfulness to others. In other words, if we don't articulate the importance of what we are trying to say to others, the information will go in one of their ears and out the other.

Here's an example: On the morning of surgery, you ask an 80-year-old pre-op patient if he has eaten anything since midnight. He says, "No." You then ask him to tell (teach) you what he did this morning, and he tells you he woke up and had his normal coffee and just a bite of a cookie. He explains he didn't "eat" anything, just had a small bite. You then tell him that the surgery will need to be canceled since he had food. The patient replies to you that if the nurse the night before had explained that he couldn't even have a small "bite" of something, he wouldn't have had it. The patient perceived "nothing to eat" as the equivalent of a full meal. You explain about the risk of aspiration, and he further shares with you that if they had explained this in detail to him last night, he wouldn't have even had the coffee! Think about it: If you didn't ask him to teach or tell you the events of his morning, this pre-op "no-no" wouldn't have been discovered. One of the best ways to ensure what others say or what you say is understood and perceived correctly is to have them teach it back.

It is important to take control of conversations when you do not understand someone or something, or if you get the impression someone else isn't in tune with your conversation. Recognize variances and deviations from what is said and what isn't said by decoding body gestures, managing your emotions, making the most of acronyms to make your communication flow, and using teach-back strategies. Do not always settle for yes/no responses when eliciting feedback. Use a Socratic approach to stimulate critical thinking and illuminate ideas (that otherwise may not even be considered). We will next discuss how we can pull all these tools together and create a road map to ensure your communications are most effective.

Your Road Map: Guiding Principles for Effective Communication

You can break down the process of communication into a simple three-step process, using the CAR acronym (which contains the aBEST approach within it):

Consideration

Action or call to action

Return on investment (ROI)

This overarching acronym can be your map (no pun intended) to clearer, more focused, and effective conversations. The CAR acronym can even be used when you're involved in an emotionally charged or controversial conversation.

Let's now *map out* (pun intended) the CAR acronym to ensure you are intertwining the aBEST approach.

Consideration

The first part of CAR is the *C*, which is to *consider* the "Five Rights for Communication Safety," including:

1. Right person to speak with

2. Right place to discuss

3. Right time to discuss

4. Right emotions in check (EI and body language)

5. Right ROI, or intent

These communication safety rights are comparable to the "Five Rights of Medication Safety" (Nursing 2012 Drug Handbook, 2012), which you may recall from nursing school. These include:

1. Right medication

2. Right dose

3. Right time

4. Right route

5. Right patient

So just as errors in medication administration are often the consequence of failing to review these "Five Rights of Medication Safety," communication errors are the consequence of failing to review the "Five Rights of Communication Safety." Always remember the "Five Rights."

Action or Call to Action

The next part of CAR is the *A*, which is the *action or call to action*. The action or call to action is what your preferred outcome is for having the conversation. Think of this as a backward approach to having a conversation. What response are you expecting to receive from the recipient by having this conversation? In other words, is the intent of your conversation to give directives, to coach, to complete a task, to seek more information, or to clarify something? So after your CAR is fueled and inspected (i.e., you reviewed your Five Rights of Communication Safety), you now must think about what action you need to take in order to get what you want from the recipient.

Let's use the following example: The provider told your patient that he can be discharged this morning. It's now almost noon, and the patient is still waiting to be discharged because the provider still hasn't entered the discharge order. The patient is dressed and ready to go. The family is waiting, but you can see their patience is running thin. Obviously, you know you need to contact the provider and ask to have the discharge order entered, so the intent of your conversation is for the provider to complete a task/directive. Sounds easy, right? Well, not so much if you know this provider doesn't like to be told what to do or has just stepped off the unit, is running a code, etc. At this point, think about what the response is that you are looking for—which, in this example, is for the provider to simply enter the order. But before you ask this, the *C* (*consideration*) helps you to reflect:

- Is this the right person to speak with? (Can the nurse practitioner write the order, or does it need to be the provider?)

- Is this the right place to discuss the situation? (The conversation is held in private and not in another patient's room.)

- Is this the right time to discuss the situation? (Is the provider in the midst of running a code or even conducting interdisciplinary rounds? Can the conversation wait another 5 minutes until the provider is done?)

- Are the right emotions in check? If the provider is known not to take direction well and lash out when asked to do something, then be prepared to approach the conversation in a nonthreatening manner. Stating "Mr. Gonzales has been waiting a very long time and is getting angry with you since you never put in *yet* another discharge order on time" can sound harsh and undermining. However, an approach that is less threatening and more meaningful to the provider would be stating something to the effect of, "… just a friendly reminder to put in the discharge order for Mr. Gonzales. I want to make sure we are respectful of his time since he and has family have been patiently waiting for the order since 8:00 this morning."

- Do you have the right ROI, or intent? (Yes, you are advocating for the patient's time and overall patient bed flow.)

The A, or the call to action, is the actual deliverable and organization of your thoughts throughout your conversation. This is the "engine" of the conversation, so aim very carefully in your approach in the fourth item above. Remember, the action, or call to action, is *what your preferred outcome* looks like from the recipent. The outcome you are seeking in this example is simply for the provider to respect your request and immediately enter the discharge order so you can properly discharge this patient.

Return on Investment

The *R* of CAR stands for the *return on investment* (ROI). The ROI measures the effectiveness of your conversation. A high ROI means the investment gain, or conversation outcome, compares favorably to the investment cost, which in the context of conversations is typically how much time you took to get your desired results. You can also consider your ROI to be high if you learned what worked or what didn't work in your approach. The benefit you are yielding is that you will continually build upon and use the prior strategies that got you the results you wanted. Bottom line: Evaluating your ROI is beneficial because you are creating a toolbox of communication strategies that will consistently help you get the results you want, when you need them the most.

The Drive Home

Let's review the *driving it back home* pointers from this chapter:

- The journey defines success; the actual destination is secondary to it.

- Common sense is subjective because there is a different perception to what people denote as "common."

- A popular model used to improve interpersonal communications is the Social Style Model.

- Each of the four styles in the Social Style Model has strengths in certain situations and opportunities when working with each other.

- The aBEST approach infuses all the core components of an effective conversation to include acronyms, body language, emotional intelligence, and scripting techniques.

- An acronym is a type of mnemonic device that assists people in remembering an image, a sentence, or a word.

- The language our body reveals can be completely opposite of the words we say. This can help or hinder our conversation and even our credibility.

- Emotional intelligence reminds us that we can't always change the adversity, but we can change they way we react to it.

- When seeking informative responses from people, we need to ask open-ended questions. Such questions should start with *what*, *why*, and *how*.

- CAR is an overarching framework for the aBEST approach and includes

  - C—Consider. Consider the "Five Rights" for Communication Safety.

- A—Action or a call to action. This is the building block of the conversation. How will you articulate what it is you're seeking from the recipient while remaining respectful?

- R—Return on investment. A high ROI indicates the conversation outcome was successful and compares favorably to the amount of time you took to get the desired results.

References

Bolton, R., & Bolton, D. G. (2009). *People styles at work—and beyond: Making bad relationships good and good relationships better.* AMACOM.

Burns, J. M. (1978). *Leadership.* New York: Harper and Row.

Centers for Medicare and Medicaid Services. Baltimore, MD. Retrieved April 14, 2014 from http://www.hcahpsonline.org

Douglass, M. E. (1993). *Manage your time, your work, yourself.* New York, NY: AMACOM.

Driver, J. (2010). *You say more than you think: A 7-day plan for using the new body language to get what you want!* New York, NY: Crown Publishers.

Frampton, S. B., Guastello, S., & Lepore, M. (2013). Compassion as the foundation of patient-centered care: The importance of compassion in action. *Journal of Effectiveness Comparative Research, (2)*5, 443–455. doi 10.2217/cer.13.54

Goleman, D. (2007). *Emotional intelligence: Why it can matter more than IQ.* New York, NY: Random House.

Karimi, L., Leggat, S. G., Donohue, L., Farrell, G., & Couper, G. E. (2013). Emotional rescue: the role of emotional intelligence and emotional labour on well-being and job-stress among community nurses. *Journal of Advanced Nursing, 70*(1), 176–186. doi: 10.1111/jan.12185

Merrill, D. W. and Reid, R. H. (1999). *Personal styles and effective performance.* New York, NY: CRC Press.

Nursing 2012 Drug Handbook. (2012). Philadelphia, PA: Lippincott Williams & Wilkins.

Psych Central. (2010). Memory and Mnemonic Devices. *Psych Central.* Retrieved from http://psychcentral.com/lib/memory-and-mnemonic-devices/0004376

Robert, G., Waite, R., Cornwell, J., Morrow, E., & Mabern, J. (2012). Understanding and improving patient experience: A national survey of training courses provided by higher education providers and healthcare organizations in England. *Nurse Education Today, 34*(1), 112–120. doi: 10.1016/j.nedt.2012

Schillinger, D., Piette, J., Grumbach, K., Wang, F., Daher, C., Wilson, C. ... Bindman, A. B. (2003). Closing the loop: Physician communication with diabetic patients who have low health literacy. *Archives of Internal Medicine, 163*(1), 83–90.

Studer, Q. (2004). *Hardwiring excellence: Purpose worthwhile work making a difference.* Baltimore, MD: Fire Starter Publishing.

TRACOM (1991). The social style profile—Technical report: Development, reliability and validity. Denver, CO: Author.

UMF Corporation. (2010). Improved environmental hygiene lowers infections and raises HCAHPS scores at Rush-Copley. Retrieved from http://www.businesswire.com/news/home/20130813005795/en/Case-Study-Published-UMF-Corporation-Supports-Role

Voltaire. (n.d.). Retrieved from http://www.brainyquote.com/quotes/quotes/v/voltaire106180.html

> *"The most important thing in communication is hearing what isn't said."*
> –Peter F. Drucker

2

Body Language Exposed

At one of my previous jobs, several directors and I were asked to attend a meeting with one of our newest senior directors, whom I'll call Mary. Before the meeting, Mary requested that each of us bring a few high-priority departmental issues to discuss. We were told that, based on these discussions, Mary would pick the top issues, which she would then prioritize in her new leadership role.

Mary was an extremely charming and charismatic leader with stellar business acumen and financial experience. Mary was also well educated, with more than 20 years of experience in healthcare executive management. In the following vignette, see if you can guess from Mary's body language whether or not she selected one of the issues I shared.

At this meeting, Mary first gave a warm introduction, asked us to introduce ourselves, and then proceeded to solicit information about our departmental issues. While my colleagues and I took turns sharing our issues, I watched how Mary's body language would change based on some of the words she heard. Some of the many topics discussed included revenue cycle, charge entry, lack of resources, staffing issues, quality improvement, relative value units (RVUs), value-based purchasing, and meaningful-use dollars.

It wasn't just Mary's facial expression that I honed in on, but the position of her upper body (as we sat around the boardroom table), whether she was writing with the pen or just dangling the pen, how often she leaned on her hand, and the direction of her eyes. For example, when my colleagues spoke to lack of specific resources, I would note Mary feverishly writing on her pad, occasionally nodding and cupping her chin with her hand. When colleagues spoke passionately about staff performance management issues, Mary would look up to the right and down to the left, sitting back in her chair.

I was one of the last of the directors to speak, and I discussed clinical quality improvement issues. As I spoke, I noted Mary looking to the right, smiling a lot, and nodding quite abundantly. After a short discussion, and as she had done with my colleagues, Mary said she would be very supportive in my endeavors. At the end of the meeting, Mary genuinely thanked us for sharing the information with her, and the meeting concluded on a positive note.

I have learned over the years that many people know just what to say, in terms of being politically correct, but most of them aren't as experienced with—or even cognizant of—what their body language is saying. When you are adept in assessing body language, you can get a better sense of what someone is thinking, even if the person isn't speaking. I watched as her body language revealed to me what she may have perceived as engaging, boring, upsetting, and so on.

Shortly after the meeting was adjourned, I quietly mentioned to one of my colleagues that I thought the issues I shared didn't make Mary's top-priority list. I also said I would be surprised if any of the staffing issues would be on the list, although 90% of us mentioned lack of staffing as an issue. He looked quite puzzled and asked me how I came to that conclusion. He reiterated how much Mary nodded and smiled to me as I spoke. He thought she appeared very engaged, especially because Mary pointed out to the group just how important my role was to the organization because I was the only director with a clinical background. (My colleagues all had backgrounds similar to Mary's.) Now, I agreed with my colleague that what she said was supportive, but I also explained to him that I found a disconnect in her body language. My colleague once again reassured me that Mary reacted no differently to me than she did to anyone else. He went on to say I was reading way too much into the situation and should be more optimistic.

So, who was right? My colleague or me? Well, the email Mary sent shortly after the meeting confirmed that I was right. None of my issues made her top-priority list, nor did any of the staffing issues. Meaningful-use dollars made the top-priority list, as well as a focus on revenue cycle improvements. Can you guess why these issues made her top-priority list? If you said her priorities were fiscal, not clinically focused, you were right.

In the Driver's Seat: Understanding and Interpreting Body Language

In this chapter, I share common and not-so-common body language tips and tidbits that can help you interpret what people are saying beyond the words they use. You can also apply this knowledge to improve your nonverbal communication strategies so that your own words and body language are congruent. Did you know that 50% to 80% of communication is nonverbal (Mehrabian, 1972, 1981)? It is so important that we not only listen to others, but that we also listen to what their gestures tell us. Body language is a two-way street; your body language can disclose to others the feelings you are suppressing, and other people's body language can disclose their suppressed feelings to you.

A considerable amount of information can be interpreted through body language gestures. For example, when you meet someone for the first time, you are already interpreting information about them, before words are even exchanged. This is because it takes only a few minutes to make a first impression. According to Mehrabian (1981), body language depicts 55% of that impression (38% comes from tone of voice; the remaining 7% from your actual words). Although our faces, eyes, and hands are the most obvious body parts that send nonverbal gestures to others, we must also acknowledge how important our less obvious body gestures are, too. Some less obvious elements of body language include the following:

- What we look at when while talking or listening.

- Our facial expressions, including the positioning of our mouths and eyebrows.

- The way we position our bodies during conversations.

- The open space we leave between others when conversing. (This is known as *proxemics,* and what makes this interesting is how our bodies fluctuate in this during conversations.)

- How and when we touch ourselves and others during conversations.

- How our bodies touch tangible objects, such as pens, cigarettes, glasses, and clothing.

- How fast we breathe, the rate of our heartbeat, and even how much we perspire.

The following sections describe how our eyes, mouths, heads, arms, hands, hand-shakes, legs, feet, and personal space specifically show meaning and rationalization. As you review each of these areas, it is important to understand that one body gesture is not an absolute interpretation. In other words, one body language gesture is just that—one suggestion for interpretation. To effectively interpret body language, all gestures need to be assessed as a whole. As Aristotle (n.d.) stated, "The whole is greater than the sum of its parts."

Body Language Traits Based on Social Style

Researchers of social psychology introduced us to the 4 social styles, as discussed in Chapter 1. Within these 4 styles, there are common denominators relative to each style's body language (Bolton & Bolton (2009); Merrill & Reid, 1999).

- *Driver social styles* will make a lot of direct eye contact and keep the space between those they are speaking to very close. This positions them to stay in control of the conversation. Driver social styles will use their hands and fingers in conversations to "point" emphasis on their key talking points.

- *Expressive social styles* make intermittent eye contact and periodically touch others while speaking in order to emphasize their speaking points. They are more likely to raise their voices when speaking and talk fast so they can keep up with all the energetic thoughts that are racing in their mind. Expressive social styles are very visual and animated. They tend to use metaphors and their hands to articulate ideas and suggestions.

- *Amiable social styles* maintain an appropriate amount of eye contact with others. They tend to stay at a distance or lean back when speaking to others because they are shy. They are soft spoken and move at a slow pace.

- *Analytical social styles* use eye contact intermittently—making more eye contact when driving a point versus less eye contact when they are deliberating about something. Their bodies often appear rigid, and they tend to keep space between themselves and the listener.

Sources: Merrill & Reid (1999); Tracom (1991); Trigon System Consultants (n.d.).

Eyes

We are naturally adept in interpreting some things just by the way we look at—or into—the eyes of others. For example, we know almost immediately when we make eye contact with others, even when we are at a significant distance from them. Although we may be at a significant distance and cannot see the details of the eyes, we know when and if eye contact is made. Now, eye contact can be good, bad, or just plain awkward, depending of the context. We can also see if someone is giving us an awkward stare, or even a clandestine type of peek. Consequently, we often make inferences just from how someone uses their eyes even before any words affirm or refute our thoughts (Body language, n.d.; Driver, 2010). See Table 2.1 for a list of various eye gestures and their meanings.

Table 2.1   The Meanings Behind Eye Gestures

Eye Gestures	Possible Inference(s)	Rationale
Viewing right	Visualizing, creating, fabricating, guessing, lying, storytelling	Looking right typically denotes creativity or some sort of exaggeration, which may be as harmless as creating a story for a child, creating an outward lie, or attempting to add more creativity to an existing fact.
Viewing right and down		Looking right and down indicates one is accessing one's feelings, which again can be a perfectly genuine response, but the genuineness depends on the context and the person.
Viewing right and up		Looking right and up is related to imagination, lying, or creativity. When accessing the right side of the brain, we use an upward eye-movement to the right side. This can be a warning sign of lying if a person is supposed to be recalling and stating facts.

Viewing left	Recalling, remembering, retrieving facts, truthfulness, self-talk, rationalizing	When recalling facts from memory, we use the left hemisphere of our brain. Looking left typically shows that one is telling the truth.
Viewing left and down		Looking down toward the left may indicate silent self-conversation or internal strategizing regarding how the person might attempt to redirect the conversation.
Viewing left and up		Looking up and to the left is a reassuring sign if signaled when the person is supposed to be recalling and stating facts.
Direct eye contact—when speaking	Honesty, faked honesty	Direct eye contact is generally regarded as a sign of honesty and truthfulness; however, practiced liars know this and will try to fake others out by using this technique.
Direct eye contact—when listening	Attentiveness, interest, attraction	When a person's eyes are directed on the speaker's eyes, this indicates the person is focused, interested, and paying attention. This is normally a sign of attraction.
Widening of the eyes	Interest, appeal, invitation	The black center of the eye, or pupil, dilates with a sense of interest. Although eyes that are widened with eyebrows raised can signify shock or surprise, they can also represent an opening and welcoming expression.
Rubbing eye or eyes	Disbelief, upset, tiredness	Rubbing both eyes, or even only one eye, can indicate disbelief, as if someone is checking their vision. This gesture can also signal someone is upset and may indicate crying is imminent. This can also mean tiredness from lack of sleep or due to boredom.

(continues)

Table 2.1 The Meanings Behind Eye Gestures (continued)

Eye Gesture	Possible Inference(s)	Rationale
Rolling of eyes	Frustration	An upward roll of the eyes signals frustration or annoyance.
Blinking frequently	Excitement, pressure	Normal eye-blink rate can be between 6 and 20 times per minute. Excessive blinking is a sign of excitement or pressure.
Blinking infrequently	Various	Infrequent blink rates can mean different things, such as boredom or intense concentration.
Eyebrow raising	Greeting, recognition, acknowledgment	Quickly raising the eyebrows is a common signal of greeting and acknowledgment. A more elaborate eyebrow flash, where eyebrows are raised for a longer time, may beckon fear and surprise.
Winking	Friendly acknowledgment, complicity (i.e., secrets or joke)	A wink is commonly a flirtatious or intimate signal, directed from one person to another. A wink can signal a shared joke or secret, hence why it is powerful.

Source: Adapted/paraphrased with permission from Businessballs.com (2014). Full source material at www.businessballs.com/body-language.htm

Mouth

The mouth can be associated with multiple body language signals because it can be touched or concealed by a person's hands, fingers, or other objects. Not only do we associate the mouth with speech, but also, as you may recall from your nursing school days, Dr. Sigmund Freud connected the mouth with infant feeding, which further connects psychologically with feelings of security, affection, love, and sex. Although more obvious mouth gestures, such as smiling, are huge components of facial body language, the extent of a person's smile has different meanings. For example, did you know that real smiles are symmetrical and produce wrinkles around the eyes and mouth, while forced smiles don't? In a forced smile, you will only see the mouth crease change (Body language, n.d.; Driver, 2010). See Table 2.2 for a list of various mouth gestures and their meanings.

Table 2.2   The Meanings Behind Mouth Gestures

Mouth Gesture	Possible Inference(s)	Rationale
"Forced" smile	Fake smile	A fake smile may indicate disapproval or feeling forced into doing something not desired.
Smiling without showing teeth	Withholding feelings or comments	The person may have a secret they are trying to disclose.
Smiling with jaw elongated	Fake smile	This is the epitome of a fake smile. The jaw is dropped low, and the mouth appears long.
Smile—head tilted, looking up	Playfulness, flirting, or teasing	When the head is tilted sideways and downward, the face is hidden, and only part of the smile shows. This is effective to draw in someone's attention.
Bottom lip salient	Upset, empathy	A salient bottom lip, or a lip that is pushed forward, shows imminent crying and upset. This also may be an overt attempt to seek sympathy or kind treatment. People who push out their bottom lip may also do so in a playful manner, or even in an authentically empathetic way.
Laughter—natural	Relaxation	Genuine laughter is a sign of relaxation. Natural laughter can change the position of the upper body or even the whole body.
Laughter—unnatural	Nervousness, cooperation	Unnatural laughter is often a signal of nervousness or stress. This can also be a subtle signal of trying to get others to cooperate.

(continues)

Table 2.2   The Meanings Behind Mouth Gestures   (continued)

Mouth Gesture	Possible Inference(s)	Rationale
Biting lip	Stress, anxiousness	Biting the lip can be caused by stress or anxiousness.
Chewing on an object	Self-comforting, flirting	Nibbling on a pen can also represent oral pleasure (so think about the message you're sending to colleagues or patients if you are chewing on the end of your pen or pencil during a conversation with them).
Pursing lips	Thoughtfulness, impatience	This often happens when you are trying to hold words in your mouth and you're trying to stop yourself from talking over someone. This can also indicate anxiousness or impatience at not being able to speak at that time.
Tongue poke	Disapproval, rejection	This gesture is similar to the reaction you have when you've tasted something gross. This is even more obvious when the nose wrinkles and the eyes squint.

Source: Adapted/paraphrased with permission from Businessballs.com/body-language.htm (2014).

Head

Because our brains are located within our heads, it guides our general body direction. Our heads are used in a lot of directional (approving and disapproving) body language and in self-protection (defensive or offensive) body language. A simple turn or tilt of our head has various meanings, and this provides significant information about what's not being said. Our heads, especially when our hands interact with them, can be dynamic in communicating all sorts of messages, both consciously and unconsciously (Body language, n.d.; Driver, 2010). See Table 2.3 for a list of various head gestures and their meanings.

Table 2.3   The Meanings Behind Head Gestures

Head Gesture	Possible Inference(s)	Rationale
Shaking head up and down	Understanding, agreement	Shaking our heads shows we are agreeing or are understanding what the other person is saying.
Shaking head up and down slowly	Attentive listening (could also be fake)	Although this gesture could authentically display the person is listening, be aware that this can be a faked signal. As with all body language signals, you must look for clusters of signals rather than relying only on a head nod. Hint: Look at the focus of the eyes to check the validity of slow head nodding.
Shaking head up and down fast	Hurry up, impatience	Shaking your head fast indicates you've heard enough and you're ready to move on to something else.
Holding head up	Neutrality, alertness	This can show attentive listening and/or that the listener has no bias in what you are saying.
Holding head up high	Superiority, fearlessness, arrogance	Keeping your head raised displays confidence and can also be valuable for demanding respect and showing authority.
Head tilted to one side	Nonthreatening, submissive, thoughtfulness	Head tilts suggest we may be considering a different view of the other person or subject. Head tilting also exposes our neck, which is a sign of trust.
Head tilted downward	Criticism	Tilting our head downward is a sign of criticism or disapproval.
Head shaking side to side	Disagreement	This gesture can indicate disagreement or disclose feelings of disbelief.
Prominent head shaking	Strong disagreement	A more pronounced shaking of the head can show how strongly we feel about someone or something.
Placing head down	Negative, embarrassment, shame	We use head-down gestures when we are responding to criticism. This gesture can indicate failure or feeling embarrassed or shamed.

(continues)

Table 2.3 The Meanings Behind Head Gestures (continued)

Head Gesture	Possible Inference(s)	Rationale
Chin up	Pride, defiance, confidence	Holding the chin up is analogous to the "head held high" signal. A chin that is naturally held up exposes the neck and is a signal of trust, strength, confidence, resilience, pride, etc. A chin that is held up also lifts the sternum, which improves airflow, expands the chest, and widens the shoulders. This can make a person's stance appear superior. An exposed neck is a sign of confidence.

Source: Adapted/paraphrased with permission from Businessballs.com/body-language.htm (2014).

Arms

Our arms can reveal a lot about our mood and feelings. For example, our crossed arms may mean we are defensive. However, it could also mean we are bored or trying to self-regulate because we feel insecure or upset. We open our arms wide to indicate we are open or accepting of others. Do you see how one body gesture is not an absolute?

Another great indicator of defensiveness or protectiveness is when our hands are placed over the top of one another and in front of our pelvic areas, or "naughty bits" (Driver, 2010). Although these notations may seem obvious as you read them in this book, it's not always so clear, especially if your attention is not focused on body language due to difficult emotional circumstances (Body language, n.d.; Driver, 2010). See Table 2.4 for a list of various arm gestures and their meanings.

Table 2.4   The Meanings Behind Arm Gestures

Arm Gesture	Possible Inference(s)	Rationale
Crossed arms	Defensiveness, reluctance, physically cold	Crossed arms are commonly shown when we feel threatened by others. We also cross our arms when they are physically cold or when we are bored.
Crossed arms with tightened fists	Hostility, defensiveness	Keeping fists tight with arms crossed in front of the chest indicates that one is feeling stubborn or aggressive, or that one has a lack of empathy. Watch out; defense is high!
Gripping own upper arms	Insecurity	When we feel afraid or unsafe, we tend to hold our arms with our hands. This is also known as self-hugging.
Hands held together behind body	Confidence, authority	This confident stance is taken by armed-forces officers, teachers, policemen, and so on.
Arms/hands covering pelvic region	Nervousness	This is another form of a protective gesture. This is even shown when we are simply trying to appear formal or ready (but still feeling nervous deep down).
Holding a drink, pen, or something else across the body while seated	Nervousness	This is a defensive gesture due to nervousness or not feeling comfortable.

Source: Adapted/paraphrased with permission from Businessballs.com/body-language.htm (2014).

Hands

Our hands are very expressive of what we are thinking or feeling. Did you know our hands contain more nerve connections to the brain than almost any other part of our body? We use our hands a lot in conscious and unconscious gesturing (Body language, n.d.). Communicating with our hands can demonstrate:

- Importance, such as pointing or poking, or slowing-down or speeding-up motions

- Illustrations, such as drawing, mimicking actions, giving signals (such as the OK sign), or trying to illustrate how big something is

- Salutations, such as greeting or saying good-bye

Driver (2010) explains our hands reveal almost as many signals as our faces do. Studying hand body language provides a lot of information. See Table 2.5 for a list of various hand gestures and their meanings.

Table 2.5   The Meanings Behind Hand Gestures

Hand Gesture	Possible Inference(s)	Rationale
Palm(s) up or open	Passive, trustworthy, appealing	This is a common gesture of "openness." This can also mean "I don't know." Be careful, however; this can easily be a faked gesture to look innocent.
Palm(s) facing the person, fingers pointing up	Defensive, instruction to stop	This looks like the stop gesture. The fingers are rigid, which indicates an authoritative instruction to stop whatever is going on.
Palm(s) down	Authority, strength, dominance, calm-down gesture	When one's lower arm moves across the body with the palm down, this is generally a sign of defiance or disagreement. It could also mean the person is asking the listener to calm down.

Palm up and moving up and down as if weighing something	Seeking an answer	This indicates that one is figuratively holding an issue, as if measuring it.
Hand(s) on heart (left side of chest)	Seeking to be believed	Although this gesture is easy to fake, the underlying meaning is to try to convince someone to believe us, whether we are being truthful or not.
Finger pointing—at a person	Aggression, threat, emphasis	Pointing at a person is very confrontational and dictatorial. This indicates a lack of social awareness or self-control, not to mention arrogance, on the part of the finger pointer.
Finger pointing—with wink	Acknowledgment, confirmation	Winking one's eye at someone while pointing a finger at them typically means one is acknowledging something. This can be a signal of positive appreciation, as if to say, "You got it."
Finger pointing—in the air	Emphasis	When someone points his finger in the air, he is generally trying to add emphasis to something.
Finger wagging—side to side	Warning, refusal	This is like saying "No," or asking the person to stop.
Finger wagging—up and down	Admonishment, emphasis	When someone is finger wagging at you, it looks like she has an imaginary yo-yo in her hand in an attempt to keep you in rhythm with what she is saying or to emphasize her point.
Hand chop	Emphasis	The hand chop can signify a person is placing a strong emphasis on a point he is trying to make or that he is attempting to end a discussion with power.

(continues)

Table 2.5   The Meanings Behind Hand Gestures   (continued)

Hand Gesture	Possible Inference(s)	Rationale
Clenched fist(s)	Resistance, aggression, determination	Clenching one's fist can indicate different feelings, such as defensiveness or negativity, depending on context. A clenched fist is an attempt to prepare oneself for battle.
Finger tips and thumbs touching each other on opposite hands (steepling)	Thoughtfulness, looking for or explaining connections, engagement	In this gesture, only the fingertips touch—each finger touches the corresponding digit of the other hand—and points upward like a tall church steeple. We often see people who perceive themselves as intellectual do this because it conveys elevated thinking.
Steepled fingers pointing forward	Thoughtfulness, defensive barrier	Similar to the preceding gesture; however, when this hand shape is pointed forward, it acts as a defensive barrier between people.
Interwoven clenched fingers	Frustration, negativity, anxiousness	Holding one's hands tightly clenched or interwoven signals emotions are high. This is especially true when hands turn red or bluish from the tight grasp.
Index finger and thumb touching at tips	Satisfaction	This is the "OK" signal.
Thumb(s) up	Positive approval, agreement	A thumbs-up means "approved." It's a positive gesture; however, it can also be done facetiously.
Thumb(s) down	Disapproval, failure	A thumbs-down means not approved or poor performance.
Thumb(s) clenched inside fist(s)	Self-comforting, frustration, insecurity	This gesture tends to indicate self-comforting. Because our thumbs are flexible, we are unconsciously disabling them by hiding them.

Hand held horizontally and rocked from side to side	Undecided, in the balance	We may see this when a decision or outcome is difficult to predict or control (as it is viewed as going one way or another).
Rubbing hands together	Anticipation	This shows positive expectations and is often seen in favorable response to rewards, activities, meals, or outcomes.
Touching or scratching the nose while speaking	Lying, exaggeration	Scratching is often exhibited when we are recounting an event or incident (or if we just have an itch!). It can also be seen as lying, as when Pinocchio's nose grew longer the more he lied.
Pinching or rubbing the nose while listening	Thoughtfulness, suppressing comment	This is an unconscious gesture of holding back information or thinking hard to recall something.
Pinching bridge of nose	Negative evaluation	We pinch the bridge of our noses when we negatively review something. This is typically done while holding a long, single blink.
Hands clamped on ears	Rejection, resistance to something	This signifies an unwillingness to hear what is being said or viewed.
Ear tugging	Indecision, self-comforting	Ear pulling or tugging can indicate indecisiveness and pondering. However, touching our bodies in various ways often signals we are seeking comfort; ear pulling is one comforting gesture.
Hands clasping head	Calamity	Clasping one's hands on one's head is like a protective helmet against a problem or a response to a panicked "Oh, no!" thought.
Hand stroking chin	Thoughtfulness	This gesture is similar to a man stroking his beard while using his thumb and index finger. It indicates that someone is giving something thoughtful consideration.

(continues)

Table 2.5   The Meanings Behind Hand Gestures   (continued)

Hand Gesture	Possible Inference(s)	Rationale
Hand supporting chin or side of face	Evaluation, tiredness, boredom	When we support our heads or chins with our hands, we are assessing or evaluating next actions, options, or reactions to something or someone.
Chin resting on thumb, index finger pointing up against face	Evaluation	This gesture is a similar, but more reliable, signal of evaluation than the full-hand support.
Neck scratching	Doubt, disbelief	When we hide our necks, we are showing feelings of distrust.
Hand clasping wrist	Frustration	Clasping a wrist, which may be behind our backs or in front of our pelvic region, can be a signal of frustration (as if we are holding ourselves back).
Running hands through hair	Flirting, exasperation	Running our hands through the hair is commonly associated with flirting, or it can be a sign to indicate we are feeling exasperation.
Hand(s) on hip(s)— "Superman" pose	Confidence, readiness, availability	We are emphasizing our presence, and we are showing our readiness for action.
Hands in pockets	Disinterest, boredom, confidence	When our thumbs are tucked in the pockets, we are typically not ready for action. When we have our thumbs held outside of our pockets, we show confidence.
Removing glasses	Desire to speak	For people who wear glasses, they will remove them for no reason other than to show others they want to speak. This gesture attracts attention to the face.

Source: Adapted/paraphrased with permission from Businessballs.com/body-language.htm (2014).

Handshakes

A firm handshake is representative of confidence and poise. Handshakes that are obnoxiously firm show a lack of respect. A firm handshake and smile are commonly used to establish a trusting relationship (Body language, n.d.; Driver, 2010).

Although many people believe confident people give firm handshakes, I know many confident people who offer timid handshakes. I often see this when men gently shake a women's hand out of respect to femininity. Many of my female colleagues, even those whom I consider to be pit bulls in the boardroom, tell me they shake other women's hands with extreme gentleness as a sign of respect. The bottom line: You should not judge a book by its cover. In this case, I mean don't judge someone simply based on the strength of his or her handshake. Rather than focusing on the strength of the handshake, I suggest looking at where the palms are facing in the handshake. This will tell you so much more. See Table 2.6 for a list of various types of handshakes and their meanings.

Table 2.6   The Meanings Behind Types of Handshakes

Gesture	Possible Inference(s)	Rationale
Handshake—palm down	Dominance	If you shake someone's hand firmly and slightly turn their palm down, you're expressing dominance. (You have the "upper hand.")
Handshake—palm up	Submission, accommodating	This method is typically used with a weak handshake, where your palm has been placed in a submissive, palm-up position by the other person's dominant hand.

(continues)

Table 2.6 The Meanings Behind Types of Handshakes (continued)

Gesture	Possible Inference(s)	Rationale
Handshake—equal and vertical	Nonthreatening, relaxed	This is typical of most hand-shakes, when no one seeks to dominate or submit to the other person.
Pumping handshake	Enthusiasm	A vigorous pumping handshake tends to indicate energy and enthusiasm.
Weak handshake	Various	Avoid the common view that a weak handshake is the sign of a weak or submissive person because it does not indicate this. Weak handshakes can be due to various aspects of personality, mood, and so on.
Firm handshake	Outward confidence	Firm handshakes are a sign of outward confidence, which could mask deceit or could indicate a strong person.
Handshake with arm clasp or holding onto the handshake	Seeking control, care	When a handshake is accompanied by the left hand clasping the other person's arm or covering the handshake, this can indicate a desire to control something. It can also mean the person is adding an extra gesture of caring.

Source: Adapted/paraphrased with permission from Businessballs.com/body-language.htm (2014).

Legs and Feet

The direction of our legs and feet provides some insight to our (and other's) feelings and moods. It is important to take into consideration that when sitting for long periods of time, it's natural for people to change their positions. As with other body language gestures, you should not judge others by the way they are sitting at any one time; instead, assess a person's posture as a whole based on the conversation. Leg gestures tend to be supported by corresponding arm signals, so review both body parts. For example, a person may cross the arms and legs for comfort reasons, but that posture may also indicate detachment or disinterest (Body language, n.d.; Driver, 2010). See Table 2.7 for a list of various leg and feet gestures and their meanings.

Table 2.7   The Meanings Behind Gestures With the Legs and Feet

Gesture	Possible Inference(s)	Rationale
Leg direction	Interest, attentiveness (according to direction)	When we are seated and interested in someone or something, the direction our feet or knees are pointing reflects where our interest is. The opposite is also true in that if our legs or knees are pointing away from something or someone, we consider them uninteresting or threatening.
Uncrossed legs in a wide, sitting position (men)	Openness	In sitting positions, men who have their legs uncrossed generally are expressing an open attitude.
Legs together in parallel position, sitting (women)	Properness	The posture is common in women who have been taught to follow traditional rules of etiquette. To many, this is the proper posture for a lady.

(continues)

Table 2.7   The Meanings Behind Gestures With the Legs and
                Feet   (continued)

Gesture	Possible Inference(s)	Rationale
Crossed legs, sitting (general)	Caution, disinterest	Crossed legs tend to indicate a degree of caution or disinterest which can be due to various reasons, ranging from feeling threatened to mild insecurity. However, many women naturally sit like this, so the key here is to pay attention to the direction of the knee. Typically, the direction of the knee will be in alignment to what the person views as most interesting (whether that is a person or even the door).
"Figure-4" leg cross	Independent, stubborn	The "Figure-4" leg cross entails the supporting leg being crossed just above the knee by the ankle or lower calf of the crossing leg. This makes a figure-4 shape. This posture portrays confidence. It exposes the pelvic area and typically causes the upper body to lean back.
"Figure-4" leg cross with hand clamp	Resistant, stubborn	Adding a hand (or hands) clamped around the knee in the plain figure-4 leg cross produces a locked, defensive, or resistant gesture.
Open legs, sitting (men)	Arrogance, combative, sexual posturing	This posture can be considered aggressive or arrogant because it requires more space to sit and makes the person appear bigger. This position could also just be physically comfortable for larger men.
Ankle lock, sitting	Defensiveness	Clasping one's ankles tightly around each other displays a defensive or uptight/nervous gesture.

Wide leg standing	Shield or protect	Standing with wide-apart legs creates a foundation to shield or protect and gives the appearance of a broad body frame. Placing the hands on the hips enhances this impression, as in a prominent Superman pose (described in Table 2.5).
Standing "at attention"	Respectful	Standing upright, legs straight, together, and parallel, body quite upright, with shoulders back and arms by the sides gives the appearance of the military "at attention" frame, which is considered respectful.
Legs inter-weaved, sitting (woman)	Insecurity, sexual posing	This tightly crossed leg is twined or wrapped around the other leg. This can be a sign of insecurity or protection. Some women may sit like this to appear long and lean.
Legs crossed, standing (scissor stance)	Insecurity, submission, engagement	Where legs are crossed and arms are not, this can indicate a submissive or steadfast agreement to stand. It can also show you're engaged, when your arms aren't crossed in front. Scissor legs can also give a shapely silhouette, hence why many celebrities and models pose like this for the paparazzi.
Feet or foot direction or pointing	Foot direction indicates direction of interest	As discussed in the knee section, the feet tend to point toward the focus of interest (or away from people or things that are not interesting). In group dynamics, if people position themselves in a triangle, or 45-degree angle, with their feet pointed outward, they are open to others joining them. When feet are directly pointing to one another, it gives the impression they are not open to others joining them.

(continues)

Table 2.7　The Meanings Behind Gestures With the Legs and Feet　(continued)

Gesture	Possible Inference(s)	Rationale
Foot forward, standing	Directed toward dominant group member	This signal can reveal a lot because it is such a small gesture. People typically direct their feet toward the person they consider the most dominant person of the group. If one foot is facing out, this may reveal the person is ready to move away from the conversation.
Shoe-play	Flirting, boredom, "My shoe just hurts!"	In certain situations dangling our shoes or slipping our feet in and out of our shoes has a sexual overtone or can even convey boredom. However, it can also simply mean that our feet are aching, and we need to relieve some of the pain while sitting.

Source: Adapted/paraphrased with permission from Businessballs.com/body-language.htm (2014).

Personal Space

Does it bother you when people stand too close to you? The amount of personal space between people can depend on many variables, such as the individual, the social norms of the culture, the situation, and the relationship between people. When personal space is violated, it can cause friction, and sometimes this violation is due to ignorance of or lack of thought about the personal space given. Hall (1966) stated there are five distinct space zones, as described in Table 2.8.

Table 2.8   The Five Space Zones

Zone	Distance	Indication	Rationale
Close intimate	0–6 inches	Lovers, married people	This is often seen when we are face-to-face with someone and are likely to kiss.
Intimate	6–18 inches	Close relation-ships	This is appropriate with our intimate relationships and close friendships. This is felt to be very threatening and invasive by people who are not in such relation-ships. Permission is often needed in order to be considered "comfortable" to both parties.
Personal	18 inches to 4 feet	Family, friends of significance	We can give a simple handshake in this zone, but then we need to take a step back.
Social	4–12 feet	Social or busi-ness casual	We can give a handshake at this zone if we reach in a little toward each other (and we don't have to step back).
Public	More than 12 feet	Private or ignoring	We do this when we are trying to avoid interaction with others who are nearby.

Source: Hall (1966).

Sometimes others may "invade" your personal space to the point of making you extremely uncomfortable. And when this invasion is of a sexual inference, this unwelcomed or uninvited gesture or conversation is known as sexual harassment. Sexual harassment is prohibited in the workplace, and anyone who feels he or she is a victim of sexual harassment may take legal action. It is important to note that *unwelcome* does not mean "involuntary." For example, many victims are fearful of retribution. Victims may choose to engage in this "unwelcomed" behavior due to fear of physical harm, job loss, or retaliation (Leskinen, Cortina & Kabat, 2011). Script 2.1 shows you how to address someone who may be making unwelcome advances.

Script 2.1 What to say when . . . you feel you are being sexually harassed.

Tell

> I need to talk to you about a serious matter, immediately and in private. Do you have a moment?

Explain

> There are times I feel very uncomfortable around you, specifically when you touch my arms or constantly rub my shoulders when you're talking to me.

Lead by example

The person apologizes:

Wow, I didn't realize this would make you so uncomfortable. I am sorry.

Your response:

I accept your apology; however, there is no excuse for your behavior. I expect you will keep your hands to yourself from this point forward.

The person undermines your accusations:

Are you kidding me? You are taking this way out of context! Don't flatter yourself.

Your response:

I thought you might respond this way, so I have an outline prepared to take to HR.

Learn the consequence

The person apologizes:

I will be sure not to touch you again. I didn't realize this was an issue.

Your response:

Thank you. Please know, if you touch me inappropriately again, I will be handing HR a log of your prior behavior, including this conversation.

The person undermines your accusations:

Oh, please. You have no evidence. It will be a 'he-said, she-said' issue.

Your response:

I'm going to let HR handle this. (Exit immediately)

Your Road Map: Improving Body Language Messaging and Interpretations

Improving body language messaging and interpretations is important because it can reveal what isn't being said. For example, have you ever wished you knew what the person was really thinking because the dichotomy of their words and actions told you something didn't make sense? I'll bet you have given others this impression at one time or another as well. Here are a few tips and tricks to help you become more engaging in conversations and to better understand what others may not be saying:

- Do not jump to conclusions. Consider all verbal and nonverbal body language gestures before you make absolute inferences.

- Motivate yourself. Becoming better at reading and enacting body language takes a great deal of time, effort, and dedication. You have to be highly motivated and want to learn.

- Practice. It is critically important that you practice how it is you want to appear to others. Practice this in both simulated (watch yourself in a mirror) and in real-world environments (take mental notes in real-time conversations).

- Know the "naughty bits" rule. How much of the pelvis area are you showing others or is someone showing you? Showing or not showing this region of the body displays the level of confidence one has for the person or situation (Driver, 2010). For example, if you (or the person you're talking to) cover this area with your hands (such as when one stands with a hand-over-top-of-hand stance), you might be indicating you're uncomfortable or you have apprehension about something or someone.

- Apply the Question-Wait-Question (QWQ) formula. Driver (2010) introduced the QWQ formula. This is a helpful formula to ensure there is two-way communication. This formula enables you to use active listening and encourages the other person to share more information. Powerful people acknowledge that sharing too much personal knowledge can actually make them look weak, so they encourage the recipient to speak more than them (Driver, 2010). Maria Shriver, at the University of Southern California's Annenberg School commencement ceremony, spoke about the "power of the pause." She explained we need to take more time to pause in conversations so we learn more from others. It is important to breathe and listen more, in lieu of stepping on people's words (Shriver, 2012).

- Use the belly button rule. Driver (2010) explains that the position of one person's belly button in relation to the other person is a great indicator of his or her interest level. For example, if a person is talking to you but has his or her belly button turned toward someone or something else, the person may not be as interested in your conversation as their words may indicate. This tip really helps you understand if a person is engaged or disengaged in your conversation.

- Look for divergence. Body language should align with the words used. For example, are you saying to someone "yes" with words while moving your head from side to side "no"? Maybe this means you don't know how to say no.

- Be a sly copycat. When body language and speech are mirrored, or copied off of one another, we establish rapport in our conversations. Mirrored body language encourages feelings of trust, and it connects people on another level because it generates an unconscious feeling of affirmation (Body language, n.d.; Driver, 2010). For example, when people display body language similar to our own, we unconsciously feel, "This person is very similar to me and agrees with me. I like this person because we are similar." The opposite effect applies to body language gestures that are not mirrored. People feel less like each other, and the engagement is less comfortable. Each person senses conflict arising because unconscious signals are mismatched. Mismatched signals can translate into unconscious feelings of disconnect, discomfort, or even rejection. The unconscious mind may perceive, "This person is not like me. I feel defensive and cautious."

- Stand confidently. You know what you want to say, but your listener doesn't. Regardless of what you say, be cognizant of your proximity to the person and the positioning of your eyes, hands, legs, mouth, and naughty bits (Body language, n.d.; Driver, 2010).

- Tone your tone. Keep your tone appropriate to the conversation. Similar to mirroring, bringing your tone down will signal others to do so as well (Driver, 2010). (See Chapter 3 on emotional intelligence.)

- Stay in the moment. Look people in the eye when you talk. Give appropriate eye contact when speaking and while listening.

- Stay in control. Stay judicious of how you position your body. When you are nervous, try not to let it show by looking uptight. Similarly, don't look so lackadaisical that you appear aloof.

- Consider what isn't being said. You can determine how effectual your conversation is by examining the listener's posture and eye contact and where they place their hands and feet during the conversation.

- Put your game face on. Some people are better at "poker faces" than others. Even if your words are appropriate in a heated conversation, make sure your eyes aren't rolling upward or you're sighing because you are really angry, bored, or frustrated (and you don't want others to know).

- Go with your gut. Don't disdain your instincts. If you feel something isn't right, you may be correct. Try to focus on the motive or why someone would be giving mismatched signals. Are they hiding something?

- Defy deception. Some people have the art of artificially controlling their outward body language to give the impression they want to create at the time. For example, a firm handshake or direct eye contact are signals that can easily be faked (Body language, n.d.; Driver, 2010).

Improving your body language messaging and interpretations will allow you to stay in control of the message you intend to deliver as well as help you to decipher what others aren't saying. A little knowledge about the subconscious can be extremely powerful, whether you are trying to involve others in conversations or simply trying to understand them.

Pulling It All Together With the CAR Framework

Now that you have a better understanding of what body gestures may be revealing and how you can use this information for improved conversations, let's organize what we learned about body messaging and interpreting using the CAR framework:

Consider	Did you assess several different body language gestures throughout the whole conversation? And did you consider it as an aggregate rather than as one body part at a time?
Action or call to action	List all the body language gestures you noted (either in yourself or in someone else) and compare them with the possible inferences described in the tables presented earlier in this chapter.
Return on investment	Did the body language match the situation, and what was said? If yes, your return on investment (ROI) was successful. If no, ask more questions in a follow-up conversation. Using the QWQ formula can help elicit more information in the follow-up conversation. This formula enforces active listening because waiting (silence) encourages a person to speak or share more information. For example, when there is a pause during conversations, we normally interpret this as our cue to speak. Silence in conversations

can be very awkward, so the power of pausing and waiting for others to reply can be extremely helpful in motiving others to talk.

time to reflect

Imagine a conversation in the break room where a male nurse is sitting across from a female nurse. His arms are crossed, and he is covering his neck. The man's feet are turned slightly away from the female nurse, toward the window. The woman's feet are directly facing the man, and she appears to be offering him information. Without having any knowledge about the conversation itself, who do you think has control of this conversation by just looking at the body gestures? If you answered the female nurse, you are correct. Who do you think feels uncomfortable or threatened? If you answered the man, you are correct.

Getting the Results You Want

Whether I am presenting at speaking engagements, caring for patients, or coaching my staff, I remain keen to my body language positioning. Certain circumstances warrant certain gestures. For example, if I have a large audience that I am about to speak to, I sometimes need to boost my confidence a tad. So prior to walking on stage, I hold my body in the high-power Superman-like pose. I lean back slightly to open my chest and place my hands on my head with my elbows out to the side for a few minutes while taking slow breaths. This posture stimulates higher levels of testosterone in my body. You may recall that testosterone is a hormone associated with power and dominance, and it suppresses cortisol, the stress hormone. In other words, simply opening my chest by placing my hands on head while taking slow breaths reduces the stress, or butterflies, I may have prior to presenting.

When I want to motivate my patients, staff, or audience to participate in my conversations, I listen! I don't multitask. I don't check my watch, email, texts, or missed calls. I focus on them by directing my belly button and feet toward them, and I make eye contact with them. I am respectful of the distance I stand from them, and I lean toward them when possible. I nod occasionally and use the head-tilt gesture to either display that I'm confused (my eyes are also squeezed together) or I'm interested in more (eyes open and raised). My arms are held wide and never crossed in front of my chest, unless I choose to drive in a nonverbal response to what I'm hearing.

I always like to encourage collaboration in my conversations. To do this, I make sure there are no barriers in our way. For example, I don't stand behind a water cooler and talk over it. I walk away from podiums; I sit next to people, at a safe distance, when possible; and I don't cover my naughty bits with my hands. If I am holding a slide advancer, I make sure it is to my side, not across my body in a defensive/protective way. If I do have to hold something, such as a chart or book, I also make sure I hold it at waist level. (To me, the higher people hold objects to their chest, the more insecure they appear.) I use my hands a lot when I speak. I carry them in an open manner, with forearms facing up, or I use finger steepling.

When I want to place emphasis on something I said, I pause and then place my hands on my hips, as in a Superman-like pose. I may also lightly fold my hands in front of me, parallel to my waist—keeping my folded hands just above my belly button yet below my chest—when I walk around the room. I bounce my folded hands in an up and down position to the same rhythm that I am speaking in order to emphasize important points. It's amazing the amount of emphasis you can place on your conversations when you move or don't move your hands. When addressing questions from the group, I also make sure my feet are in a triangular position so that others feel welcomed into the conversation, as appropriate.

If I am going to have a conversation with someone new, I smile genuinely to them and offer a firm handshake with my palm facing to the side. I always give a firm handshake with a slight squeeze at the end as I repeat the person's name. (Side note: I repeat the name for my benefit, not theirs. It simply helps me remember it.) Another tidbit I often use to help my memory is to make sure my arms and legs are unfolded when I'm listening. Pease and Pease (2006) found that when a group of volunteers sat with their arms and legs unfolded during a lecture, they remembered 38% more than a group that attended the same lecture and sat with folded arms and legs.

When I agree with what people are saying, I'm a copycat at heart. In other words, I mirror their body positioning and/or the speed of their voice. I truly believe this makes people feel understood and respected. When I don't like or trust what people are saying, I hone in on the microgestures, such as feet placement, eye directions, and other small facial expressions.

When my students carry a conversation too far and I am trying to redirect them, instead of yelling over them, I begin to speak while keeping my voice low. If I speak in the same monotone that I would if I kept my lips closed and said, "Um-hum," in an authoritative manner, I sound stern, but not threatening, and I get a better response than I do when I try to excitedly say, "OK, everyone, settle down. OK, shhhhhh!!!"

time to reflect

One way to mirror is with the speed of your voice. The next time you have a discussion with a family member or friend, try to first match the pace of their speaking and then gently change your pace—either slower or faster—to see if the other person follows you. Try this multiple times, but not in an obvious way. Subtle changes in tone are far more genuine than changing your tone in an inappropriate, awkward manner.

Changing the speed of your conversation is also a great way to approach conflict. Think of a time when you were very angry with someone or about something. You might have been yelling and so hot that steam was coming from your ears. Think about how you would have felt when someone else, who wasn't the cause of your anger, approached you.

Would it have made a difference to you if you had been approached by someone with a nonthreatening, very soft, and mild-mannered voice who said, "Calm down. I'm here to help you," or would a mild-mannered voice have angered you even more? Would you initially have thought, "This person just doesn't get it"? Or are you someone who would have related better to someone who said, "Calm down! I'm here to help you," in a voice that mirrored your ranting but was nonthreatening and genuine? Think about it.

By focusing on your verbal and nonverbal language when communicating with others, you can better direct the conversation toward getting the results you want. We only have a small window of opportunity to leave a good impression, so we must learn how to control our nonverbal gestures.

The Drive Home

Let's review the *driving it back home* pointers from this chapter:

- Body language signals are relative.

- Body language gestures can have different meanings to various people and in various settings.

- It is important to be aware that just because someone looks to the left or to the right doesn't mean they are being creative or recalling facts; you need to be aware of all subtle and not-so-subtle hand, eye, and body posturing.

- Collecting and analyzing all the body language cues provides a much more impressive and accurate depiction of what's not being said than focusing on one body gesture only.

- Body language is about constantly being mindful of the signals people are giving.

- Body language is not just reading the signals in other people. It enables us to have better self-awareness and self-control. Body language helps us understand thoughts and feelings in ourselves and in others.

- Microgestures are small gestures such as contracted pupils, eyebrow lifts, and twitches at the corner of the mouth. These microgestures help us to make more informed interpretations of what others are feeling. Remember, we cannot control them; therefore, they are extremely useful in reading body language.

- Mirroring, or being a copycat, is not simply mimicking someone. Mirroring is the ability to position your body similarly to that of the other person in order to help them feel more comfortable with you.

References

Aristotle. (n.d.). Retrieved from https://www.goodreads.com/quotes/20103-the-whole-is-greater-than-the-sum-of-its-parts

Body language. (n.d). Retrieved from http://www.businessballs.com/body-language.htm

Bolton, R. & Bolton, D. G. (2009). *People styles at work—and beyond: Making bad relationships good and good relationships better.* AMACOM.

Driver, J. (2010). *You say more than you think: A 7-day plan for using the new body language to get what you want!* New York, NY: Crown Publishers.

Drucker, P. (n.d.). Retrieved from http://www.brainyquote.com/quotes/authors/p/peter_drucker.html

Hall, E. T. (1966). *The hidden dimension.* New York, NY: Anchor Books.

Leskinen, E. A., Cortina, L. M., & Kabat, D. B. (2011). Gender harassment: broadening our understanding of sex-based harassment at work. *Law and Human Behavior, 35*(1), 25–39. doi: 10.1007/s10979-010-9241-5

Mehrabian, A. (1972). *Nonverbal communication.* New Brunswick: Aldine Transaction.

Mehrabian, A. (1981). *Silent messages: Implicit communication of emotions and attitudes.* Belmont, CA: Wadsworth.

Merrill, D. W. and Reid, R. H. (1999). *Personal styles and effective performance.* New York, NY: CRC Press.

Pease, B., & Pease, A. (2006). *The definitive book on body language.* New York, NY: Bantam.

Shriver, M. (2012). USC Annenberg School of Communication Commencement speech. Retrieved from https://www.youtube.com/watch?v=A5xLcLIIXg.U

TRACOM. (1991). The social style profile—Technical report: Development, reliability and validity. Denver, CO: Author.

Trigon System Consultants. (n.d.) Retrieved from http://www.softed.com/Resources/Docs/SSW0.4.pdf

3

The Emotionally Intelligent and Emotionally Competent Nurse

Did you know your emotions have a physical basis in the brain? This phenomenon can best be explained by understanding the way the brain processes emotions (see Figure 3.1). Typically, when one of our five senses receives an external stimulus, it sends the signal to the thalamus where the signal is deciphered in the visual cortex. The visual cortex analyzes and categorizes the information and sends the signal to the neocortex, which is the "thinking" brain that helps us to problem solve, strategize, and analyze information. From the neocortex, the signal is sent to the amygdala, which is commonly known as the brain's emotional command center. The amygdala organizes behavioral, autonomic, and hormonal responses to a variety of situations, including those emotions that produce disgust, fear, or anger. In addition, it plays a role in processing odors and pheromones, which are associated with our sexual and maternal behaviors. Stimulation of the amygdala leads to emotional responses (Goleman, 1998).

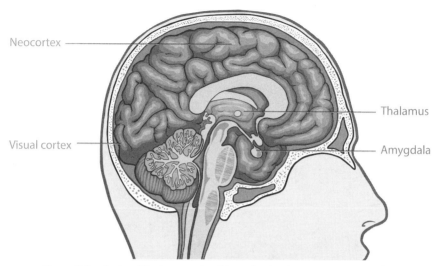

Figure 3.1   A simplified example of how the brain processes emotions

When an external stimulus triggers emotions, it sends the signal from the external stimulus directly to the amygdala. This happens before the brain can process the signal into a rational response. For example, you walk into your patient's room—a patient who just had leg surgery—and see the color red all over the foot of the bed. Your heart starts pumping hard; you're nervous, shaking, and panicking. You're thinking "Oh no! The patient is bleeding out!" This "oh-no" feeling can happen within a few milliseconds! This knee-jerk reaction happened before you could rationally process it. Basically, you were a victim to your amygdala being hijacked! In this example, by the time you calm yourself down and assess the situation, you realize the patient, who *was* resting comfortably prior to you entering her room, is now, based on your response, just as panicked as you. Your response triggered such strong and quick emotions that it didn't allow time for the family to explain to you that they passed a large cup of red juice over the foot of the bed and accidently spilled it.

Intense emotions are a physiologic, neurologic response to tenacious stimuli. Note what your emotions are telling you so you can learn to manage your reactions (before you respond irrationally). This will help you to regulate your emotions and stay poised and under control (Goleman, 1995).

Emotional intelligence (EI) pulls from numerous segments of emotional, behavioral, and communications theories, such as neuro-linguistic programming. By developing our EI, we can become more productive and efficacious at what we do. We help others to be more productive and successful, too. The method and results of EI development contain many rudiments known to reduce stress for individuals and organizations, which include reducing conflict, cultivating relationships, and increasing continuity and synchronization (Delcourt, Gremler, Van Riel, & Van Birgelen, 2013). EI also plays a significant role in our ability to have critical conversations. For example, an emotionally intelligent person is less opt to lash out at someone, even when that person is inappropriately yelling at them. This is because a person with EI is aware of his or her feelings, and this awareness controls the temptation to yell back.

The Driver's Seat: Understanding Your Emotions and Your Intelligence

Lazarus (1991) describes emotions as brief events or "episodes" that we direct toward someone or something in response to how we feel about people, situations, or outcomes. We experience joy, fear, anger, and other emotional episodes as they relate to tasks, customers, coworkers, patients, or even something like a new electronic medical record (EMR). Emotions also stem from our experiences. Emotions can change our physiological conditions, such as blood pressure, heart rate, and perspiration, as well as cause changes in our behavior. Behavioral changes can include facial expression, tone of voice, and eye movement. These emotional reactions are involuntary and often occur unconsciously. (See Chapter 2 for more information.)

Working With People Means Working With Emotions

We all come to work dealing with emotions that stem from situations that happen in our personal lives. These emotions can include anger, sadness, and joyfulness, to name a few. For some nurses, they can set their personal emotions aside and not allow these feelings to interfere with the new emotions placed on them during work. Paradoxically, there are those nurses who just can't seem to separate the emotions that they bring to work from the emotions that arise during the course of their work day. Whether nurses separate their work emotions from their personal emotions or not, there are limitations to each. For example, if a nurse shows up to work angry because her husband forgot to take out the trash and now their garage will smell horrifically for the party they have coming up, this anger maybe wrongfully displaced on a colleague by yelling at them over an issue that they normally would have been more rational about. On the other hand, if a nurse leaves her anger behind, she may appear rigid or stoic when a colleague comes to her about an issue.

Increasing EI in the healthcare setting means acknowledging that emotions will always surface, and you not only need to be aware of them, but you also need to do something smart with them. People vary immensely in the skill with which they use and react to their emotions, as well as others' emotions. This is very important when placed in a leadership position. Godse and Thingujam (2010) posited a strong relationship between EI and transformational leadership, and EI and conflict resolution and effective management. Case in point, the unit nurse leader may be a genius in IV skills or critical-thinking skills, but a failure in terms of managing staff.

Sadly, negative emotions are often found in healthcare organizations, so it is important we learn how to cope with such feelings. After all, negative emotions can be contagious and even metastasize throughout the organization faster than you can take someone's pulse. Know what situations cause your negative emotions so when they surface, you can implement a strategy to disrupt the cycle. The earlier you adopt a strategy, the easier it becomes to move past it.

Is Being Emotionally Intelligent Enough? The Need for Emotional Competency

Emotionally intelligent people are clearly adept in identifying emotions, but having EI isn't enough. You not only need to have emotional intelligence, but you also need to be emotionally competent. What is the difference? Clearly put, emotional competence (EC) is the application of EI, whereas EI is the ability to identify emotions (not always applying it). Emotional competence describes a person's ability to express emotions in real time. Although this term stems from EI, emotional competence determines a person's ability to connect effectively and consistently with others. (Goleman, 1998).

A person who has emotional intelligence "knows" about the different personality styles. Conversely, a person who has emotional intelligence and competence knows and applies certain techniques to cultivate better relationships (see Table 3.1).

Table 3.1   Using the Social Style Model to Foster Relationships

Social Style	How to Connect Better With This Group
Driver Styles	Allow them control in decision-making.
	Focus on results and efficiency.
	Remain objective.
Analytical Styles	Provide factual and detailed information.
	Don't rush them.
	Support their reasoning.
Expressive Styles	Express enthusiasm.
	Be accepting of the relationship they are trying to build with you.
	Give compliments and praise.

(continues)

Table 3.1   Using the Social Style Model to Foster
             Relationships   (continued)

Social Style	How to Connect Better With This Group
Amiable Styles	Be sensitive.
	Be sensitive to them.
	Ask them open-ended questions. Otherwise, they will try to answer you based on how you want them to answer.

Sources: Social Styles (n.d.); Merrill & Reed (1999).

The Impact of Emotional Intelligence and Emotional Competence on the Healthcare Environment

Using EI in healthcare is vital because it gives awareness to the importance of introspection. For example, when your nursing supervisor assumes all the credit for your hard work on the unit, your first emotional response might be anger or irritation. If you "turn on" your emotional intelligence and competence, though, you can venture into your conscious mind and think about a healthier reaction than anger. A more respectable approach may be to assert your right for the credit you deserve (see Script 3.1).

Understanding and applying EI is very powerful because it will help you stay in control of your emotions. Although your subconscious is automated with immediate responses, your conscious mind can redirect it into a more positive manner.

Godse and Thingujam (2010) state that there is a link between EI, employee retention, and good fiscal stewardship. According to American Association of Colleges of Nursing (AACN, 2012)

> It is expected that the number of employed nurses will grow from 2.74 million in 2010 to 3.45 million in 2020, an increase of 712,000 or 26%. The projections further explain the need for 495,500 replacements in the nursing workforce bringing the total number of job opening for nurses due to growth and replacements to 1.2 million by 2020. (para 3)

If it costs up to $100,000 to recruit, orient, and backfill a nursing position with overtime or agency use (depending on the specialty), then a hospital staffed with only 200 nurses can expect to spend millions per year on new hires (Blake, 2006). An emotional competence and stress reduction program can cut turnover by almost 50% (Cherniss & Goleman, 2001). Emotional competencies are reported to be better predictors of workplace success and should be counted more heavily than one's intellectual ability score (Goleman, 2007). Research has shown the following EI success stories:

- The Hay Group reported that 44 Fortune 500 companies discovered that sales people who scored high in EI doubled their revenue compared to those with mediocre EI scores.

- Rozell, Pettijohn, and Parker (2002) found correlation between EI and work performance in a sample of people who sold medical devices. In this study, EI was a reliable predictor of who had high work performance.

- A large metropolitan hospital implemented EI assessments and, within 18 months, decreased the critical care nursing attrition from 65% to 15% (Petrides & Sevdalis, 2010).

- The Johnson & Johnson Consumer & Personal Care Group (JJC&PC Group) conducted a global study of 358 of its managers to determine if there were certain leadership skills and competencies that differentiated high-performing managers from average managers. Results of this study demonstrated that managers with high EI competencies were better performing managers (Cavallo & Brienza, 2001).

Script 3.1 What to say when... you need to tell your supervisor someone else took credit for your work.

Tell

To your nurse manager:

Tony, I would like to speak with you about something a little uncomfortable. I am very supportive of teamwork, so I am concerned when my colleagues don't work well as a team. When is a good time to meet?

Your nurse manager is supportive:

Sure, let's meet now.

Your nurse manager downplays your concern:

You know, I don't like tattletales and other juvenile behavior. We are a team, after all.

Explain

Your response:

Specifically, I am concerned about Connie's comments in today's meeting when she said her abstract was accepted for podium presentation at this year's regional Nursing Excellence conference.

Your response:

I agree we are a team. As a member of the team, I don't like it when hard work is not recognized or when it is undermined. Team members shouldn't disrespect their teammates.

Lead by example

Your nurse manager is supportive:

Right. What is the problem?

Your response:

I came up with the abstract's idea a few months ago. I told Connie all about my idea in hopes of working with her on this, but she said my idea wasn't strong enough to submit for the conference. I have a few emails here to show you I originated the idea. I'm sad that she took my idea and didn't include me in her plans. I feel betrayed. And I thought it was important that you knew the truth.

Your nurse manager is unsupportive:

I'm sure Connie didn't mean to disrespect you. You also have to consider she could have built upon your original idea, making it completely different.

Your response:

I told Connie all about my idea in hopes to work with her on this, but she said my idea wasn't strong enough to submit for the conference. I have a few emails here to show you I originated the idea, and that was the idea she submitted. I'm sad that she took my idea and didn't include me in her plans. I feel betrayed. And I thought it was important that you knew how much work I put into this. I just wanted you to be aware of her behavior and my contributions.

Learn the consequence

Your nurse manager is receptive:

I'll speak with Connie if you'd like. I'm sorry you were slighted."

Your response:

Thank you for listening and for you support. I would like to have a meeting with you and Connie to discuss this.

Your nurse manager is unreceptive:

I think you're taking this out of context. It's not that big of a deal.

Your response:

I'm concerned other nurses may not submit ideas in the future because the unit is working in silos and there's an unhealthy atmosphere of competitiveness.

How Is EI Measured?

Several tests are available to measure EI, and each focuses on different categories. Some of these EI tests include Emotional and Social Competency Inventory (ESCI), Mayer-Salovey-Caruso Emotional Intelligence Test (MSCEIT), Six Seconds Emotional Intelligence Test (SEI), and Emotional Quotient Inventory 2.0 (EQ-i 2.0).

- **Emotional and Social Competency Inventory (ESCI) by Hay Group.** Using Goleman's model, the ECSI measures a spectrum of critical competencies shown to affect workplace performance. The ECSI is a "multi-rater," so the test-taker receives feedback from several people. The ESCI is the latest version of the original Emotional Competency Inventory (ECI) by Richard Boyatzis and Daniel Goleman (Sixseconds, 2011).

- **Mayer-Salovey-Caruso Emotional Intelligence Test (MSCEIT).** The MSCEIT measures one's ability to identify, use, understand, know, and solve emotional problems by asking a series of objective questions. This testing measures the intelligence behind the emotions of perceiving, using, understanding, and managing feelings. The MSCEIT test is considered an "ability test." In other words, it evaluates responses according to a criterion of correctness in lieu of self-assessments (Sixseconds, 2011).

- **Six Seconds Emotional Intelligence Test (SEI).** This test measures eight basic skills, such as emotional literacy, navigating emotions, intrinsic motivation, and empathy (Sixseconds, 2011, para 5).

- **Emotional Quotient Inventory 2.0 (EQ-i 2.0).** EQ i 2.0 is a newer tool based on the EQ i by Reuven Bar On. This new tool measures self-perception, self-expression, decision-making, and stress management.

EI Versus the Myers-Briggs Type Indicator

Emotions, thoughts, and behaviors determine a person's unique personality. Personality refers to biases in how one behaves, for example, if they prefer to be around people or not. It doesn't; however, identify their thinking patterns like EI does. EI identifies the thinking patterns behind the decisions made (Goleman, 2007). In the Myers-Briggs Testing Indicator (MBTI), there are four psychological scales used (Myers, McCaulley, Quenk, & Hammer, 1998):

- **Extroversion–Introversion:** This describes the energy flow of an individual. For example, people who are extroverts receive energy from being actively involved in events. They like to be around people and feel they energize other people. Extroverts enjoy action and are forerunners in making things happen. They understand a problem more efficiently when they can talk out loud about it and when others include their thoughts and perceptions. On the other hand, Introverts prefer self-examination and self-discovery. These individuals tend to conceal their feelings. Introverts prefer to work alone, and they learn better by watching others rather than participating (Myers, McCaulley, Quenk, & Hammer, 1998).

- **Sensing–Intuition:** This describes how people learn information. Sensing people use their five physical senses (sight, hearing, touch, taste, and smell) to understand things. Sensing people relish real-life examples and hands-on applications. They learn best when they can first see the pragmatic side of what is being taught. Intuitive people rely on an unconscious reasoning that propels them to do something without telling us why or how, also known as a gut instinct. They learn based on their feelings. Intuitive people tend to use their imagination in order to understand and learn things (Myers, McCaulley, Quenk, & Hammer, 1998).

- **Thinking–Feeling:** This describes how people make decisions and choices. Thinking people use logic, objective principles, and impersonal facts. Thinking people will ask the question, "Why?" and analyze the pros and cons. They tend to be consistent and logical in making choices. Feeling people prefer harmony and do their best to help others. They make their

best decisions by weighing what other people care about and always consider others' points-of-view (Myers, McCaulley, Quenk, & Hammer, 1998).

- **Judging–Perceiving:** This describes how people deal with the world. Judging people prefer an orderly way of life and like to have things settled and
  organized. They like control, structure, rules, and organization. Perceiving
  people prefer a flexible and spontaneous way of life. They like to understand and adapt to situations rather than organize them. Perceiving people
  are flexible, are open to new experiences, and like to explore (Myers, Mc-
  Caulley, Quenk, & Hammer, 1998).

Personality tests typically distinguish only these four categories of temperament.
This is important to understand because they do not measure how someone's
behavior is portrayed. Specifically, let's look at a nurse who is interviewing for
a sales position for a medical device company. The owner of the medical sales
company knows he wants a nurse who exemplifies an extrovert personality to
fill the sales position, but he cannot tell from a temperament test which nurse
will be *persistent* from those who would be perceived as *insistent*. It is more
desirable for sales people to have persistence, as this is described as having
the energy, drive, and thick skin to develop and close new business. It is less
desirable to have an insistent sales person, or one who may turn off prospective
buyers because they are too pushy or just cannot stop calling on someone who
is simply not interested.

Let's pretend you need to hire a nurse for a role that requires one to have the
characteristics of an extrovert, sensor, thinker, and judger (ESTJ). Although this
person (ESTJ) will be outgoing, pragmatic, and consistent and use logic when
making decisions, we don't know from their MBTI if they would turn draconian
and mutilate anyone they interact with when they are faced with problems and
stress. We cannot predict behaviors based on personalities. We all know people
who are fun, energetic, and outgoing; however, that doesn't necessarily equate
that they will be successful in the workplace. Even people who are energetic
and fun can make errors in judgment due to their behaviors when making
decisions. They can wind up handling situations in a very aggressive approach,
which can be intimidating to others. This can turn an organization's culture of

safety into a culture of fear. As an example, have you ever worked with a nurse leader who is typically fun and energetic, but when someone or something goes awry, you know you better hide because their emotional outbreak is coming? It's crazy how some nurse leaders transition from the good to the bad and to the ugly—and without any time for the rest of us to take cover! This example helps to explain why people with similar personality styles can't successfully perform the same job. The MBTI does not measure emotional intelligence (Thompson, 2006).

An employee with high EI and EC can manage emotions well, communicate effectively, lead change, solve problems, and use humor to build rapport when faced with adversity. These people also embody genuine empathy, remain optimistic, and are talented at educating and influencing others. They have a unique ability to maintain their composure in chaotic situations, and this is what often separates high performers from low performers.

time to reflect

As a staff nurse, manager, or nurse executive, you might have asked yourself some of the following questions:

- Why do certain nurses seem to get into more accidents than others?

- Why do some nurses ignore the policies and procedures in the organization?

- Why do some nurses use illegal drugs during work?

- Why do some nurses cause confrontation and issues?

- Why do some nurses have higher patient satisfaction recognition whereas other clinically competent nurses struggle to build any type of rapport with patients (even though they seem to genuinely try)?

Think about it. In many cases, the answer lies in the nurses' EI and EC IQs rather than their personality types.

≣REAL WORLD | EI, PATIENT SATISFACTION, AND
PHYSICIAN BURNOUT

Using a multisource data collection, Weng et al. (2011) "…assessed the factors
associated with job satisfaction. It found that higher EI was significantly associated with less burnout and higher job satisfaction. In addition, less burnout was
not only associated with higher levels of patient satisfaction, but also with higher
levels of job satisfaction" (p. 841).

Your Road Map: Improving Your Emotional Intelligence and Emotional Competence

Did you know IQ peaks around age 17 and remains constant throughout adulthood? In contrast to this, EI can be continually developed, and this rises steadily
in adulthood according to Sze, Goodkind, Gyurak, and Levenson (2012).
Research also shows the presence of EI can predict a person's work performance
and career (Goleman, 1998). The EQ-i model posits the best way to increase
EI is to build on existing strengths rather than to focus on rectifying deficits
(Joseph & Newman, 2010). Let's first look at ways to improve EI and EC. We'll
then look at some ways to control common emotions.

Improving EI and EC

To improve self-awareness:

- **Journal your feelings.** This simple act can improve your mood and self-
  awareness.

- **Slow down.** When you experience strong emotions, try to slow down.
  Examine what exactly triggered this emotion. Although you can't control
  the situation, you can control your reaction to it.

To improve self-regulation:

- **Know your values.** What values are most relevant to you? What values will you not compromise? Examine your own personal code of ethics. Understanding what is most important to you will help you make good choices.

- **Hold yourself accountable and own problems.** Don't blame problems on other people. Make a commitment to confess mistakes and and accept consequences. By doing so, you will earn respect.

- **Practice being calm.** The next time you find yourself in a challenging situation, be aware of how you act. Practice deep-breathing exercises and think through your emotions.

To improve motivation:

- **Reexamine why you're a nurse.** When you're faced with adversity, it's easy to forget what you really loved about nursing, so reflect back to why you went into the nursing profession in the first place. This often helps you look at your situation in a more positive light.

- **Know where you stand.** Look in the mirror and determine how motivated you are to lead change. Think about what motivates you and how you can motivate others.

- **Be encouraging.** Motivated nurses are usually sanguine, no matter what issues they face. The next time you are faced with an issue, problem, or failure, try finding something positive about it. Although you may feel you can only find something trivial or small, it is still considered positive, so look for it.

To improve social awareness:

- **Put yourself in someone else's shoes.** Take time to look at situations from another's perspective. This can shed a completely different light on the situation and provide conflict resolution.

- **Pay attention to body language.** Body gestures can reveal to others how people really feel about a situation. Learning to read body language can be a real asset as a nurse because you can learn more about how someone feels without them disclosing it. (See Chapter 2.)

- **Respond to other's feelings.** You ask your nurse colleague to work late for you because you're running late for work. Although she agrees, you can hear the disappointment in her voice. Respond by addressing her feelings. Tell her you appreciate that she is willing to stay for you and that you're just as upset about getting to work late. Promise to pay it forward when she needs you (and keep your word).

To improve relationship management:

- **Learn how to resolve conflict.** Nurses must know how to resolve conflicts between their colleagues, patients, and doctors. Learning conflict resolution skills can halt gossip, backstabbing, and other toxic behaviors. This skill is vital if you want to succeed in any area of nursing. See Script 3.2 for a way to handle gossiping in the workplace.

- **Improve your communication skills.** The next time you're in a conversation, pay attention to how much you're listening versus speaking. (See the QWQ formula in Chapter 2.)

- **Learn how to recognize others' accomplishments.** Recognize and share accomplishments directly with your patients, colleagues, and leaders, as appropriate. Remember to always commend in public and coach in private.

Controlling Common Emotions

To be effective, nurses must know how their emotions and actions affect the people around them. The proficient EI and EC nurse relates well to others and is often viewed as successful. Some of the overarching emotions, such as frustration, worry, anger, dislike, or disappointment, are hard to overcome, but you can do it if you consistently work through them. Let's review strategies to overcome these complex emotions.

Frustration. Frustration usually occurs when you feel stuck or trapped. For example, you just arrived at work and a patient or family rudely approaches with issues you literally just walked into. It can be very frustrating trying to fix a problem or issue that you had nothing to do with. Keeping your frustration levels at a minimum is key to optimal outcomes. Here's how:

- **Stop.** This allows you to assess the situation. Stop and ask yourself why you feel frustrated. Write it down, if needed, and be clear and specific with what is causing the angst. Subsequently, think of one positive thing about your challenging situation. For instance, if the doctor placed you on hold for a long time, then perhaps a positive outcome of this is that you had time to prepare your question(s) for the call or even that you had time to stand still a few moments. This positive way of thinking can improve your mood greatly.

- **Reflect.** Recall the last time your were frustrated by someone or something. Did frustration solve your problem? Probably not. In other words, move forward, not back; there is no point in doing so.

Now take a look at Script 3.3, which shows how you might handle this kind of situation of responding to a family's issue.

Script 3.2 What to say when…
you need to ask a colleague to stop gossiping.

Tell

To your coworker:

Colin, do you have a minute? I need to speak with you in private. Someone is going around the unit telling everyone that I'm dating our new surgeon, Dr. Pete.

Explain

Your coworker plays dumb:

I have no idea what you're talking about.

Your response:

I wish whoever is saying this would stop. Can you help me in stopping this?

Your coworker is confrontational:

It's no big deal!

Your response:

This may be true, but it's no one's business. We don't have the right to share each other's private information.

Your coworker is defensive:

Do you know who is telling everyone?

Your response:

Why do you care if I know who it is? It doesn't matter who; I just need the gossip to stop.

Lead by example

Your coworker plays dumb:

Wow, that's a shame. Sorry to hear this, but there is nothing I can do.

Your response:

If you hear someone saying this, I really need you to tell them it's none of their business and to stop spreading gossip.

Your coworker is confrontational:

There are bigger issues at hand. Your love life isn't so important. Don't worry about gossip.

Your response:

We need to respect each other's privacy.

Your coworker is defensive:

Sorry, I don't have anything to do with it.

Your response:

Well, if you know who is spreading the gossip, it would really mean a lot to me to if you would tell them to stop.

Your coworker plays dumb, or is confrontational or defensive.

Your response:

I'm sure this wasn't done maliciously, but I'd appreciate your help in stopping the gossip. If it continues, I will need to take further action and report that I'm being harassed.

Learn the consequence

Script 3.3 What to say when....
you need to apologize to patients or their families.

Tell

To the patient/family:

I apologize your appointment is running 2 hours behind and no one has given you an update as to when you will be seen. I would like to help in finding a solution. First, it is important that I listen to your concerns. (Allow them to vent. Use the HEARD acronym.)

Hear the family:

We had other doctor appointments lined up today, and now we are late because of the disorganization in appointment scheduling.

Explain

Empathize with the patient/family:

I would react similarly if I were in your shoes. (Validate their feelings.)

Apologize to the patient/family:

I am very sorry, and I feel horrible that you have been here waiting for 2 hours.

L ead by example

Patient/family is confrontational:

> I want this fixed! My whole day is a mess now.

Resolve:

> Do you have any ideas or solutions in order to remedy this situation?

If yes, consider the patient/family response. If no, offer a contingency plan:

> Although I can't replace the time you lost and the inconvenience of rescheduling your other appointments, I would like to earn your trust back by offering to let you see another provider. Or I promise to continue to update you every 15 minutes about the estimated time you will be seen. We will be sure to give you the same time and attention that we are giving the current cause of this delay. Safety is our top priority.

Patient/family is accepting:

> Well, it's not your fault.

Diagnose:

> Unfortunately, emergencies happen. Being negligent of other patients' time is not acceptable. Once again, I apologize for this oversight of not keeping you well informed. In the meantime, I'd like to offer you a complimentary refreshment in the cafeteria. When you return, I will update you with the status.

L earn the consequence

Patient/family is still angry:

> I'll never come back here again!

Your response:

> Once again, I am very sorry for not keeping you well informed. In the meantime, I'd like to offer you a complimentary refreshment in the cafeteria. When you return, I will update you with the status. Unfortunately, emergencies happen. Being negligent in updating you about your appointment time is unacceptable. You can be sure you will be receiving the most comprehensive care when you are seen and given the same time and attention.

Worry/nervousness. Nurses care for sicker patients and yet are still asked to do more, with less. This can easily get out of control, if you allow it. Worry will not only affect your mental health, but also your productivity. Try these tips to overcome worry:

- **Avoid the worry and anxiety.** Take yourself out of the situation. For example, if nurses start to gossip about impending layoffs, avoid the conversation so you don't worry with them.

- **Breathe.** Breathe in through your nose and out through your mouth for approximately 5 seconds in duration. Take 5 deep breaths. This technique helps slow your breathing and your heart rate.

- **Concentrate on how to progress the situation.** If you fear being laid off, don't sit and worry. Instead, show how valuable you are by brainstorming ideas that consist of small wins you can help implement for your unit.

- **Start a "worry" log.** Document in a personal notebook the situations that worry you and schedule time to deal with them later. This practice enables you to put these worries to the side and focus on other important issues. By putting worries aside, you know that you'll deal with them at a more appropriate time. When it comes time to deal with them, assess patterns and take action to overcome them.

Now consider Script 3.4, which provides a sample conversation you might have when asking your supervisor for help with your workload.

Anger and aggravation. Anger is a destructive emotion that many nurses experience in the workplace. Unfortunately, there are numerous reasons why egregious situations occur, and this can violate workplace rights and professional values. What makes anger even more toxic is when it is mismanaged. Nurses tend to take their anger out on each other, and this leads to even more destruction (Dellasega & Volpe, 2013). If you have trouble managing your temper at work, then learning to control it is one of the best things you can do (especially if you want to keep your job and sanity). Try these suggestions from Dellasega & Volpe (2013) to control your anger:

- **Watch for early signs of anger.** We all know when anger is building, so learn to recognize the signs as soon as they begin. When dealing with anger, remember, you can choose how you react to something or someone that angers you, even though you can't change the genesis of the situation. You need to stay in control, because it is easy to become angry, but deflecting this anger appropriately is what differentiates your successes from failures.

- **Take a break.** Try shutting your eyes for a few minutes and take deep breaths. This will interject your angry thoughts and place you into a more positive conduit.

- **Look in a mirror.** Think about how and what you look like when you're angry. Is this the person you want others to see you as? Would you want to be around or interact with the person you're envisioning? Probably not.

In addition, see Script 3.5 for how to deal with someone who is angry.

Script 3.4 What to say when... you need to ask your supervisor for help with your workload.

Tell

To your nurse manager:

> Beverly, I am realizing my eagerness to "do more" has gotten the best of me. I would like to speak with you to discuss some solutions. When can we meet?

Your nurse manager is disappointed:

> What? I was really counting on you to help me out. I should have known you would drop the ball.

Your response:

> I have accepted more than I can handle, and it is important to me that I sustain my typical high performance. There is just more work than hours in the day. I don't believe this is because of my inability. I believe it's the workload. You may not be aware my current responsibilities include...

Your nurse manager understands:

> I appreciated your eagerness to help out. What are your thoughts?

Your response:

> First, I would like your help in setting priorities on each project.

Explain

Lead by example

Your nurse manager is open to suggestions:

> Where do we begin?

Your response:

> I would like your help in setting priorities on each project. I would also like to incorporate some other staff members to take accountability on the projects. If everyone pitches in, we can obtain more creativity and have a better chance at meeting our deadline.

Your nurse manager is disappointed:

> So, I guess this is just another mess for me to clean up?

Your response:

> I can arrange a meeting on Monday to discuss the projects with the group and take the lead in delegating to staff.

Learn the consequence

Your nurse manager is receptive:

> I'm glad you brought this to my attention.

Your response:

> I would like to express my thankfulness for your support.

Your nurse manager is unreceptive:

> Are you sure you can at least handle that?

Your response:

> I am working beyond full capacity, where safety and quality could be compromised. I would like to think you would appreciate that I recognize my own strengths and weaknesses. This has been a learning opportunity for me, and your support would be appreciated.

Script 3.5 What to say when....
you need to deal with an angry physician.

Tell

To the physician:

Dr. Chou, I am aware you are angry with surgical throughput. (Allow him to vent and then restate the issue in a simplified manner). So, if I understand you correctly, you are frustrated because we have been running behind on our surgical cases all week.

The physician is rational:

Yes, I just want organization and timeliness in my OR.

Your response:

I appreciate your concern. I understand that delays in surgical cases cause a lot of issues. I want to find a remedy also.

The physician remains angry:

Yes, my OR times should not be so convoluted. You need to get your act together and fix this.

Your response:

I appreciate your concern. I understand that delays in surgical cases cause a lot of issues. But your anger toward me is not the answer to this problem. We need to work together, not against each other.

Explain

Lead by example

The physician apologizes:

Look, I know your trying, but it's all very frustrating that something so easy is so difficult around here.

Your response:

I will contact these departments and see if there is a simplified approach; if not, I will arrange meetings. I know you're busy. I'd really appreciate your support on this.

The physician remains angry:

I'm here to operate, not to play cruise director!

Your response:

There are multiple touch points where the cases are backing up. We need to work with housekeeping, admissions, and transport to improve the throughput. I will contact these departments and see if there is a simplified approach; if not, I will arrange meetings. Your presence is key to moving this forward. Can I count on you as part of this team approach?

Learn the consequence

The physician is supportive:

Start making the calls. Let me know what I need to do.

Your response:

I will start making the calls after our last case today. I am looking forward to working with you on this.

The physician remains unsupportive:

Why do I have to do everything? What do they pay you to do around here, anyway?

Your response:

I will start making the calls after our last case today. If you can support me on this, we will have a more productive outcome. I will not tolerate your outbursts and will contact the leadership team on how to proceed in this. I hope you will reconsider working with me.

Dislike. Sadly, we have all worked with someone we didn't like. Whether it is their attitude, their work ethic, or even the amount of perfume they wear (see Script 3.6), it is often tough to work with certain types of people. Fortunately, with the right strategies, you can still have a productive working relationship with someone you dislike:

- **Be respectful.** Take the higher echelon and treat the person you dislike with basic respect and courtesy.

- **Be mindful.** Determine why you don't like this person. Is it their behavior, who they hang in the breakroom with, or the tone of their voice? Think about why you have these feelings. Although there is no simple solution to dealing with dislike, bringing mindfulness to the process can help.

- **Be assertive.** Whatever the reasoning is behind why you dislike working with someone, remember, you're in control of how you react to them. The truth isn't always easy to state, but peppering your conversation with empathy and respect will make the conversation a little easier.

Disappointment. If you've just suffered a major disappointment, such as your nurse manager's negative comments on your annual work evaluation, you can easily get very down on yourself. This may prevent you from going above and beyond in the care of your patients. Here are some proactive steps you can take to cope with disappointment:

- **Know your core values.** Take a moment to consider what values are most important to you. Are you disappointed because you violated your own core values or because you feel you let someone or something violate your core values?

- **Respond early.** If your gut tells you that you need space or distance from someone or something, take some space. Once you have space, reflect on things that make you happy. This reflection won't necessarily make you happy instantaneously, but it will help you to think about more positive things than what is disappointing you at the moment.

In addition, consider having a conversation with your manager, as shown in Script 3.7.

Leading With EI and EC

According to Goleman, Boyzatzis, and McKee (2002), the aptitudes of leadership, unlike academic or technical skills, are learned in life. If you are weak in leadership, you can get better at virtually any point in life with the right effort. Getting better requires motivation, a clear idea of what you need to improve, and consistent practice. For example, good leaders are excellent listeners.

Let's assume that you need to become a better listener because you have a habit of interrupting people mid-sentence and often completely hijack the discussion. The first step is to become aware of the moments when you do this and stop yourself. (Review the QWQ formula in Chapter 2.) Conversely, you might have to deal with someone who constantly interrupts you. This can be incredibly annoying, but if you control your emotions, you will better be able to help the person decrease this behavior. See Script 3.8 for an example of how you might address such a situation.

Another skill that good leaders possess is helping others stay in a positive emotional state. Leaders who attain the best results get people to laugh three times more often than do mediocre leaders (Goleman, Boyzatzis & McKee, 2005). Laughter signals relaxation and enjoyment, so these people are more inclined to be focused and productive.

In Maria Shriver's 2012 commencement speech at USC's Annenberg School of Communication, she states, "Have the courage to press the pause button." Maria's advice is a testament to how we should stop worrying about what's next and notice what's happening in the moment. She further states, "Whenever you are in doubt, pause. Take a moment. Look at all of your options. Check your intention. Have a conversation with your heart. And then always take the high road" (Shriver, 2012). Shriver's "Power of the Pause" provides a superlative approach to self-managing. Any time you stop to assess what you're feeling, you raise your self-awareness, enhance your relationships, and increase your ability to make a positive difference.

Script 3.6 What to say when... you need to take the "fumes" out of someone who wears too much perfume/cologne.

Tell

To your coworker:

I'd like to ask you something in private. Do you have a moment? (When in private, continue.) If I wore too much perfume, would you tell me?

Your coworker doesn't take the hint:

Yes, I'd tell you, why do you ask?

Your response:

Well, I appreciate that, and that's why I wanted to bring this to your attention. I find your perfume strong and thought you might want to know.

Your coworker takes the hint:

Yes. Are you saying I am wearing too much?

Your response:

Yes, and I thought you might want to know, just as I would want someone to tell me.

Explain

Lead by example

Your coworker is offended:

You should really mind your own business.

Your response:

I don't mean to cross the line. I just thought if I mentioned this, you might wear less. I'm sure you are not aware how strong the scent is, but I thought you'd rather hear this from me than from others. You're not alone. We all have times when we aren't aware that we put too much on.

Your coworker is embarrassed:

I spilled it, and it ran all over my clothes. That's why it's so strong.

Your response:

I understand. It happens. Please be sure to let me know if I'm ever wearing too much, too, ok?

Your coworker is embarrassed:

I probably won't wear any tomorrow!

Your response:

I'm glad we're able to have open discussions like this. Thank you for understanding.

Learn the consequence

Your coworker is offended:

I know how much and what I put on my body. Maybe you should pay more attention to the outfits you wear than my scent!

Your response:

I am respectful to you and ask that you are respectful to me by not wearing such a strong perfume. It is giving me headaches. If you don't, I will have to take this issue to our manager.

Script 3.7 What to say when...

you want to optimize your annual evaluation.

Tell

To your nurse manager:

I enjoy what I do, and I am looking forward to reviewing my performance with you.

Your manager is positive:

I've been really impressed by your work ethic this past year.

Your response:

Thank you for the recognition of my hard work.

Your manager is positive:

What goals do you have for next year?

Explain

Your manager is negative:

I have concerns about your work performance, specifically your tardiness.

Your response if you agree:

I understand, and I'm ready to work on an action plan.

Your response if you disagree:

I don't understand how you came to this. Could you elaborate?

Your manager is negative:

If you continue to be late, you will lose your job!

Lead by example

Your response if you understand:

(Restate your understanding.) I will make sure I clock in on time, which is only up to 7 minutes before the time of my shift; otherwise, I am considered late. And if I clock out 7 minutes after my shift is over, I understand that is unapproved overtime, and I am subject to disciplinary action.

Your response if you disagree:

Can you show me how many times I was actually late?

Your response:

I want to continue to work hard, and I would appreciate your support in allowing me to take some management courses next year to be considered for promotion.

Learn the consequence

Your manager is negative:

I expect more from you. I expect you to be on time.

Your response if you agree:

I understand if I continue to be late or go into overtime, you will need to start formal disciplinary actions.

Your response if you disagree:

I will expect then for you to contact me when I am not in compliance since I don't see this reflected on the time clock.

Your manager is positive:

I will be happy to sign you up for some professional development courses.

Your response:

Thank you for your support. I'm looking forward to another great year.

time to reflect

Two nurses on different units each had an argument with their boss at work. On returning home, the first nurse, who wasn't emotionally intelligent, started shouting at her kids because they were shouting at one another. The nurse's actions were based on her emotions because she didn't stop to think that her outburst at her kids was really a displacement of her feelings about the argument she had with her boss. When the second nurse returned home and found that the kids were shouting at each other, she calmed herself down by thinking, "Well, why should I shout at the kids? They are not the ones to blame for my feelings. The main reason I am feeling bad is because of the argument at work, not my kids." The second nurse recognized her emotions, thought about them, and then acted in an emotionally intelligent way. How would you react in a similar situation?

Understanding the Oz Principles and Emotions

Connors, Smith, and Hickman (2004) introduced *The Oz Principle* based on the morale of the story "The Wizard of Oz." This philosophy propels staff to overcome adversity to achieve the results they desire by being accountable for their actions. Similar to Dorothy's search for the Wizard of Oz for guidance, staff also look to a "wizard" to rescue them from issues or conflicts that happen at work. The connection between the Wizard of Oz story and workplace confrontation is that the search for a wizard is really just a distraction or excuse for the ugly truth that needs to be revealed—which is often the lack of individual and/or organizational accountability in dealing with issues head on. When the core problem(s) is not addressed, a toxic cycle of blame, overlook, or ignorance will fester, and no improvements will be made.

Individuals with EI and EC own accountability and manage issues with a "See It, Own It, Solve It, and Do It" approach (Connors, Smith, & Hickman, 2004). The first step, See It, means acknowledging there is a problem; to Own It is to take responsibility for the issue or problem; Solve It means to find solutions; and, as a concluding step, Do It drives the implementation of the solution(s) identified, while also being cognizant of behaviors and emotions of themselves and others.

Beware of victimization. Just as Glenda, the good witch from the movie *The Wizard of Oz* explained to Dorothy that she always had the power to find her way back home, she just had to find the power for herself, you need to stay in control of your emotions, especially when faced with adversities, such as gossip. (Scripts 3.9 and 3.10 show you how to address such an adversity.) Do not fall victim to following the yellow brick road in hopes a wizard will fix all the problems. Remember, even when you feel powerless, you do have choices. You gain nothing from feeling as if you're a victim of circumstance. This might seem minute, but if you realize you are choosing to do something—even staying in a job you enjoy—you relinquish the feeling of powerlessness (Connors, Smith, & Hickman, 2004). When you make the choice to do nothing, you are actually doing something.

Take control. If you come in to your workplace with a poor attitude or always see "them" (that is, executive leadership or any other group with power in decision-making) as wrong and you as right, you are the one at fault. Attitude is a matter of perspective, and perspective is significant. As discussed in the book *The Oz Principle,* hold yourself accountable to situations by asking, "What else can you do to achieve the results you desire or overcome the circumstance that plagues you?" (Connors, Smith, & Hickman, 2004). In other words, it's not always "them," and, even if it is, the power to change your thoughts into positive ones is within your control.

Being right isn't what is most important. Don't fixate on being right. Remember those kids you went to school with who were labeled as know-it-alls? Well, in the workplace, actions do speak louder than words. You can prove your worth by not focusing on *being right all the time,* but by focusing on being perceived as someone who helps out, promotes solution-oriented problem-solving, and gets things done. You don't have to be right every time to be perceived as effective and appreciated, but you do have to be helpful.

Script 3.8 What to say when...
you need to confront a habitual interrupter.

T ell

To your coworker:

Paige, I have a problem I'd like your help with. Do you have a moment to talk in private?

E xplain

Your coworker is receptive:

Sure, what's up?

Your response:

When I talk, I like to get to my point, but I find it difficult when I can't finish my sentences. Although I do appreciate your insight, it's when you chime in while I'm in mid-sentence that I easily lose track of where I was going with the conversation to begin with.

Your coworker is defensive:

I'm really busy. I can't help you.

Your response:

This will only take a few minutes. I'd really appreciate your time. Look, when I talk, I like to get to my point, but I find it difficult when I can't finish my sentences. Although I do appreciate your insight, it's when you chime in while I'm in mid-sentence that I easily lose track of where I was going with the conversation to begin with.

Lead by example

Your coworker is receptive:

I didn't realize I did that to you. I guess I do this a lot?

Your response:

I'm noticing a pattern more and more and thought I should bring this to your attention.

Your coworker is defensive:

Are you seriously taking up my time to tell me this?

Your response:

When I am energetic about other people's conversations, I've noticed that I also chime in too early, and I'm trying to wait for pauses before I express my thoughts. I'd really appreciate it if you could help me do this, and I can offer you the same—if you're accepting.

Learn the consequence

Your coworker apologizes:

I am sorry. I don't even know I'm doing this until after I do it and only when there is a look of awkwardness on the person I interrupted!

Your response:

What if when I see that you are ready to chime in too early I hold up my finger in a "wait your turn" fashion, but discreetly, of course?

Your coworker denies it:

I think you are just oversensitive.

Your response: (give examples)

Paige, you interrupted me yesterday during the safety huddle. I was ready to explain how many patients left the ED before being seen, but before I could give the stats, you interjected with how full the ICU was. If you continue to interrupt me, I'm going to announce that you are interrupting me in our next conversation so that you'll become more aware of this.

Script 3.9 What to say when... the "rumor mill" or gossip involves you—and you don't know who started it.

T ell

To your nurse manager:

Kelly, I've heard some of my colleagues have been complaining to you that I'm not pulling my weight on the unit.

Your nurse manager is negative:

Yes, I have heard this, and I, too, am becoming concerned about your work.

Your response:

As you know, I have been working with the education committee very closely to meet the deadline, and I thought it was important that I focus on this project. Am I correct?

Your nurse manager is positive:

No, I haven't heard this.

Your response:

As you know, I've been working with the education committee very closely to meet our deadline, like you asked me. I think my colleagues may not know you asked me to work on this project in lieu of doing some of my other duties, and this is causing them to think I'm not pulling my weight. I am very concerned about this.

E xplain

Lead by example

Your nurse manager is supportive:

I've been very busy myself. I know how difficult it is to balance everything.

Your response:

I would appreciate it if you could share with our team your expectations on meeting the education committee's project deadline and my role in facilitating this so they don't feel this way about me.

Your nurse manager is negative:

I didn't think that asking you to do this would be so difficult for you to balance.

Your response:

There just isn't enough time in the day for one person to complete all the tasks. Even if you replaced me with another person, I am confident they would feel stretched as well. I'd like to propose that Tara or another colleague work with me in finishing the education project. If I can get help, I can balance my tasks better.

Learn the consequence

Your nurse manager is receptive:

That sounds like a plan. Thank you for bringing this to my attention.

Your response:

I understand you are very busy. I want to help you get this communication out asap, so do you mind if I sent everyone an email and cc you on it? I really appreciate you discussing this with me.

Your nurse manager is negative:

I think you should complete this on your own. This would be a good lesson in time management.

Your response:

If my workload cannot be shared with everyone, then I will have to withdraw my efforts with the education committee. Respectfully, this has become a compromise to my work ethic, but I do want to thank you for the opportunity.

Script 3.10 What to say when... the "rumor mill" or gossip involves you—and you know who started it.

T ell

To your coworker:

Jen, I overheard you complaining to the nurses yesterday in the break room that you feel like I'm not pulling my weight on the unit. I was standing outside the break room and was very upset you were talking about me like this.

Your coworker denies it:

It wasn't me who said it. It was everyone else.

Your response:

Well, I was pretty sure I heard your voice. I wish you would help me by putting out these terrible rumors that are causing more tension and decreased morale in our unit.

Your coworker confirms it:

Yea, I just feel like you expect all of us to do everything. Everyone agreed, and I wasn't the only one saying something. You just happened to hear me.

Your response:

Can you help me understand why you are having such a discussion about me and why you didn't approach me directly? I feel like you are undermining me and attempting to persuade others to think less of me. This is causing a decrease in our unit morale and unnecessary tension in our unit.

E xplain

Lead by
  example

Learn the
  consequence

Your coworker is defensive:

Well, it wasn't me. I just don't want to get involved.

Your response:

Please help me. I'm asking for your help in putting out rumors and gossip, not in getting involved in them. I'm sure you'd expect the same thing if you were in my shoes. I would do the right thing and am just asking you to do the same thing, too.

Your coworker apologizes:

I'm sorry I allowed this behavior. I'll speak more positive next time. I feel awful.

Your response:

I accept your apology. I think we can go forward from here.

Your coworker is threatening:

Look, everyone on the unit feels this way. Maybe if you pulled your weight, you wouldn't be the topic of discussion.

Your response:

Should you ever question my workload, I would appreciate you coming directly to me instead of discussing it with our colleagues. I find gossiping about others is both unprofessional and a form of bullying.

Your coworker is unapologetic:

Whatever. Are we done? You're wasting my time.

Your response:

I'm taking your actions further and will discuss this with our supervisor since your conduct is very unprofessional.

Understanding the Damage of Emotional *In*competence

Nurse leaders rarely fail in the workplace because they lack clinical skills. Many nurse leaders fail because of emotional shortcomings, and this leads to lost trust in their relationships with others (Clancy, 2012). They have autocratic leadership styles, are poor at reducing conflict and build a culture of fear. Many managers assume their perceptions should apply to everyone.

Many people assume that what we feel is good for us must be good for others. Because most people in leadership positions are driven to excel, this bias can be interpreted that all good employees also want to continue to excel and be promoted. Leaders with strong emotional intelligence and emotional competence understand that their bias and perceptions are not the panacea.

The Drive Home

Let's review the *driving it back home* pointers from this chapter:

- Goleman (1995) identified the five key domains of EI as self-awareness, self-regulation and management, motivation, social awareness, and relationship management.

- Responses that require emotion are sent to the amygdala, or the brain's emotional command center. The amygdala organizes behavioral, autonomic, and hormonal responses to a variety of situations, including those emotions that produce disgust, fear, or anger.

- It is very important to be aware of what you are feeling. For example, know when you are about to be on the verge of "losing control" of a situation.

- Feelings have an impact on just about everyone we interact with. Nurses need to be able to read emotional clues from patients, colleagues, and staff.

- Controlling emotions requires you to also be empathetic to others. You need to have finesse in relating to what others are feeling. This will help you to better understand them.

- Recognizing emotions is not the same as understanding emotions.

References

American Association of Colleges of Nursing. (2012). Current and projected shortage indicators. Retrieved from http://www.aacn.nche.edu/media-relations/fact-sheets/nursing-shortage

Aristotle. (n.d.). Retrieved from http://www.quoteworld.org/quotes/594

Blake, R. (2006). Employee retention: What employee turnover really costs your company. Retrieved from www.webpronews.com/expenarticles/2006/07/24/employee- retention-what-employee-turn-over-really-costs-your-company

Cavallo, K., & Brienza, D. (2001). Emotional competence and leadership excellence at Johnson & Johnson: The Emotional Intelligence and Leadership Study Consortium for research on Emotional Intelligence in organizations. Retrieved from www.eiconsortium.org

Cherniss, C. & Goleman, D. (Eds). (2001). *The emotionally intelligent workplace: How to select for, measure, and improve emotional intelligence in individuals, groups, and organizations.* From the Consortium for Research on emotional intelligence in organizations. San Francisco, CA: Jossey-Bass.

Clancy, C. (2012). *Nursing leadership: Discovering the what, who, why and where.* Retrieved http://nursing.advanceweb.com/Archives/Article-Archives/Nursing-Leadership.aspx

Connors, R., Smith, T., & Hickman, C. R. (2004). *The Oz principle: Getting results through individual and organizational accountability.* New York, N.Y: Portfolio.

Delcourt, C., Gremler, D. D., Van Riel, A. C. R., & Van Birgelen, M. (2013). Effects of perceived employee emotional competence on customer satisfaction and loyalty: the mediating role of rapport, *Journal of Service Management, 24*(1), 5–24.

Dellasega, C. & Volpe, R. L. (2013). *Toxic Nursing: Managing Bullying, Bad Attitudes, and Total Turmoil.* Indianapolis, IN: Sigma Theta Tau International.

Godse, A. S., & Thingujam, N. S. (2010). Perceived emotional intelligence and conflict resolution styles among information technology professionals: Testing the mediating role of personality. *Singapore Management Review, 32*(1), 69–83.

Goleman, D. (1995). *Emotional intelligence.* New York, NY: *Bantam.*

Goleman, D. (1998). *Working with emotional intelligence.* New York, NY: Bantam.

Goleman, D. (2007). *Emotional intelligence: Why it can matter more than IQ.* New York, NY: Random House.

Goleman, D., Boyzatzis, R., & McKee, A. (2002). *Harvard Business Review on what makes a leader.* Boston, MA: Harvard Business School Press.

Goleman, D., Boyzatzis, R., & McKee, A. (2005). *Primal leadership: realizing the power of emotional intelligence.* Boston, MA: Harvard Business School Press.

Joseph, D. L., & Newman, D. A. (2010). Emotional intelligence: An integrative meta-analysis and cascading model. *Journal of Applied Psychology, 95*(1), 54-78. doi: 10.1037/a0017286

Lazarus, R. S. (1991). *Emotion & adaptation.* New York, NY: Oxford University Press.

Mayer, J. D. & Salovey, P. (1997). What is emotional intelligence? In P. Salovey, & D. Sluyter (Eds.), *Emotional development and emotional intelligence: Education implication.* New York, NY: Basic Books.

Merrill, D. W. and Reid, R. H. (1999). Personal styles and effective performance. New York: CRC Press.

Myers, I. B., McCaulley, M., Quenk, N., & Hammer, A. (1998). *MBTI handbook: A guide to the development and use of the Myers-Briggs Type Indicator* (3rd ed.). Mountain View, CA: Consulting Psychologists Press.

Petrides, K. V., & Sevdalis, N. (2010). Emotional intelligence and nursing: Comment on Smith, Profetto-McGrath, and Cummings (2009). *International Journal of Nursing Studies, 47,* 526–528.

Rozell, E. J., Pettijohn, C. E., & Parker, R. S. (2002). An empirical evaluation of emotional intelligence: The impact on management development. *Journal of Management Development, 21*(4), 272–289.

Shriver, M. (2012). USC Annenberg School of Communication commencement speech. Retrieved from https://www.youtube.com/watch?v=A5xLcLIIXqU

Sixseconds (2013). Six Seconds Emotional Intelligence Assessment (SEI). Retrieved from http://www.6seconds.org/tools/sei/

Sze, J. A., Goodkind, M. S., Gyurak, A., Levenson, R. W. (2012). Aging and emotion recognition: Not just a losing matter. *Psychology and Aging, 27*(4), 940–950. doi: 10.1037/a0029367

Thompson, H. L. (2006). "Exploring the Interface of the Type and Emotional Intelligence Landscapes," Bulletin of Psychological Type (29)3, 14-19. Retrieved from https://hpsys.com/PDFs/Type_%20and_EI_Landscapes2.pdf

Weng, H. C., Hung, C. M., Liu, Y. T., Cheng, Y. J., Yen, C. Y., Chang, C. C., & Huang, C. K. (2011). Associations between emotional intelligence and doctor burnout, job satisfaction and patient satisfaction. *Medical Education, 45*(8) 835–842. doi: 10.1111/j.1365-2923.2011.03985.x

> *"It is better to keep your mouth closed
> and let people think you are a fool than
> to open it and remove all doubt."*
> –Mark Twain

4

Impromptu Scripting Techniques

To script or not to script; that is a burning question in healthcare. Although I have come across a lot of controversy on this topic from fellow colleagues, I favor the idea to a degree. Critics complain that scripting is robotic and staged; however, it really boils down to how it was said. Think about how many times you use scripting and don't even realize it. For example, think about what you say when you come across an old friend or colleague by surprise. As smiles and delight fill the air around you, have any of the following phrases ever just come rolling out of your mouth—without any thought or pretense:

- "Hello, how are you?"

- "Hey, how have you been?"

- "Oh my goodness, how have you been?"

- "Hi, it's been so long…?"

Chances are high that you have either said these exact phrases, or you have said something very similar to these phrases. Regardless of whether you are talking to someone you haven't seen in a while or when conversing in day-to-day conversations, you have probably used scripting without even knowing it.

Have you ever noticed that you don't have to put much thought into a greeting such as, "Hello, how are you?" or your nonverbal gestures, such as your smile or the way your elbows go into your waist and palms face up, in an open, welcoming approach. Or perhaps you put your hands to your cheeks or cover your mouth, in an "I'm speechless" manner. Imagine if you could have the same natural response when you are faced with a less desirable situation. Wouldn't that make life a little easier?

In my leadership experiences, I have found it to be invaluable to hardwire some scripts. I try to hardwire new phrases for new situations almost every day. I don't reinvent the wheel; I just build upon what is already working well and adapt new situations to it. I reevaluate its effectiveness and then test its applicability to varying personality types, as we discussed in Chapter 1.

According to Wikipedia ("Scripting," 2014), scripting is a set of messages, "phrases, or sentences that provide the language that goes into a specific conversation" without creating much thought in forming words. Scripts can involve conversation ice-breakers, starters, and key speaking points. Scripts are also beneficial for changing topics, redirecting, or even ending conversations. The value of scripting is that it enables leaders to naturally deliver thoughtful, appropriate responses or phrases. Scripts can't be imposed. You must have ownership of a script and truly believe it in order to deliver it with true authenticity. Otherwise you sound rehearsed. Scripting also helps to deliver a consistent, service-oriented response, which is especially important in healthcare settings.

The Driver's Seat: Using Impromptu Scripts and Acronyms for Recollection

Have you ever entered into a potentially difficult conversation with an employee, patient, family, or executive and felt like a deer in the headlights in terms of what to say and what to avoid saying? Many of us have. Searching for just the right words or phrases in a highly emotional and/or serious situation increases your stress levels, which decreases your ability to think logically or insightfully.

As discussed in Chapter 3, your emotions can cause strong signals from your senses, which trigger a prompt emotional response before you've been able to respond rationally (Goleman, 1998). This is why using scripts as a *guide* in your everyday conversations can be very advantageous. In many cases, scripting will deter an out-of-control feeling or a knee-jerk response that is a detriment to a desired outcome. Table 4.1 shows some examples of scripting in complex leadership and management situations. Remember, though, that the expectation is that you aren't memorizing these scripts. You are becoming familiar with them and using them as a guide in responding to various emotionally charged situations.

Table 4.1 Using Scripting to Address Challenging Situations

What to Say When Pressured	What Not to Say	Rationale
"I would like to think this over first. I have some time at _____ to discuss this."	"Well, you may have time to discuss this, but I don't."	This script gives you time to cool off, calm down, or even just think about the problem and solution.
"I'd really like to help you with your patient, but I'm working with Mrs. Smith right now. I just can't leave my current responsibilities."	"No."	Just saying "no" sounds cold and standoffish. Providing a short explanation as to why you can't do something provides understanding to barriers.

(continues)

Table 4.1   Using Scripting to Address Challenging Situations
(continued)

What to Say When Pressured	What Not to Say	Rationale
"I'm just finishing something up right now. Can I stop by your unit when I'm done?"	"I don't have time to talk to you."	This response is just plain rude, whether you're talking in person or on the phone. Explain why at this time you cannot talk and suggest a better time for you.
"I'm prioritizing my time on _____ right now."	"That's not my job."	When approached with tasks that are not within your primary role (and you don't have time to help out), reinforce your primary responsibilities.

What to Say When Uncertain or Confused	What Not to Say	Rationale
"Could your clarify your comment about _____?"	"This may sound dumb, but…"	Be clear in what you're thinking, respectfully. This provides credibility so you present your ideas with confidence.
"I trust your judgment."	"We shall see."	What you're saying is "You have my permission. I believe in you."
"I will find out," or "I will look into this."	"I don't know."	This is a more savvy way of understating you don't have an answer yet, but you will help obtain one.
"What I hear you saying is _____."	"Aha."	Paraphrase what you heard. You'll likely get more detail when you do this.

What to Say When Feeling Confident or Appreciative	What Not to Say	Rationale
"Thank you."	"OK."	This is common courtesy. Whether given in private or public, a sincere "thanks" creates benevolence.
"I'm on it."	"I guess I'll have to do it."	You're saying, "Relax. Don't worry about a thing. I'll see to it personally." That response can defuse just about anyone.
"My pleasure," or "I'm happy to help."	"No problem."	This gives the notion that you are happy to help or assist and that it wasn't a "problem" for you. If someone asks you for directions, is that a problem, or are you happy to help them?

Your Road Map: Scripting Techniques for Acronyms, Body Language, and Emotional Intelligence

To elicit better responses from others, nurses need to ask open-ended questions. Scripting questions with acronyms can be a helpful tool in reminding you to use open-ended questions. You may recall "therapeutic communication skills" from your nursing school days. Well, that speaks to open-ended questions, but sometimes it's easy to forget to use them and you end up asking closed questions. An open-ended question removes bias and helps gauge whether someone's body gestures are appropriate to the words they use. Open-ended questions can confirm or deny what was perceived and understood. Using words like *what, why, where,* and *how* helps ensure your questions are for the purpose of seeking information.

Acronyms

Nurses cannot underestimate what others understand when we converse, so various scripting techniques, such as acronyms, can aid us. Specifically, the

American Nurses Association (ANA) has endorsed the SBAR acronym in nursing language. According to the Joint Commission (2006), "poor communication accounts for more than 60% of the root causes of sentinel events." The use of the SBAR acronym ensures that healthcare providers are delivering safe communications during all patient handoffs. Patient handoffs provides the critical information needed about the patient, such as the transfer of the responsibility for care from one healthcare provider to another. This acronym reminds nurses to use open-ended questions when discussing a patient's situation, background, assessment, and recommendation (SBAR):

Situation	A concise statement of the problem
Background	Pertinent and brief information related to the situation
Assessment	Analysis and considerations of options— what you found/think
Recommendation	Action requested/recommended—what you want

Source: Kaiser Permanente of Colorado (2004), para 2.

Acronyms With Scripting Techniques

Piggybacking off the SBAR concept, we can use acronyms to help us elicit feedback from others. For example, 3WITH helps you to remember to ask open-ended questions. Specifically, 3WITH stands for choosing the three words that start with *W,* such as *what, why,* or *where.* The *I* stands for "in what way," the *T* represents "tell me more" or "talk with me more about this," and the *H* stands for "help, how, hear"—again using the three to remember that there are three options. I easily recall 3WITH when I need to quickly craft an open-ended question. In using 3WITH, you can ask an opened-ended question using any of the following words:

- *"Why* did that happen?"

- *"What* did you do?"

- *"Where* did this stem from?"

- *"In what way...?"*

- *"Tell* me more about…."

- *"Help* me understand…." or *"How* did this happen?" or "I'm *hearing* you say…."

Take a moment to review Script 4.1, which shows how you can incorporate the 3WITH process when working with a patient that you feel is being disrespectful.

Do you see how easily the patient's demands could have initially been interpreted as being disrespectful to the nurse? By continually asking open-end questions, we can unveil what's really going on with someone, rather than jumping to conclusions. Try not to leave too much to perception. This can easily become distorted by biases and lack of understanding. The 3WITH acronym can help you remember what the beginning words are to form an open-ended question.

Script 4.1 What to say when... you think a patient isn't being respectful to you (using the 3WITH acronym).

Tell

To the patient:

John, as the doctor just explained, you are going to be discharged to home today, so please help me understand why you are asking me to brush your teeth and wash you today?

Explain

The patient is disrespectful:

Well, I have been brushing my teeth every day—along with washing myself and feeding myself. Don't you nurses take care of patients anymore? I have Medicare insurance, so you're getting paid to do your job.

Your response:

(Ask open-ended questions to unveil what's not being said.) John, it is important that you take care of yourself when you can. Why do you think nurses need to do basic hygiene care if a patient is more than capable?

The patient responds:

I thought nurses were supposed to take care of sick people. You haven't done any of this for me. I'm once again left to do everything myself. You nurses these days aren't as good as they were years ago. A good nurse then would have attended to me more.

Your response:

Nurses do care for the sick and assist patients when needed. Tell me more, John. I'm not sure I understand why you're so upset.

The patient responds:

Look, I just wanted my ol' teeth brushed. (Silence.) Ah geez, ok, well, my brother was in this very same hospital and had his teeth brushed, and they washed him. He said how comforting it was, and I'm getting the raw end of the stick. He just said to me this morning that his car accident years ago was much more serious than why I am here. But, of course, he always has one on me.

Your response:

I'm sorry you are feeling this way. It sounds like your brother couldn't do basic care for himself when he was hospitalized. Fortunately, you are strong enough to be independent. Tell me how you feel about your independence.

The patient responds:

Hey, you know, I have to be independent. I'm all I got. The wife passed years ago, and the kids live across the country. I have friends and neighbors, but it's not the same as when my wife was here.

Your response:

I see. So in your situation, independence isn't always what you want. Please correct me, but what I'm hearing is that you may have wanted me to brush your teeth just so you could take a little break from doing everything all by yourself?

(continues)

Lead by
example

Script 4.1 What to say when… you think a patient isn't being respectful to you (using the 3WITH acronym). *(continued)*

Learn the consequence

The patient responds:

Well, everyday I have to do everything alone, and I guess I let my brother's comments make me feel even more alone. (Pause.) Hey, thank you for talking to me. Getting old isn't easy.

Your response:

I'm happy I could be here for you and talk this through. What else can I do for you, John? I have the time.

The patient responds:

Brush my teeth? (Patient laughs and affirms his comment was meant to make the nurse smile.)

Body Language With Acronyms and Scripting Techniques

After you have asked one of the open-ended questions using the 3WITH acronym, you look at specific body gestures to see correlations. As an example, let's pretend we think someone isn't being honest with us. Let's examine what body gestures are likely to be displayed.

Body language assessment of eyes. In a person who is dishonest, the obvious expression will be a distressed look, accentuated with eyebrows raised up and inward. This is similar to how someone appears when he or she is shocked or angry. The person will have a "wasn't me" type of appearance. A subtler cue to discern if a person is recalling a fact versus making something up is based on how their eyes flow during the conversation flow. When people remember concrete details, you will notice their eyes moving to the left if they are right-handed. When right-handed people make up stories or are dishonest, you will notice their eyes travel to the right. Left-handed people will move their eyes to the left when being dishonest. Eye blinking will also happen more frequently if they are dishonest, and they tend to clench their knuckles. You may find dishonest people gripping something tight, like the arms of a chair, their arms or hands, or other nearby objects until their knuckles turn colors. They do not even realize what they are doing, but now you do. Another tactic you will note is that dishonest people try to "block out" the truth, by rubbing their eyes throughout the conversation. People who aren't honest may also deliberately try to make direct eye contact with you to seem more sincere. This is a way of "proving" that they're telling the truth. Don't fall for it (Driver, 2010)!

Body language assessment of nose. Dishonest people touch their nose more often than someone who experiences the occasional itch. They are also likely to cover their mouths with a hand or place their hands near their mouth, almost as if they're trying conceal the fabrications coming from their mouth.

Body language overview. Driver (2010) explains that it is natural to mirror the behavior of others with whom we are having a conversation with; it helps build rapport. When people are dishonest, mirroring decreases as they spend more effort on hiding the truth for the listener. An example is when they lean away from you during the conversation. A dishonest person will be more likely to lean backward, which is a sign they are uncomfortable with sharing more information than needed. Honest people will tend to lean toward you.

Someone who is dishonest will also tend to be limited and stiff. The person's hands might touch their face, ear, or the back of the neck, or they might keep their arms folded, legs locked, and not move their hands. They tend to avoid hand gestures, yet they often uncomfortably play with their hair, adjust a tie, or fidget with a shirt cuff. Also, consider how much they talk when you become more silent. It is very hard for dishonest people to avoid filling the silence that is created by you. They want you to believe their lies. Because their is no feedback when silence is present, they attempt to fill in the silence void—watch for this!

Now, consider Script 4.2, which will show you how best to deal with a colleague's dishonest behavior.

Emotional Intelligence With Acronyms and Scripting

Using the 2BROKE Acronym to Recognize Fibbers

A helpful acronym to help you remember body gestures of someone fabricating is the acronym 2BROKE. This acronym represents the:

2B	Blinking and brow movements
R	Right-sided eye movements (if the person is right handed)
O	Opposite mirroring
K	Knuckles clenched
E	Edgy (fidgety, nose rubbing, staring, no silence)

Obviously, 2BROKE doesn't include all the suggested body language gestures indicated earlier, but it gives you a quick-and-dirty overview to look at potential signs of someone who is a fibber.

Script 4.2 What to say when...
you are confronting a colleague's dishonest behavior.

Tell

To your coworker:

> Shane, telling our boss you had to leave the meeting early because of an issue with one of your patients is wrong—we both know that. If our boss asks me about this, he will easily catch me in a lie since the chart doesn't reflect your story.

Explain

Your coworker gives you the guilt trip:

> Look, you know this interview is extremely important to me. I wouldn't ask you to do this unless it was that important.

Your response:

> I want to help you out. I understand you needed to leave the mandatory meeting to take the phone call about your upcoming job interview at hospital ABC. I really hope you get the job. I think you'll probably be a lot happier there. In the meantime, I need this job, and I'm afraid our manager will take action against me when she finds out I'm covering for you.

Lead by
example

Your coworker continues with the guilt trip:

> Just say it is something about the family—something we don't document. Say anything like that. Please?

Your response:

> I can tell our manager I knew you had to step out, but I'm not comfortable telling her it was a patient-care issue. I will just tell her I'm not really sure what was going on—since I really don't know what happened on your phone call.

Learn the
consequence

Your coworker is relentless and thankful:

> That is fine, I really owe you one. Thanks again!

Your response:

> I can do this, this one time for you. I don't like to be placed in this difficult situation. Please don't ask me to cover again. It's not because I don't want to help you, it's because I need this job. I appreciate you understanding my situation, too.

Techniques

Acronyms and scripting techniques are only as good in conversations as the level of emotional intelligence (EI) and emotional competence (EC) you have. In other words, you may have hard-wired how to formulate open-ended questions, but if you insistently ask these questions, with no regard to your emotions or the persons that you are speaking to, these questions can be useless if emotions are running high. You are more likely to receive no response than even a simple yes or no answer, if you or the person you're speaking to is emotionally unstable. Let's review the components of EI when infused with acronyms and scripting techniques.

Self-awareness. Know your emotions and examine your undertones when speaking and listening to others. Being self-aware keeps you in check with how your emotions affect you and others (Goleman, 2007). As a nurse, this means having a clear picture of your strengths and weaknesses and ensures you are behaving with modesty and humbleness (Crompton, 2010). LEARN is a proactive, self-reflective way to stay respectful to others and maintain your integrity:

Listen

Empathize

Ask questions

Recognize yourself and others

No interruptions

Self-regulation. Nurses who control their emotions rarely attack others, make hasty or emotionally based decisions, stereotype people, or show disrespect. Self-regulation keeps us in tune with our emotions and in control with our emotions. This element of EI, according to Goleman (1998), covers a leader's commitment to personal accountability. Using active listening skills and asking clarifying questions ensures you that your communications are effective. To become aware of your emotions and how you regulate your emotions, ask yourself the following open-ended questions using some of the 3WITH acronym described earlier in this chapter:

- *How* and what am I feeling?

- *How* long have I have I felt this way?

- *What* feelings are manifesting in my body (for example, clenching my teeth, feeling tired, headache, stomachache)?

By asking yourself these simple questions, you are rationalizing your emotions and gaining better control of your emotions because you are logically thinking them through rather than just blurting out the first thing you think of (which is usually not the most appropriate thought, thanks to our amygdala). You might recall that the amygdala, or the emotional center of the brain, is the trigger point for how you respond to certain situations. For example, when these circuits perceive a threat, such as your emotional response to forgetting to administer digoxin on time, they flood the body with stress hormones. These stress hormones shunt blood away from the organs to the limbs, and this causes that awful panic feeling.

The response is also cognitive and determines the extent you worry or become upset, frustrated, or angered. That means that you don't have as much energy for what you are supposed to be doing or want to be doing. Moreover, you are more likely to resort to old, immature behaviors that can cause you regret and embarrassment (Goleman, 1998). For example, when something upsets us in the workplace, we all know how easy it would be to simply yell or cry as if we were toddlers; however, we know we must stay professional and poised. Unfortunately, not everyone in the workplace remains professional when things don't go their way. This is why having a high EI is so important.

time to reflect

Examples of statements you may unconsciously think that tell you your amygdala is being hijacked include the following:

- What was I thinking? I'm such an idiot.

- I'll never get this project done.

- That's it; I can't take it anymore!

- This place is just toxic and chaotic.

- No one ever cares about me around this place.

- If they don't want to listen to me, then—oh well.

- I'll never be nice to him again.

Where is your responsibility in those statements? The answer is that you have none. You are placing it on the other people. To correct your thought process and take control of your emotions, you would take responsibility and say something along these lines:

- I am angry.

- I am worried.

What other kinds of statements might you make that show you are taking responsibility?

Motivation. Self-motivated nurses work steadily toward their goals, and they have extremely high standards for the care they deliver to their patients. Motivated leaders inspire their associates and lead by example. Therefore, it's important to hardwire high-impact, motivational words into your everyday conversations (see Table 4.2).

Table 4.2 High-Impact, Motivational Words and How to Use Them

High-Impact, Motivational Word	Example of Use
Positive	I am **positive** about our choice.
Fabulous	That is a **fabulous** idea.
Absolutely	I **absolutely** agree….
Certainly	I can **certainly** assist you….
Wonderful	That is a **wonderful** alternative….
Fantastic	What a **fantastic** solution.
Completely	I **completely** agree with your concern.
Indeed	**Indeed**, this will help….
Unquestionably	That is **unquestionably** the solution.
Definitely	I am **definitely** interested.

Social awareness. Nurses need to be aware of their surroundings, which includes patients, families, and colleagues. Read facial expressions and examine other nonverbal signals that can create a better understanding of your individual employee's mood, feelings, and comfort level. For nurses, having empathy is critical to delivering nursing excellence and quality care. Nurses with empathy have the ability to put themselves in someone else's situation. They help in the professional development of other nurses on their units, resolve conflict, and actively listen. To begin practicing empathy, you need to become aware of other people's emotions.

Most nurses understand that patients and even colleagues don't always tell us how they are really feeling about something. Think about the standard greetings in the workplace, such as, "Hello. How are you today?" The receiver responds with "Fine," or "Good, thank you," regardless of how they are actually feeling. So how do nurses become aware of others' true feelings? The answer is by asking open-ended questions. The responses to open-ended questions can help you read between the lines of what the receiver is saying versus how they are really feeling. A few open-ended questions can include:

- "Tell me more about that."

- "What type of resolution do you think would work best?"

- "How can I help you?"

Nurses who have experienced emotional extremes due to personal experiences are more likely to be empathetic to others (Lombardo & Eyre, 2011). When nurses are empathetic, they understand how others feel because they have experienced something similar and have felt similar emotions. When nurses haven't experienced this breadth of emotions, it is more difficult to find empathy for others. What is even more concerning is when nurses have experienced consistently high amounts of stress and become victims of compassion fatigue (Lombardo & Eyre, 2011). It is vitally important to understand where physiological empathy ends and where pathological empathy begins. Signs and symptoms of this include exhaustion, decreased ability to feel sympathy or empathy, and increased levels of anger and irritability.

Here are a few scripts and phrases to increase your empathy and social awareness:

- **"I imagine…"** This tells your listener that you're just exercising your imagination and not trying to be judgmental.

    Example: "When I came in I *imagined* the patient would be sitting up. I don't know about you, but I have to admit I was optimistic about him reaching that goal."

- **"That reminds me…"** This transition-type phrase helps to connect topics, especially when you would like to change the subject, but keep the conversation flowing. This is useful to even completely redirect the conversation.

    Example: *"That reminds me* of when I went down to the lab. Did you know there is a new process for obtaining blood gases?"

- **"Let's pretend…"** This phrase invites others to join you in leaving reality behind for a short time. This is also great to gain permission to play devil's advocate or show an opposing side to a situation without appearing threatening or judgmental.

  Example: "I see you are in a lot of pain, so while your medication is beginning to work, *let's pretend* we are on a sunny beach on a beautiful day," or "*Let's pretend* our boss says no to the proposal; we can always remind him what happened the last time he said no and _____ happened."

- **"I would like to…"** Sometimes you might feel left out of a conversation, so using a phrase like this opens the door to showing interest.

  Example: "Although I don't work in the labor and delivery unit, *I would like to.*"

Relationship management. Attaining a clear picture of yourself and others will help in conflict management, team building, communication, and productivity. Nurses who are adept in the social skills component of EI are proficient communicators. They're just as open to hearing bad news as good news, and they're experts at motivating their teams to support them and be excited about a new initiative. Nurses who have noble social skills are also good at leading change and resolving conflicts in a diplomatic way; they set an example with their own behaviors.

It is incredibly important to never undermine someone's thoughts or feelings. It is acceptable to agree to disagree, but it is unacceptable to be disrespectful or judgmental. For example, you want to *avoid* saying things like:

- "I understand how you're feeling, *but* I don't think you understand."

- "I can understand why you feel that way, *but* you're wrong."

- "I appreciate what you are telling me, *but* I think you are really off base."

Improve your relationship management by using the following sample scripting tips:

- **"…just kidding…"** This is the best way to backtrack out of something that was inappropriate or perceived as inappropriate to the listener. The key, however, is that you say this phrase before your listeners react verbally. Look at the nonverbal language as a cue for how they perceived it.

  For example, a patient who is being prepped for surgery is telling jokes. With good intent you join them by saying, "This is my first day in the OR, and you are my first patient…." [The patient suddenly glares at you and isn't in a laughing mood anymore.] You can quickly say *"Just kidding!* I have been here for 15 years and have assisted in hundreds of these surgeries. I can assure you, you are in good hands and I was only trying make you comfortable by joining you in the joking."

- **"I can relate to…"** Sometimes the best way to relate to someone or something is to restate their story from an experience you had to show commonalities as to how they felt about an experience.

  Example: "I can't imagine how you felt when awaiting the diagnosis about your sister, but *I can relate to* being scared about things, like when we thought my brother would have to have his leg amputated."

- **"I don't know too much about that, so I'm guessing it's similar to…"** This is the perfect transition-type phrase to keep a conversation going, even when you have no knowledge of a topic. It's okay to admit your ignorance. Use this phrase to fill in the gap.

> Avoid using the word *but.* When you say that word, you're drawing negative attention and discounting all the information mentioned before the word *but.* For example, "I like your scrub top, but I like the one you wore yesterday." Replace the word *but* with *and* or *so.* This keeps the conversation positive. For example, "I like your scrub top, and I like the one you wore yesterday, too."

Example: *"I don't know too much about that since I never worked in the cath lab, so I'm guessing it's similar to* my unit in terms of its unique challenges."

The goal is to work to truly understand why someone is feeling a particular way. A person's resistance to an idea could be indicative of them having a different perception. Perhaps it is one you haven't thought of? In other words, treat the other person's feelings as information that you need to process. Here are some suggested scripts for how to comfort the emotions of others:

- "Tell me why you feel that way."

- "What aspect of the project/idea/decision makes you feel that way?"

- "What is it that you need?"

- "I understand that you feel this way. How can we gain your support in the decision?"

- "I can see that you are very uncomfortable with the decision. Tell me more."

- "I know you are hesitant and that you only want us to be successful."

- "I hear the concern in what you are saying, and I appreciate it."

- "I haven't experienced what you are feeling. I imagine it is not easy."

Think for a moment how someone would respond to these statements. Although you are considering their needs and helping them to achieve their goals, you're also benefiting by empowering them and helping them feel validated. It's truly a win-win situation.

Conflict management is a complex skill set to develop because it requires you to revisit the conflict in order to find remedy. I think a common approach used by many in resolving conflict is to obey the Golden Rule. You may recall the Golden Rule reminds us to treat others as we wish to be treated. Alessandra and O'Conner (1996), authors of *The Platinum Rule*, offer a different approach.

These business experts suggest that we treat others as they would like to be treated (not as we would want to be treated). How would we know what other people want? Well, think about the 4 social styles of people we discussed in previous chapters. For example, if you have an Amiable style, or focus on emotions and feelings, then trying to resolve conflict with a Driving style will not appreciate your coddling as remedy (Merrill & Reid, 1999). They would prefer a direct, quick, and specific resolution. We need to remember that we all have different needs, wants, and desires. We cannot always internalize issues that affect others. We need to think about how we can best serve others in their way, not ours. The ability to manage conflict is invaluable because it will help you become a better leader, coworker, and nurse.

time to reflect

To improve your conflict-management skills, consider:

- Setting "ground rules" for the conversation (such as no interruptions, providing for individual considerations)

- Asking open-ended questions to get to the genesis of the conflict

- Allowing people to share their feelings and concerns without judgment

What else might you do to improve you conflict-management skills?

Pulling It All Together With the CAR Framework

We reviewed in prior chapters how the aBEST framework infuses acronyms, body language, emotional intelligence, and scripting techniques for more effective communications. In this chapter, we reviewed how helpful acronyms can be used to deliver comprehensive conversations (i.e., SBAR and 3WITH) or when looking for an easy way to recall what body gestures can be indicative of someone who is being dishonest (i.e., 2BROKE). In addition to using acronyms, we reviewed the relevance of emotions, body gestures, and sample scripting to achieve desired outcomes.

At a more definite level, we can apply the CAR framework within the aBEST principles. This helps us think through the specifics of how, why, where, and when we will engage others in conversations. More specifically:

Consider. The C in the CAR framework reminds you to consider the 5 Rights for Communication Safety (as discussed in Chapter 1). This helps you to make sure you're speaking to the right person, at the right place, at the right time, and with the right emotions in check. These emotions are dependent upon our emotional intelligence and emotional competence as well as our ability to interpret the meaning of body gestures during conversations. Conducting conversations at the right time can be further assessed in regard to our emotional sensitivity, as shown in Figure 4.1).

Action or call to Action. The action or call to action allows us to plan the layout of the conversation. What specific acronyms, or scripting techniques, will you use and why? Maybe delivering the same message to two different people would prompt you to say it differently to each person due to varying personality styles. As we discussed in Chapter 1, the Social Style Model helps us understand why our thoughts, feelings, and interactions with others are perceived differently. This is why we need to carefully plan how we will execute conversations based on people's varying personality styles.

Return on investment. Understanding your return on investment (ROI) prior to having a conversation is key. This basically asks you about the genesis of the conservation, or why you're having the conversation to begin with. Understanding your ROI will also help you determine what a successful conversation would look like to you. What is the result you are seeking from the conversation? If you have an understanding of what it is you're seeking from the conversation, you can better prepare which acroynms and scripting techniques to use. Analyzing your ROI brings awareness to the importance of how the conversation is perceived. Think of the ROI as your investment. In other words, if your emotions are running high and you allow your initial emotional reactions to drive your behavior, you are at risk of having poor outcomes. Is this worth investing in? We have all experienced moments when we said or did something less than desirable and punished ourselves with negative thoughts and self-talk. But

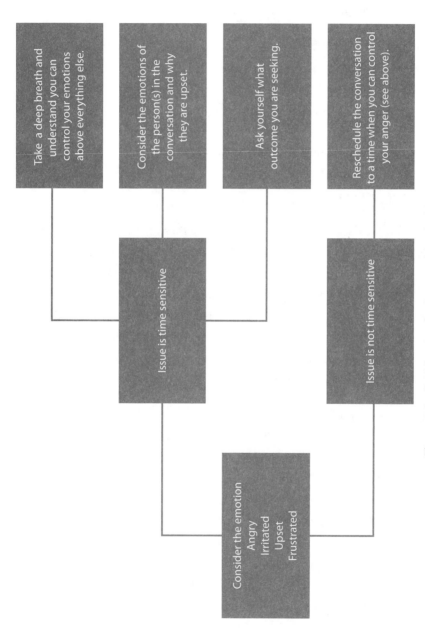

Figure 4.1 Decision tree for time-sensitive decisions

when we consider the importance of the ROI in conversations, we can learn to reframe our negative self-talk into positive talk to keep us focused and on track. For example, alternatives to the negative self-talk phrases include:

- "I made an honest mistake. This is frustrating, but I can undoubtedly fix it."

- "I need to refocus on the priorities and ask for help."

- "I need to take a pause so my frustration doesn't prevent me from doing a good job."

- "I'm not in a good mood today."

- "My ideas aren't always the ones chosen. Maybe I should get feedback on that idea."

- "Let me make sure I fully understand the goal/initiative. What else can I do to help get us there?"

- "He may be someone who doesn't want a friendly relationship with me, and that's okay."

time to reflect

Know when you are being reactive in thought versus when you're proactive.

Reactive Statements	Proactive Statements
Well, I did what I could...	I will consider or search for alternatives.
It's just who I am.	I can make a different choice.
She makes me so mad.	I can control my feelings.
I have to do that.	I will choose an appropriate retort.
I can't _____.	I prefer to _____.

What other reactive and proactive statements can you think of?

Responding to Bad News

You have been asked to work on a very important project for the Magnet application. You work with an elite group of nurses and put in a lot of time and effort. After 1 month and countless hours of blood, sweat, and tears, your group submits this assignment to the chief nursing officer (CNO). The CNO reviews the project and sends it back to the group with more corrections than you had expected. There wasn't even one positive comment made! What is happening upon receiving this news?

Feeling:	Are you angry or scared? Embarrassed?
Thinking:	What is your initial thought? How does this tie in with how you are feeling? What did you say to the CNO? How was that received?
Physical Reaction:	Is your heart racing? Are you breathing faster than normal? Did you lose your appetite?
Behavior:	Did you punch a wall? Put your head down? Cry?

A typical first response to bad news may look like the following:

Nurse:	"But _____ [CNO], we spent a lot of time on this. (Feeling: victim)"
CNO:	"This is not the level of work I was expecting from this team."
Nurse:	"I beg to differ. You don't understand how much effort we put into this. This is crazy, I just can't believe this. I don't know what will make you happy." (Feelings: angry, confused, and upset)

Now, look at what an emotionally competent nurse might say:

Nurse: (taking a deep breath and remaining calm)	"It is important to our team that we are successful on this project. I would like clarification on a few of your comments. When is a good time to set up a meeting?" (Feelings: optimistic and positive)

During the meeting, the emotionally competent nurse will calmly repeat the CNO's complaints back to him or her to make sure that everything is being understood properly. Making steady eye contact and speaking in a nonaggressive tone, the nurse will say: "So, what you're saying is _____," or "To clarify _____." Put the criticisms in your own words. The goal here is to take the focus away from any personality clash and place it directly on substantive disputes.

And if what the CNO is saying is truly unreasonable, this tactic may shine a harsh light on the initial critique. Be very careful to stay factual and avoid the temptation to exaggerate. If the CNO claims your work will deliver mediocre results, don't say, "So what you're saying is that our work is not good enough for the Magnet document." If you overstate the case, you'll come off as someone who's defensive rather than a practical person who's authentically looking to get to the bottom of the problem. Rational treatise really is the best antidote to unfair criticism. More often than not, it wins out, as long as the people involved are open and willing to finding the best course.

It's often best to manage immediate situations by remaining calm, getting your critic to repeat the comments, and then clarifying verbally that you understand them. You may spot that the criticism is based on a misunderstanding or a different perspective, in which case it is reasonably straightforward to iron this out. In more complicated situations, particularly when your critic is your boss, you need to schedule an "offline" meeting to discuss the criticism.

The Drive Home

Let's review the *driving it back home* pointers from this chapter:

- Hardwiring positive and motivating scripts can help deter future amygdala hijacking, which results in improved communication and relationship management (Goleman, 1998).

- Weaving scripting into open-ended questions helps you remember what words to use, removes bias, and helps you gauge whether someone's body gestures are appropriate to the words they use.

- 3WITH stands for choosing any three of the words that start with *W*, such as *what, why,* and *where*. In addition to remembering there are three words that start with the letter *W*, the *I* stands for "in what way," the *T* stands for "tell me more," and the *H* stands for "help, how, hear," again using the number 3.

- To see if someone isn't telling the truth, remember 2BROKE. This represents that you might see the following body language gestures: 2 Bs (blinking and brow movements), R (right-sided eye movements), O (opposite mirroring), K (knuckles clenched), and E (edgy—fidgety, nose rubbing, staring).

- In order to resolve conflict, we need to consider how we can best serve others in their way, not ours.

- Within the CAR framework, you need to

    - Consider (C) if you are speaking to the right person, at the right place, at the right time, with the right emotions in check (EI and body language), and with the right ROI or intent.

    - Action (A) reminds you to think about which action or approach is best suited for which individual due to varying social styles. One size doesn't always fit all.

    - Return on investment (R) reminds you to think about what the outcome is you're looking for before having a conversation. We don't always think about what we are seeking as a final result of conversations, so our ROI may end up in the red. Reframe any negative self-talk so that it becomes positive and leads to a productive action. If you lash out at other people, what ROI is that getting you? Not much, other than possibly embarrassment or even the cost of your job.

References

Alessandra, T. & O'Conner, M. J. (1996). The Platinum Rule. Retrieved from http://www.alessandra.com/dobusiness.htm

Crompton, M. (2010). Improving self-awareness increases your emotional intelligence. Retrieved from http://www.peoriamagazines.com/ibi/2010/apr/improving-self-awareness-increases-your-emotional-intelligence

Driver, J. (2010). *You say more than you think: A 7-day plan for using the new body language to get what you want!* New York, NY: Crown Publishers.

Goleman, D. (1998). *Working with emotional intelligence.* New York, NY: Bantam.

Goleman, D. (2007). *Emotional intelligence: Why it can matter more than IQ.* New York, NY: Random House.

Joint Commission. (2006.). Root causes of sentinel events, all categories. Retrieved from http://www.jointcommission.org/NR/rdonlyres/ FA465646-5F5F-4543-AC8F-E8AF6571E372/0/root_cause_se.jpg

Kaiser Permanente of Colorado. SBAR Technique for Communication: A Situational Briefing Model report to physician about a critical situation [Institute for Healthcare Improvement web site] Evergreen Colorado USA 2004, Retrieved from http://www.ihi.org/knowledge/Pages/Tools/SBARTechnique-forCommunicationASituationalBriefingModel.aspx

Lombardo, B., & Eyre, C. (2011). Compassion Fatigue: A Nurse's Primer, *OJIN: The Online Journal of Issues in Nursing (16),*1, doi: 10.3912/OJIN.Vol16No01Man03

Merrill, D. W. & Reid, R. H. (1999). *Personal styles and effective performance.* New York, NY: CRC Press.

Scripting. (2014). In *Wikipedia.* Retrieved from http://en.wikipedia.org/wiki/Scripting_language

Twain, M. (n.d.). Retrieved from http://www.brainyquote.com/quotes/quotes/m/marktwain122650.html.

> *"If your actions inspire others to dream more, learn more, do more and become more, you are a leader."*
> –John Quincy Adams

5

Interprofessional Coaching Conversations

In lieu of common buzzwords, such as *courageous* or *difficult,* I purposely used the term *coaching* in this chapter's title to describe hard-to-have conversations. That's because I firmly believe almost all conversations have the potential for coaching. Coaching conversations are not one direction either; all conversations, even if you are the only person talking, are two directional. Although providing corrective action is a coaching moment for the listener, it is also a coaching moment for yourself.

For example, an upset patient speaks to the nurse manager of the unit because her nurse hasn't been responding timely to her numerous call button requests. A wise nurse leader will prepare how he or she will deliver this coaching conversation to the nurse, as well as take time after the conversation to reflect on what he or she (the nurse manager) could have improved upon during the conversation and what worked well. It is important to emphasize that coaching conversations are not limited to vertical, or nurse-leader-to-staff conversations, but can also be applied horizontally, that is, between colleagues.

Planning and self-reflection are really at the core of the *R* (return on investment, or ROI) in the CAR framework. The ROI reminds you to explore what your investment is for having the conversation in the first place. Whatever that investment is (e.g., providing education or direction, asking for feedback), you learn something when you take a moment to reflect on your strengths and weaknesses in the conversation. In other words, your ROI gives you a chance to "look in the mirror" and note what you can improve upon and what worked well. With this reflection, you can continually improve your conversations, especially when you need to have hard-to-have ones. Hard-to-have conversations run the gamut, including:

- Talking to a coworker about a problem he or she is having and that is affecting your work

- Giving your nurse manager feedback when he or she is doing something that's demotivating you

- Critiquing a colleague

- Talking to a colleague, doctor, or patient who is not keeping up his or her end of the bargain

- Confronting a coworker or colleague about disrespectful behavior, such as discrimination

- Pointing out someone's shortcomings that are affecting patient care (e.g., noticing a colleague didn't wash their hands)

When faced with the prospect of having hard-to-have conversations such as the ones just described, it can be helpful to have scripts in place. For example, Scripts 5.1 and 5.2 address two of the conversations above.

time to reflect

Do you find yourself looking to blame someone or even yourself when things don't go right? The next time you find yourself stuck in blame, ask yourself:

- What feelings am I not expressing?

- Has the other person acknowledged my feelings?

Try using a role-reversal approach and ask yourself:

- "What would they say I'm contributing?"

Work through your feelings and any distortions or gaps in your perceptions. Share the impact by saying something such as, "Although this was probably not your intention, I felt uncomfortable when I heard you say _____." This shows you are taking responsibility for your contribution.

You also need to describe how your contributions affect situations. For example, you can say things like, "There are a few things that I've done [or not done] that have made this situation harder," or "I'm apprehensive in bringing this up, yet at the same time, it's important to me that we discuss _____."

Remember, a real conversation is an interactive process in which you are constantly listening. Listening transmutes the conversation by shifting the goal of the conversation from trying to persuade someone to actually learning from them. Moreover, when you listen, you potentially increase how the other person listens to you. If you ever find that others aren't listening to you, consider whether you need to spend more time listening to them. Or maybe you are "trying" to listen to them, but your body gestures show them you're really not. Make sure you consider all variables that may affect how the conversation is going.

Script 5.1 What to say when... you want to ask your manager to stop micromanaging you.

T ell

To your nurse manager:

> Judy, I would like to speak with you about our mutual involvement in [insert name of project if this is a one-time instance or a trend that you are noticing]. I appreciate that you asked me to take the lead on this. I'm just hoping you can explain why I need to obtain your approval before moving onto the next level.

Your nurse manager is understanding:

> I didn't realize I was doing this. You're right, I don't need to approve this at every level.

Your response:

> Great, thank you. I'll still keep you abreast of my progress, though.

Your nurse manager is defensive:

> Well, I just want to make sure you're on the right track.

Your response:

> I appreciate your concern. But I'm afraid you aren't comfortable with my judgment.

E xplain

Lead by example

Your nurse manager is understanding:

How should we proceed?

Your response:

Moving forward, I'd like to send you a summary of how I will complete the next section of the project, and you can give me feedback. Does that sound reasonable?

Your nurse manager is defensive:

I never said I was uncomfortable with your judgment. Like I said, I just want to make sure you're on target. This is a big proposal.

Your response:

I was hoping I could be more instrumental in the decision-making process. I would like to complete [insert task] and then gain your insight. Is it acceptable from this point forward that I meet with you [insert time] and at that time you can provide further guidance, instead of me submitting this every day for your approval?

Learn the consequence

Your nurse manager is receptive:

Great, that sounds reasonable.

Your response:

Thank you for your support. I really appreciate it. I'll send you a meeting request today.

Your nurse manager is unreceptive:

I need to think about this.

Your response:

I respect that. Is there anything else I can do in the meantime? (If the manager is unreceptive, ask more open-ended questions to understand why he or she needs to be so involved in every aspect of the initiative(s) at hand. The consequence may be that you will need to continue working in this way.)

Script 5.2 What to say when… a coworker isn't respectful of diversity.

Tell

To your coworker:

John, I was told you didn't think Shweta (coworker) could handle the project since she was from India.

Explain

Your coworker denies it:

No, I didn't!

Your response:

I'm glad this source was incorrect because that was a very offensive comment.

Your coworker says he was joking:

Oh, come on, it was funny.

Your response:

I'm sure that was your intent, but it was offensive, not funny.

Your coworker says he did:

Well, it's true!

Your response:

Your personal feelings have nothing to do with her performance. Your accusation is inappropriate.

Lead by example

Your coworker denies it.

Your response:

It's a shame people feel the need to undermine others because of varied backgrounds. I hope you would join me in confronting staff who do this and even report it.

Your coworker says he was joking.

Your response:

Can you share with me why I thought your comment was so inappropriate? (Teach back)

Your coworker says he did and apologizes.

Your response:

If I ever hear such a comment again, I will report you on that occurrence and provide documentation on this prior occurrence and this conversation as well.

Learn the consequence

Your response:

(At this point, either take further action or move forward. Either way, you showed John his accusations are not tolerated.)

Formal and Informal Nurse Leadership Training

Regardless of the topic or circumstances, some types of conversations are awkward and hard to initiate, especially when emotions are elevated or the conversation involves someone you sincerely like (or dislike). Most people tend to avoid these conversations completely, which actually makes things worse. They tend to think that the situation will improve or the other person will change his or her behaviors, but this rarely happens. At other times, people use the ready-fire approach (as described in Chapter 1) to deal with the conversation, but this often makes the situation worse.

A better alternative is to learn the skills necessary to have effective conversations and then facilitate the dialogue with grace and finesse. Regardless of your title, you *are* a leader. All nurses are leaders, whether formal or informal (Clancy, 2012). Therefore, when issues arise, it is your professional responsibility to come with a solution-oriented approach to problem solving, not a problem-oriented approach. If nurses constantly run to those in formal leadership roles to seek answers to their problems, they are missing big opportunities to be viewed as leaders.

It has been vastly published that many healthcare organizations are not investing resources in leadership training for nurses (Curtis, Fintan, & de Vries, 2011; Sherman, Bishop, Eggenberger & Karden, 2007; Shirey, 2006; Swearingen, 2009). This is proven in the answer to this question: According to a recent Gallup poll, what is the number-one reason why more than 1 million people employed in the United States leave their jobs? Answer: Poor relationships with their managers or bosses (Ripper, 2013). Formal nurse leaders are encouraged to meet monthly or bimonthly, also known as "rounding with staff," to identify any gaps in processes or systems, establish relationships, show appreciation, and, ultimately, build trust (see Appendix B). In addition to rounding with staff, formal leaders can also round with other departmental managers or directors (see Appendix B).

Replacing Certainty With Curiosity

One key element you can adopt to improve your leadership skills is to move from a place of certainty to a place of curiosity in your conversations. You need to move from what you think is certainty, such as:

- "How can they think that?"

- "How can they be so unreasonable?"

to a more curious thought process such as:

- "I wonder what information they have that I don't."

- "How do they see things so that it makes sense to them?"

This way of thinking isn't so easy, but you need to negotiate with yourself in order to find this place of curiosity in your thoughts. In order to do this, you must first realize that understanding someone doesn't mean you are agreeing with the person. You need to respect each other's views, which you can do by realizing each person's stories have different information and different interpretations, thus both make sense to each of you and at the same time.

Simply acknowledging this earns you a lot of respect. For example, saying something such as, "Now that we understand each other, what is a good way to approach this?" doesn't mean that you are giving in to someone; it simply opens the door for finding resolution. This method also helps to separate blame from contributions in conversations. Blame is about judging others and draws on negativity. When you ask the question, "Who is to blame?" you essentially ask three negative questions:

- Who is responsible for the problem?

- Were they incompetent, unreasonable, or unethical?

- What punitive action is now warranted for their actions?

Although being punitive may be appropriate in some bureaucratic situations, it is really just a substitute for figuring out the root cause, or what really happened and why. On the other hand, contribution is an approach that helps you understand situations; it's also more positive. To show contribution, you can ask questions such as, "How have we each contributed to this condition?" or "What can we do to move forward?"

> Learn from conversations when emotions run high:
>
> **Don't**
> - Disguise a claim as a question.
> - Use questions to cross-examine.
> - Let your body show that you are in opposition of them.
>
> **Do**
> - Ask open-ended questions using 3WITH, such as
>   "Tell me more."
>   "Help me understand better."
>   "What would that look like?"
>   "What information might you have that I don't?"
>   "How do you see it differently?"
>
> In order to clarify what you are learning, paraphrase what you've heard.

The primary undertaking of a hard-to-have conversation is not to persuade, or get one over on the other person. It is to demonstrate what you see and why you see things certain ways, explain how you feel about things, and come to a resolution. Likewise, it is important to understand others' points of view.

When you acknowledge feelings, you aren't necessarily agreeing with others; you are simply showing respect and learning from conversations. Why? Well, because you can't move the conversation in a more positive direction until the other person feels he or she is heard and understood—remember the Platinum Rule (discussed in chapter 4)! This solidifies the importance of being cognizant to when you are playing the sly fox in conversations versus the cool cat. You play the sly fox when your amygdala is hijacked or when you don't have control of your emotions. You use words that are general, undermining, toxic, dramatic, or made up. When you play the cool cat, you stick to the facts, acknowledge your feelings and the feelings of those around you, and seek resolution respectfully.

For example, let's look at a conversation taking place between a CCU nursing director, Dr. Kelly, and a CCU medical director, Dr. Smith. They are both in formal leadership titles, working at the same hospital. In this conversation, Dr. Smith appears antagonistic toward Dr. Kelly, and she constantly reacts to his intonations. Dr. Smith's mistakes are highlighted in brackets in this conversation.

Dr. Smith:	"Look Dr. Kelly, everybody knows [Generalization] that this process-improvement project is supposed to be finished by the end of June. The only reason we are not going to meet the deadline is because of your slow [Toxic word] nursing department."
Dr. Kelly:	"Well, first of all, my nursing team is not slow. They have a much better record than other teams around here. Besides, the reason we cannot make the deadline is because we didn't have the resources…"
Dr. Smith:	"Somehow I knew you were going to use that as an excuse [Undermining Dr. Kelly]. I am not quite sure if this is true [Undermining himself], but I heard that the executive team gave you

three extra people to work on this part of the
project [Mixing facts with fiction].”

Dr. Kelly: “That's not true. I needed people with specific
skill sets, and we rotated the nursing team members for this.”

Dr. Smith: “The fact is that you think you can get anything
you want around here for this little part of a big
project and still be able to fall back on excuses
why it's not done on time [Condescending].”

Dr. Kelly: “I cannot believe this! I feel that I am being mar-
ginalized here.”

Dr. Smith   “It is absolutely clear [Extreme language] that
the reason your team is failing [Toxic word] is
because they lack a strong nursing leader [Un-
dermining]!”

Obviously, Dr. Smith needs to use less extreme remarks and stick to facts, not
his assumptions. Here are a a few suggestions that he can use:

- *Don't generalize* by suggesting “everybody.” Instead, he should speak from
  what he sees and leave out information that is hearsay from others.
  Suggestion:
  “As you know, we were given a deadline of June. I worry we will not
  make the deadline as I look at our progress to date.”

- *Stick to the facts* and don't make personal views or perceptions the facts.
  Suggestions:
  “As I understand…”
  “There have been some developments that I believe you might not be
  aware of….”
  “In my opinion….”

- *Don't undermine himself* by stating he doesn't know whether the things he is saying are even true.

   Suggestions:

   "I have heard from two people that…."

   "Can you tell me more about…."

- *Don't undermine others.*

   Ask thought-provoking questions such as:

   "What can we do to solve this"

   "Help me understand why you choose _____ instead of _____."

   "How did you come to the conclusion that…."

- *Stick to the facts at hand,* not the ones he makes up. Also, he shouldn't be so dramatic and condescending. In lieu of stating, "The fact is [insert story or perception]," or, "It is clear that _____," he should simply state, "From what you said, my understanding is _____."

time to reflect

Have you ever had a conversation so heated that you have simply walked away from it? Are the outcomes better when this happens? Have you ever told the person why you were walking away? Does giving an explanation help? The next time you walk away from an emotionally heated conversation, try the following:

- Explain why you are walking away. Otherwise, you may be giving the person the notion that they must be right because you have nothing else to say.

- Explain what hasn't been met and what you need for resolution. This gives the other person clear insight as to what your expectations are.

- Be willing to accept the consequences.

What else might you do?

Moving from a place of certainty to a place of curiosity can greatly improve your conversations as well as your leadership style. Regardless of whether we are formal or informal nurse leaders, improving our leadership skills is a shared responsibility. Refining our leadership skills is truly a journey to excellence. As I described in Chapter 1, the actual destination of the journey is secondary to the journey itself. We need to learn from others, and, even more importantly, we need to learn from our own experiences. Stay in a mindset of striving for progress, not just perfection. Remember, perfection is perception—everyone views it differently.

Hard-to-Have Conversations as a Reverse Hourglass

I describe hard-to-have conversations with the understanding that the receiver already knows there is an issue that needs to be discussed. Unlike other conversation approaches discussed in prior chapters, where the focus is on understanding the differences, a hard-to-have conversation is a more direct approach. Just like any story or movie, hard-to-have conversations have a beginning, a middle, and an end. The beginning provides the structure, or the intent or purpose, of the conversation. The middle shares the journey of experiences, perceptions, and feelings. At the end of the conversation, the parties should reach an agreement that satisfies mutual interests. If you've prepared for the conversation by following a structured process and remained in a resourceful emotional state, then the likelihood of reaching a desired outcome is high.

Keep in mind that when you're having a hard-to-have conversation, craft the amount of time you devote to each section as a reverse hourglass (see Figure 5.1). The beginning of the conversation should be relatively brief. After all, you are introducing or even reintroducing the issue. The middle of the conversation takes the most time because this is where listening to and understanding each other's issues and concerns takes place. The end of the conversation is the moving forward approach and wraps up the conversation.

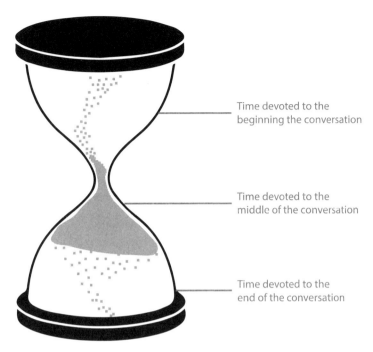

Figure 5.1 How to craft a hard-to-have conversation

Most of my colleagues share that just starting the conversation is often what is most difficult for them. They ask, "How do I even bring up an uncomfortable topic?" I usually explain that if they are feeling a little apprehensive, chances are high that the other person is, too. It is very important to have structure in a conversation. The following examples can make starting the conversation a little easier:

- "I want to suggest a way to discuss _____ that provides us both time to think and respond to what's being said. I'm open to the possibility that I've either missed something or in some way contributed to this, so I'd like to hear your reactions to what I'm going to share, and I'd also appreciate your perspective."

- "Here's how I thought we'd begin: I'll start by describing my perspective, such as what I remember about what happened, and then you can share your reaction to this with me."

- "It's important to me that I share how I'm feeling and the impact it had on me, and I'd like to hear your thoughts on that. I'd then like to explore ways we could ensure that when we work together in the future, we work effectively."

In addition, use the CAR framework to make sure you have *considered* (C) your emotional state and the intent of the conversation, as well as reviewed the 5 Rights of Communication. Make sure you have a solid *action* plan (A) that is structured for clear delivery, and you are aware of body language gestures. Finally, acknowledge what your *ROI* (R) is, and revisit your action plan and what the outcome is you're seeking. Remember to ready, aim, and re-aim before you fire up your conversation.

The Driver's Seat: Understanding the aBEST Approach in Coaching Conversations

To demonstrate the difference the aBEST approach can make when addressing difficult situations, read the following vignette and a typical response and then compare the same vignette using the aBEST approach to the conversation.

> You are a nurse manager (NM) of a primary care pediatric practice. On a dreary day in mid-November, you take on a full patient assignment because you have three registered nurse (RN) call outs, and you're also trying to run flu clinic and meet payroll deadlines. In passing, Dr. Todd, the medical practice director, instructs you to have an immediate conversation with one of your RNs named Susie.
>
> According to Dr. Todd, Susie is experiencing many difficulties in obtaining proper head measurements. He irately informs you that Susie is consistently making errors in documenting and in

obtaining a head circumferance. He undermines your managerial skills by asking how you could possibly allow someone so incompetent to work at the practice. After he abruptly tells you to "Fix it or else...," he storms off before you can respond.

You're left feeling angry because he doesn't acknowledge how much you have on your plate right now, embarrassed because you've not noticed her skills were "that bad", and apprehensive because discipline is the most awkward part of your roles and responsibilities. You are simply not a fan of conflict.

In response to Dr. Todd's direction, let's assume the nurse manager responds in self-preservation or a knee-jerk management reaction and goes straight to Susie in an attempt to "fix it," per Dr. Todd's demand. Here is an example of a typical response:

NM: "Susie, our medical director informed me that you are not obtaining head circumferences correctly." (This is stated with arms crossed in front of chest in an accusatory manner.)

Susie: "I'm taking the measurements correctly. What is he talking about? What patient? When?" (She rolls her eyes and crosses her arms in front of her chest.)

NM: "But Dr. Todd says otherwise." (Places hand on chin with arm still crossed over chest, looking perplexed.) "You know I have a full patient load today, too, and a million other tasks at hand. I really don't need this right now."

Susie: "I don't know what else to tell you. I know what I'm doing, and he never said anything to me." (Hands on both hips with weight shifted to the right hip, expressing that she is defensive.)

NM: Feeling Susie's defense, the NM backs down and says,
       "Okay, well, just make sure you double-check yourself,
       especially around Dr. Todd." (Stated in a skeptical tone of
       voice and talking as she is walking away.)

Does this sort of dialogue sound familiar? Do you think that was an effective
conversation? If yes, then you need to read more. If you see opportunities in this
scenario, you're on target.

Your Road Map: Applying the aBEST Approach in Coaching Conversations

Engaging in coaching conversations can help others make better contributions
toward a goal, enhance the performer's capability in both their competence
and commitment, and improve relationships with the performer. Utilizing the
aBEST approach ensures your words are appropriate to your body gestures and
to your emotions. We will now take a closer look at how the aBEST approach
can be used more effectively in coaching conversations by incorporating the
CAR acronym.

Pulling It All Together With the CAR Acronym

Let's apply the CAR framework within the aBEST approach to make a hard-to-
have conversation a little easier on you. You may recall the CAR acronym is the
framework behind the aBEST approach. Let's begin with the *C* and *consider* the
5 Rights for Communication Safety, as described in Chapter 1.

- **Right person:** Are you sure the RN named by the doctor is the RN at
  fault? Who else might need to know about the conversation before it takes
  place? If you speak up, who or what else will this affect? How important
  is it that you bring this up? What would happen if you didn't have the
  conversation?

- **Right place:** Coach in private, commend in public. Because this is a coaching session, plan for the conversation to take place in a private setting. Has this person been given the opportunity to discover the issue on her own, and does the person recognize it as an issue? Can this issue be brought up via email or some other medium? Does this conversation need to be had face-to-face?

- **Right time:** Is now an appropiate time for the conversation? (In other words, will taking the RN aside disrupt patient flow?) Is the issue current or one that occurred some time ago?

- **Right emotion:** Consider your emotions and the emotions of the RN. When elevated moods are present, the chances of an effective conversation decrease. Control your emotions! Have you thought through enough what the real problem is so you can articulate it well? If you bring up this issue, do you have an action plan, or are you just going to rant and rave because you feel like it?

- **Right ROI:** What is the outcome you are seeking (for example, educational, disciplinary, informational)? Are you willing to experience the emotion that might come as a result of speaking about this topic? Have you thought through why this person might be behaving this way? What external or internal factors are affecting this person? What are her motivations? Is the behavior you are proposing as a substitute possible for this individual to accomplish or learn?

Next is the *A. Action or a call to action* reminds you to think through the action plan. For example, how will you structure this impeding difficult conversation? Because the preceding vignette is a good example of a coaching session, the TELL approach (described in the next section) is appropriate to implement.

The final part of the CAR framework is the *R, ROI*. As discussed in the "consider" section, this is the area where you need to dig deeper into not only identifying the outcome you are seeking to this conversation, but also how this outcome will provide resolution. In other words, are you looking for the RN to just agree with you, or are you looking for her not to agree with you but to want to improve her performance? If you answered that you want her to improve her performance, then prepare to help her develop an action plan. This is key to finding resolution and in driving an effective conversation.

Pulling It All Together With the TELL Acronym

Now that you've reviewed the CAR framework, it's time to apply the TELL acronym and learn how to make the conversation between Susie and her nurse manager more effective:

T   *Tell or talk about* what has been observed or the issue at hand. For example, don't be the sly fox and state, "Your hostility and negativity are demoralizing!" as this would only trigger an emotional response. Instead, state, "When you're not engaged, _____."

E   *Explain* the observation or issue that is a problem and extract the person's story of the account. When stating how you feel about the situation, avoid "You make me feel" statements in favor of "I feel." Being assertive means you can choose your reactions, even if others are being unreasonable. The goal is to keep the conversation factual and calm by describing feelings rather than acting them out. Be specific: "I'm angry," "I'm worried," or "I'm annoyed."

L   *Lead* by example. In other words, show Susie what good performance should look like. Articulate the desired new behavior while avoiding blame, judgment, or condescension. The key is to ask for a positive change, not a negative one. For example, "Susie, please try to be more open to the opinions of others by asking open-ended questions," is more powerful than "Stop being so critical!"

L   *Learn* the consequence. Be clear with Susie what the performance improvement plan (PIP) will be (if applicable) or what the consequence is if she continues the same performance. If the behavior doesn't change or the conversation is disciplinary, then use the negative consequence. If you do introduce the negative, be sure you're prepared to carry it out or you'll lose credibility. For example, state, "If you will work with me on this, then I am confident that both you and the team will benefit. If not, I will be forced to start formal disciplinary action according to our human resource policy."

Keep in mind that the body language section is bringing to your attention key points only. Remember to consider all gestures before making concrete assessments.

In the following tables, you will note that by reviewing and assessing Susie's body language and keeping her own emotions in check, the nurse manager (NM) effectively exhibited a coaching approach more than a reprimanding approach.

Table 5.1 Using the Tell or Talk Component of the TELL Acronym to Improve Conversations

Body Language NM	Body Language RN	Emotional Intelligence/ Competence NM	Emotional Intelligence/ Competence RN	Scripting Techniques	Conversation
Has eye contact. Relaxed and places arm out to direct RN into an office.	Has eye contact. Grabs a pad and pen, runs hands through hair while walking to the office.	Remains in control of her emotions.	Feeling a little uneasy, questioning what this "talk" is about.	NM is considerate of RN's time.	NM: "Susie, do you have a few minutes to talk"? Susie says, "Yes."
Hands are lightly folded on top of the table, with midsection turned toward RN.	Hands folded across chest, legs wrapped around chair legs.	Remains in control of her emotions.	Feeling more uncomfortable and defensive.	NM is straightforward, to the point.	NM: "Let's sit down here. Susie, it has come to my attention that you're not obtaining head circumferences correctly."

Table 5.2 Using the Explain Component of the TELL Acronym to Improve Conversations

Body Language NM	Body Language RN	Emotional Intelligence/ Competence NM	Emotional Intelligence/ Competence RN	Scripting Techniques	Conversation
Has eye contact. Leans in to Susie; belly button faces RN. Hands placed in front in a steeple.	Has eye contact. Remains with arms crossed and legs wrapped around chair.	Remains in control of her emotions.	Feeling more uncomfortable with the accusation, but appreciates her hard work is recognized.	NM remains positive and validates RN's contributions to the office.	NM: "Susie, you have been a great asset to us for the past 3 months of your employment. You come to work on time; you're happy; and you work hard. I was quite shocked to hear from a colleague that you are having difficulty with this task. Can you share with me your thoughts on this?"
Hands are lightly folded on top of the table, with midsection turned toward RN.	Hands are now cupping her neck, and she is leaning toward the NM. RN's legs are wrapped around chair legs.	Remains in control of her emotions and observes that RN's body language indicates that she is upset.	Emotions of worry prevail; anger does not.		RN: "I am shocked, too. No one ever said this to me before. Am I being fired? Who said this?"

Table 5.2 Using the Explain Component of the TELL Acronym to Improve Conversations   (continued)

Body Language NM	Body Language RN	Emotional Intelligence/ Competence NM	Emotional Intelligence/ Competence RN	Scripting Techniques	Conversation
Palms open and face up, revealing openness. Her midsection is turned toward RN.	Hands are now cupping her neck, and she is leaning toward the NM. RN's legs are wrapped around chair legs. Looks to the left often.	Remains in control of her emotions and senses RN is upset.	Emotions of worry prevail; anger does not.	Motivating	NM: "I didn't receive permission to share who said this, but it is more important that we iden-
			Emotions of inquisi- tive nature begin, and RN is recalling how she usu- ally performs head measurements.	Positive Acknowledges RN's feelings by stating she isn't being fired.	tify where the mistake is, if any, and how we can fix it. You are not being fired. I know it is not your intention to take in- accurate measurements. Let's work together on an action plan."

Table 5.3 Using the Lead Component of the TELL Acronym to Improve Conversations

Body Language		Emotional Intelligence/ Competence		Scripting Techniques	Conversation
NM	RN	NM	RN		
Has eye contact. Maintains open arms and remains confident by standing tall and approachable.	Has eye contact. Arms are initially crossed in front of her, but as the teaching begins, she begins to lean toward the teaching, and her naughty bits are directly facing the tape measure the NM is holding.	Remains in control of her emotions and is confident.	Feeling uncomfortable but then begins to look interested at the way the NM is measuring.	NM is straightforward in her conversation and teaching. NM is not punitive.	NM:"I want to perform the head circumference in front of you on the next patient. Let's go bring the patient back to the exam room." (Preps patient and performs head circumference measurement.) After the patient leaves, RN identifies that she measures heads on the eyebrow and at the top of the occipital bone, not above the eyebrow and at the largest spot on the back of the head. RN clearly articulates her knowledge deficit and where she can improve.

Table 5.4   Using the Learn Component of the TELL Acronym to Improve Conversations

Body Language NM	Body Language RN	Emotional Intelligence/ Competence NM	Emotional Intelligence/ Competence RN	Scripting Techniques	Conversation
Has eye contact.

Maintains open arms and remains confident by standing tall and approachable. | Has eye contact.

Arms are initially crossed in front of her, but as the teaching begins, she begins to lean toward the teaching, and her naughty bits are directly facing the tape measure the NM is holding. | Remains control of her emotions and is confident. | Feeling uncomfortable, but then begins to look interested at the way the NM is measuring. | NM is straightforward in her conversation and teaching. NM is not punitive. | NM: "Susie, I will watch how you perform the next head circumference measurement and will provide feedback. I will also watch the next three measurements. Please know, this is considered a coaching session, based on our performance management policy. I strongly encourage you to ask me for help if you are uncertain of anything. I will be periodically checking you to ensure this practice is sustained. If you do not continue in this manner, we will move toward disciplinary action. Can you share with me what you understood from our conversation, and do you have any further questions?"

RN correctly paraphrases her understanding of the problem and the resolution. |

When Emotions Take Over Conversations

We've all been there. We finally found strength to have a coaching conversation, and just as we began to talk about the intent of the conversation, the person immediately began to cry or became angry or defensive. High emotions are contagious. To protect yourself, get vaccinated. This is not to say you should become completely immune to others' emotions and appear robotic; you can sympathize. But don't fall victim to having your emotions hijacked. It is important to remain calm and composed in the face of the other person's emotion. By doing so, you may help the person regain some control of his or her emotions. Also, keep a matter-of-fact response—without judgment or disapproval. This can help to de-escalate the emotion. Here are a few scripting suggestions to deal with common emotions:

> **Coaching Conversations: The 6 Rules of Etiquette**
> - Don't judge others, blame others, and fault others.
> - What you would like for yourself, give to another.
> - Change your perspective. This changes your perception.
> - It's not what you say, but how you say it.
> - Perception is someone's reality until proven otherwise.
> - Feelings aren't right or wrong—they are feelings.

- **Crying:** "I can see you are upset. I will give you a moment to compose yourself before we continue."

- **Anger:** "I understand that this situation is difficult and frustrating. If you need a minute, please take it. We're going to work through this issue to resolution so I need you to remain calm."

- **Blame:** "I understand that there are other people involved; however right now this conversation is about you and me. Those other employees will be dealt with in the same respectful manner that I am dealing with you right now."

- **Bringing up past complaints:** "I understand that you have other concerns, and we can schedule time to talk about them at another time. Right now, we will focus on _____, which is what I brought you in here for."

time to reflect

One of the best ways to prepare for hard-to-have conversations is to ask yourself questions and reflect on your responses. Through this process, you can explore possible issues before they catch you by surprise.

- What makes you nervous about this conversation?

- What are you most worried about?

- What personal issues come to mind as you anticipate this conversation?

- What hot topics come to mind around this conversation?

- When have you handled a difficult conversation well? Poorly? How might your attitude, affect, or behavior have played a role in those circumstances?

- What would you most like to happen in this upcoming conversation? What might you do that would contribute to this happening? What might you do that would impede it?

Overcoming Conversation Traps

Being clear and direct is far more respectful than attempting to soften hard-to-have conversations. I once overhead a colleague of mine calling one of her direct reports into her office to discuss tardiness. Her office was adjacent to mine, and I couldn't help but overhear this conversation. As her employee walked into her office, my colleague began the conversation with, "Oh, I love your shoes today. You look so nice." She then continued the conversation with, "So, I am really worried about your tardiness. What is up with you lately? You'd better get your act together." Without even giving her employee a minute to speak, my colleague concluded the conversation with, "Oh, and hey, by the way, thanks again for running that blood down to the lab for me."

I call this a conversation-sandwich error. My colleague started off being nice, delivered the bad news, and then was positive once again. I am completely in favor of positive feedback; however, when you need to deliver serious conversations about behaviors, you need to keep the conversation direct and focused. Positive conversations are for reinforcing positive behaviors and should not be woven into hard-to-have conversations because it is much too confusing.

Paradoxically, I've heard conversations that sound like a battlefield is right in front of me. Some people enter the conversation so heated that there is absolutely no room for anything positive. Their adrenalin is in overdrive, and absolutely no resolution is found—only more issues are uncovered. In the fog of a hard-to-have conversation, it's easy to forget that you don't have access to anyone's intentions but your own. It is important to remember all parties involved are dealing with high emotions and ambiguity. So, if you get stuck, a convenient phrase to say is, "I'm realizing as we talk that I don't fully understand how you see this problem." This respectful observation can be very powerful in redirecting the conversation back to its original purpose.

The bottom line is that you need to keep sight of the goal. Go into conversations with a clear and realistic preferred outcome. Know how you want your *relationship* to be. Remember, winning is not a realistic outcome, because the other person is unlikely to accept an outcome of losing.

The Drive Home

Let's review the *driving it back home* pointers from this chapter:

- The CAR approach is a framework for conversations and can help infuse the aBEST approach into the conversation.

- Each person involved in the situation has a different story about what happened. Your goal is not to judge who's right and wrong, but to manage the situation for a better outcome.

- Paraphrase or summarize what you interpreted from someone for clarity. This also tells them you were listening and you care.

- Confrontation, denial, and tears are all possible outcomes of difficult conversations. Although you can't direct the other person's reactions, you can anticipate them and be emotionally prepared.

- The TELL acronym is a reminder to describe the intent of the conversation, explain why the behavior or action must change, show what good behavior or action looks like, and know the consequence if the behavior is not improved.

- Stay consistent in your delivery of hard-to-have conversations. Don't let your conversation become a sandwich; in other words, don't start positive, then go into the real reason why you're having the conversation, and then attempt to end on a positive note. It is best to deliver the message with consistency throughout.

- The best feedback is straightforward and simple.

- The best way to ensure that expectations set forth will be hardwired is to consistently follow up on progress.

References

Adams, J. Q. (n.d.). Retrieved from http://www.brainyquote.com/quotes/authors/j/john_quincy_adams.html

Clancy, C. (2012). Nursing leadership. Discovering the what, who, why and where. Retreived from http://nursing.advanceweb.com/Archives/Article-Archives/Nursing-Leadership.aspx

Curtis, E. A., Fintan, K., & de Vries, J. (2011). Developing leadership in nursing: the impact of education and training, *British Journal of Nursing, (20)*6, 344–352.

Ripper, B. (2013). The big, bad boss: Poor management costly. Retrieved from http://thebusinesstimes.com/the-big-bad-boss-poor-management-costly

Sherman, R., Bishop, M., Eggenberger, T., & Karden, R. (2007). Development of a leadership competency model from insights shared by nurse managers. *Journal of Nursing Administration, 37*(2), 85–94.

Shirey, M. R. (2006). Authentic leaders creating healthy work environments for nursing practice. *American Journal of Critical Care, 15*(3), 256–276.

Swearingen, S. (2009). A journey to leadership: Designing a nursing leadership development program. *Journal of Continuing Education Nursing, 40*(3) 107–112. doi: 10.3928/00220124-20090301-02

6

Improving the Patient Experience

Is healthcare customer oriented or patient centered? When people mention the words "customer service" and are referencing patients, I can feel tightness in my chest (I like to think I'm emotionally intelligent, so I do remain calm). Since when are patients *customers?*

Many leaders have tried to achieve a culture of customer service in healthcare organizations and have failed because the frontline resistance was insurmountable. Much of that resistance has centered on the language and delivery of the message. Many caregivers cannot accept the proposition that a patient can also be a customer. I don't know about you, but the last time I checked into a hotel, I wasn't there seeking pain management, let alone checking in to obtain medical care. When I check into a hotel, I am a customer. I have expectations. For example, I expect friendly concierge or front desk staff, a clean room, and well-stocked towels. I can assure you that when I check into a hotel, my expectations have nothing to do with the hotel scheduling my upcoming medical procedures, setting up doctor appointments, assessing my pain, or arranging provider referrals.

I do believe the hotel industry, as well as the food and service industries, sheds light in healthcare on service excellence initiatives; however, I do not believe we should compare the two as apples to apples. Consider that, in the service industry, customers are always viewed as right; in healthcare, however, the patients cannot be always viewed as right. For example, when I work telephone triage, I receive so many calls from parents who "know" the ear pain their child is experiencing is an ear infection and they "know" their child needs an antibiotic. If we allow patients and families to assume such diagnostic roles, then our current state of overprescribing antibiotics would take on a whole new level. Patients and families are extremely instrumental in the diagnostic process; however, they do not have a license to diagnosis and prescribe. (For a script on how to handle a situation like this, see Script 6.1.)

Take, for instance, the Disney Leadership Institute. The Disney approach to customer service has received a positive reception among many healthcare leaders who are interested in providing a quality service experience. Disney does an unparalleled job of preparing its cast members to create a magical experience that guests expect (Disney Institute, 2001). Disney's orientation program communicates the company's culture; it defines the heritage and traditions of the company and inspires enthusiasm of employees. Disney also accepts corrective criticism from guests about any poor behavior that is executed from the cast. Disney also emphasizes the importance of and provides prompt and courteous service recovery. The Disney Guidelines for guest service are succinct and clearly defined. They clearly explain the responsibilities of cast members and hold them accountable.

Script 6.1 What to say when... you are dealing with angry patients or families.

Tell

To the patient's parent:

> I understand you are dissatisfied with the care you are receiving on our telephone triage line. It is our first priority to ensure you that we are providing safe, high-quality service to everyone we care for. (Allow the caller to vent.)

Explain

The patient's parent is angry:

> I have four children, and I know when my children have an ear infection. I don't need an appointment. I need to get an antibiotic for my child!

Your response:

> I know it is very difficult to see your child in pain. You are correct that antibiotics are a good choice for certain diagnoses; however, an antibiotic is not the appropriate treatment if your child has an outer ear infection. (Explain swimmer's ear.) We can only determine the cause of the pain by examining your child's ear.

Lead by **e**xample

The patient's parent remains angry:

> You try dealing with a screaming child in pain! I know this cry, and it's not swimmer's ear!

Your response:

> Keeping your child comfortable is very important. (Review the treatment plan with anti-inflammatory medications, warm compress, etc.) It's important we treat your child with the best medication. I highly encourage you to bring your child in for an appointment. I have an appointment available today for you.

Learn the **c**onsequence

The patient's parent remains angry:

> Do you know how difficult it is for me to bring all my children out to the doctor's?

Your response:

> It is very important we examine the cause of your child's pain. Can you make the appointment today?

Additionally, Disney clearly distinguishes to all employees the expectations of onstage versus backstage areas. This creates a clarity about "being on" when guests are present versus being oneself, which may include behaviors that do not conform to Disney's guidelines (Disney Institute, 2001). This same "onstage" expectation is predominantly important in terms of delivering patient-centered care and improving the patient experience. Patients do not want to hear staff complaining in the cafeteria, outside of patient rooms, or in hallways. Expectations about caregiver conduct should be shaped by the fact that our environment usually includes patients and their families. Therefore, great customer service should be emulated to great patient-centered care. The two are inextricably linked and cannot be discussed in isolation.

First things first, we should work toward an improved patient experience because it is the right thing to do. Using patient surveys as a guide can help ensure that we are doing the right thing, yet this is just a guide and not an absolute. Patients should feel that their feedback is not only welcomed but also considered. Coaching ourselves to make time to listen to patients authentically is mutually beneficial. The work done up front to address patient needs pays off in huge dividends down the road. Patients who feel heard are less likely to monopolize the time we can devote to them.

The Driver's Seat: Reaping the Benefits of Engaged Employees and Engaged Patients

Many healthcare organizations understand the value of an engaged workforce. Heightened staff morale and engagement harnesses staff benevolence, which improves patient satisfaction. If staff feel engaged and respected, they are more likely to go the extra mile for their patients. For example, a patient survey question asks a patient about how quiet the unit was at night during his or her stay. Night shift staff who are engaged are more likely to be proactive in bringing forward issues that may otherwise cause a patient to answer that question with a poor rating (Lindberg & Kimberlain, 2008).

Moreover, evidence of better outcomes and lower costs has been found with patients who feel engaged. Engaged patients have improved knowledge, skills, and awareness to help manage their care (Hibbard, Greene, & Overton, 2013). A framework in which both staff and patients are active in decision-making may lead to breakthroughs in consistently achieving positive patient experiences. For example, a new mom explains to the nurse that her infant won't sleep through the night because the baby is sleeping all day and not waking for feeds. Mom states she is frustrated with the lack of sleep she has been getting and would like to start adding rice cereal to the infant's formula. The nurse listens intently and is not judgmental. In lieu of the nurse just telling Mom this *"could hurt the baby,"* the nurse takes time to clearly explain to Mom how the extra caloric intake of the rice cereal could be harmful to the infant's gut and reviews the other risk factors in detail. Both mom and nurse then review the feeding scheduling to develop a better daytime schedule that decreases the frequency of nighttime feeds. Mom feels more empowered and more knowledgeable in the care of her baby because she felt comfortable discussing her issues with the nurse. Had the nurse not taken time to explain the effects, the mom may have still given the cereal. Engaging patients, or in this case, the family, is vital to improving the quality of care provided.

When Mistakes Happen

According to the Disney Institute (2001), when service failure occurs, emotions rise, and customers pay more attention to how they are treated than the recourse itself. This is why it is imperative that the person should be acknowledged as the issue is being acknowledged. Disney recognizes that a service failure may not always be a fault within their control. Even with this acknowledgment, however, Disney still accepts it as the company's problem to remedy.

For that reason, the Disney Institute (2001) recommends using the HEARD acronym as a means of providing consistent service recovery. HEARD is a great acronym for service recovery in healthcare, too. It reminds us the first part of service recovery is to make sure the patient is heard. Let's look at this acronym with the aBEST approach woven through the HEARD acronym for service recovery:

Hear
Allow the patient to explain his or her whole story. Do not interrupt the story. There is more you can do than just listen. You can make sure you are listening not only to the words, but also the body language (and your own body language, too). Even if you feel the patient is making a personal attack on you, control your emotions! This does not give someone permission to be disrespectful to you, but to remind you to stay calm.

Body language check: Don't look defensive by standing with your arms crossed in front of you or hiding your naughty bits (Driver, 2010) with your hands. Pay attention to where your feet are positioned and how you are holding your arms. Your body language should convey warmth, although you don't necessarily have to be comfortable or familiar with a person or situation. Relaxed posture, open body position, sitting or standing in an appropriate proximity, and other generally relaxed behaviors are appropriate ways of showing warmth. Be genuine, or else there will be no recovery from the service failure.

Empathize
By empathizing with patients, you create an emotional relationship that shows you are authentic in your willingness and ability to help. Consider scripts that validate feelings, such as, "I understand we haven't done our best to meet your needs," "I understand this

is very difficult for you," or "I see why you would be upset."

Body language check: Your body language must mirror your words. Are your feet pointing toward the patient or, if you're sitting, are your knees facing them? How is your tone? Bring your pitch down so that you don't sound condescending.

Apologize   The power of a sincere apology should never be underestimated. Be authentic in your apology, even if you personally have nothing to do with the issue. You still represent the organization, so take ownership. Consider starting with any of these statements:

"Please accept my apology on behalf of the organization."

"I apologize for this inconvenience/ misunderstanding/miscommunication/ experience."

"I'm so sorry we disappointed you. Our intent is to always provide you with excellent service."

Body language check: Keep eye contact with the person and listen intently.

Resolve   Promptness is very important to recovery. Issues need to be worked on instantly. Consider statements such as, "How can I help make a difference or improve this situation for you?" If the person doesn't have an answer, state, "Here is what I think should do to improve this situation … What are your thoughts on this?" or, "Thank you for bringing this to my attention. Your comments will help us to make improvements."

Body language check: Again, your body language must mirror your words. Are your feet pointing toward the patient or, if you're sitting, are your knees facing them? How is your tone? Bring your pitch down so that you don't sound condescending.

Diagnose   Eradicate any personal guilt or guilt of others and inspect the processes as they relate to the service failure. Patients will be more forgiving if you're genuine in your efforts to improve their experience.

Body language check: Body language that conveys sincerity is much like that which conveys honesty. It is characterized by steady eye contact, relaxed but poised body posture, and leaning toward or reaching out toward the other person or people.

THE REAL WORLD | EMBRACING CRITICAL CONVERSATIONS AS A MEANS TO IMPROVE PATIENT CARE

At PeaceHealth St. Joseph Medical Center, administrators created a "Safe to Speak Up" campaign to promote communication and transparency in the organization. They wanted to create a safe environment where staff felt empowered to have honest and transparent communication. This campaign embraces critical conversations among caregivers, which is the cornerstone for superior patient-centered care.

Perception Is Reality

Perception is reality—bottom line. Perception remains the golden rule of patient satisfaction, like it or not. The patient's perception of care is—especially for the purposes of the Hospital Consumer Assessment of Healthcare Providers and Systems (HCAHPS) survey—a strong reality. For example, you and your colleagues may be clinically excellent, but patients may perceive you as too busy, aloof in their care, or lacking in compassion. So, how can you change this perception? After all, it may not be your reality, but it is the patients'.

A nurse's perception, or even an entire healthcare system's perception, of service excellence only has meaning if the patient's perception authenticates it. What helps (and also hinders) is that perceptions can change as the patient moves through the patient experience. For example, you may have provided excellent care as evidenced by verbal affirmations from the patient, but when patient satisfaction scores come back, the criteria in nurse-patient communication was ranked low. How could this be?

Well, *you* may have provided excellent care, but did *all* of your colleagues (in terms of the patient's perception)? There may be a lot of assumptions that haven't even been considered in the root cause of poor patient perceptions. For example, perhaps the patient mistakenly identified a disgruntled and stressed-out nursing student as his primary nurse during his stay. And even though 100% of the RN care was indeed superior, the patient is still reflecting on when the nursing student was unsympathetic to him. Although you can't anticipate and change the perception of every patient who passes through your care, there are several important pulse points you can reflect on to improve the design of an effective patient satisfaction system.

> There is no "one size fits all" approach to improving the patient experience, and what may work really well in one setting or situation might not work so well in another. Consistently evaluate and reevaluate strategies by asking patients, families, frontline staff, and other applicable key stakeholders for their ideas and suggestions.

First, in designing an effective patient satisfaction system, nurses need to understand patient perceptions are not based on objective facts. Perceptions are biased and influenced by previous experiences, education, and expectations. Perceptions are also built on the premise of the Platinum Rule, which reminds us that people want to be treated as they wish to be treated, not the way you wish to be treated (Alessandra & O'Connor, 1996). Moreover, many patients enter a health care experience with certain anticipations and fears based on patient value propositions. Patient value propositions are those things that are considered truths based on patient prior experiences or from stories shared by friends and family. All this information leads patients to drawing their own conclusions, regardless of whether there is actual evidence to support any of it.

Second, because perception prevails, it is imperative that nurses speak highly of their health care organizations so that the organization can work toward being the preferred choice of health care services within their market (Rivers & Glover, 2008). If patients have the expectation that they are entering a prominent health care establishment, they are already likely to give the benefit of any doubt when issues surface. When patients are entering a health care establishment with a poor reputation overall, but they trust their provider, every little issue seems like a big issue to them. From the lack of parking spaces to the rude registrar, the patients' perceptions are already diminished, regardless of the superior clinical care rendered. Also, because the average patient cannot judge the total quality of the health care experience until after her or she is discharged, any perceived negativity violates the little trust they had to begin with.

When trust in a health care system is damaged, it requires significant effort to fix it. In many cases, the patient's sense of trust is irreparable. An effective patient satisfaction system allows for the timely identification of negative perceptions that might have not come to light during the patient/provider encounter. Nurse engagement and hourly rounding is critical. Every individual health care member within an organization plays an important role in the patient experience. Everyone needs to do due diligence in establishing a sound relationship with every patient in the organization's care, even if your encounter with a patient is nothing more than passing in the hall. The same is true for demonstrating respect for your colleagues and your organization as a whole (Rivers & Glover, 2008).

Finally, consumerism is blooming and maturing rapidly in healthcare. I define consumerism as the personal happiness one experiences as one buys and consumes goods and services. Over the years, the expenditures in healthcare related to achieving high-quality care have increased while public satisfaction and trust have decreased. This is largely due to the fact that many of these efforts are not focused on those things that drive patient happiness. The need to be responsive to patient-driven consumerism increases only as it becomes more apparent to patients that they have the right to be happy with the services they receive/ purchase. An effective patient satisfaction system takes into account the significance of the patient's personal happiness with the organization's services at large.

Your Road Map: Communicate, Communicate, Communicate

Most realtors tell their clients "location, location, location" is the cardinal rule in the world of real estate. Well, communication is paramount in the healthcare sector. Healthcare is based on relationships, and successful relationships are based on a cornerstone of good communication.

Nurses should strive to establish a trusting relationship with patient and family members. Trust can begin to grow in the first few minutes of a basic introduction—and can be scorned in that time as well. For example, nurses introduce themselves to patients and families by offering their names and explanations of their roles. This sounds easy right? Well, it is, but it's not always done correctly. The missing link in this example is failing to ask the patients and families for their names. Developing a give-and-take type relationship is cardinal to a trusting relationship. In other words, how can trust be established if you feel like someone isn't taking time to learn about you and those around you? Taking a deeper dive, nurses many times introduce themselves to patients and families yet fail to ask *and use* the patient's *preferred* name. Think about it: How often do you ask your patients about their preferred names, or do you more commonly address them as Mr./Ms. and then are corrected by them before you even ask their preference? Be proactive by getting to know your patients on a higher level than just as "the patient."

Nurses can also improve communication with patients by utilizing many communication tools that have been shown to increase patient satisfaction (Baker, 2010; Studer, 2004; Woodard, 2009). These communication tools include AIDET for handling the patient greeting, whiteboards, hourly rounding, bedside shift change, discharge phone calls, and understanding the nurse's role in patient satisfaction surveys; SPIKES for delivering difficult news; and the aBEST approach. Chapter 7 expands on these tools in a universal staff approach. This chapter focuses mainly on the nurse's role.

AIDET

You may recall from Chapter 1 that AIDET, an acronym coined by Studer (n.d.), is an evidence-based communication model that provides a framework for communication with patients, families, and other healthcare providers. Using AIDET can lead to better patient satisfaction, staff satisfaction, and clinical outcomes (Studer, 2004). Consider the following example:

Acknowledge   Greet people with a smile, maintain appropriate eye contact, and demonstrate a warm, receptive attitude with everyone you meet. Be mindful, however, that direct eye contact may be disrespectful in some cultures, so look for cues from your patient. A handshake or simple nod of the head is a universal sign of acknowledgment.

Example Acknowledgment Statements:

"Good morning/afternoon, Ms. _____. We've been expecting you, and we're glad you are here."

"Good morning/afternoon, Mr. _____. Welcome to Hospital ABC. We want to make your visit with us as convenient as possible. Would you please confirm that we have your most current information in this document?"

Introduce

Introduce yourself by offering your name, title, and experience.

Example Introductory Statements:

"My name is _____, and I will be conducting your test today. I am a certified registered nurse, and I do about six of these procedures a day. Do you have any questions before we begin?"

"Mr./Ms./Mrs. _____ (or preferred name), you will be seeing Dr. _____ today. He is an excellent cardiothoracic surgeon. He is renowned for his bedside manner and for thoroughly answering all questions. You are fortunate that he is your surgeon."

Duration

Keep the patient informed of meals, tests, procedures, and so on. Explain how long a procedure will take, how long the patient might have to wait, or, if you are walking with someone, how long it will take to reach your destination.

Example Duration Statement:

"Dr. _____ has had to attend to an emergency right now. He wanted you to know that it may be approximately 20 minutes before he can see you. Are you able to wait, or would you like me to schedule an appointment for tomorrow?"

Explanation   Explain to patients what they can expect before,
                 during, and after a test or procedure.

                 Example Explanation Statement:

                 "The test takes about 45 minutes from preparing
                 you to your recovery. The first step requires you
                 to drink this solution and then, as required for
                 this test, we'll have you wait 20 minutes before
                 we take a blood sample. Would you like to read a
                 magazine or listen to your music while you wait?"

Thank You   Sincerely thank patients, families, and visitors for
                 choosing your hospital and for trusting you to
                 provide care. Always be polite and use direct eye
                 contact. Although you may be using an interpret-
                 er, body language can also help put the patient at
                 ease and develop trust in the staff.

                 Example Thank You Statement:

                 "Thank you for choosing Hospital ABC and
                 trusting us to provide your healthcare needs. It
                 has been a privilege to care for you."

                 "Thank you for calling us. Is there anything else I
                 can do for you? I have the time."

Notice that the AIDET approach is a warm, comprehensive greeting that includes crucial pieces of information designed to specifically help gain the trust
of others.

Whiteboards

The placement of whiteboards in patient rooms is an increasingly common tactic used to improve communication (Niraj et al., 2010). These boards allow any number of providers to communicate a wide range of information. Whiteboards should be placed in clear view of patients from their hospital beds. Whiteboards need erasable pens attached to them. Be proactive in the usage of the whiteboard by ensuring there is always a supply of erasable pens available at the nursing station to replace missing fading ones.

Creating whiteboard "templates," or structured formats, is a more effective approach to ensuring both important and accurate information gets included, such as the patient's goals for the day. Blank whiteboards lead to less standardization in practice and fail to create reminders for providers to both write and review the content. Also, make sure the care team continually updates the whiteboard. By leaving it empty or outdated, it sends the message to the patient that the staff is not paying attention to detail, they're too busy, or they simply don't think it's important enough to update it. Remember, the clinical team passes by the whiteboard many times a day, whereas the patient is basically staring at it all day. Pay attention to details such as this because the patients and families sure are.

I hope some of these tips are already hardwired into your daily practice; however, you'd be surprised how many nurses don't hardwire this. When I'm facilitating speaking engagements on the patient experience with nurses in my audience, I often ask, "How many of the nurses in the audience write down goals on the whiteboard?" Almost every nurse raises a hand immediately as if to say, "Of course!" But when I clarify, "How many nurses write down the patient's goal, not the patient care goal?" I don't see so many raised hands.

As an example, a nurse's goal in the NICU may be to advance tube feeding by 2 ccs every other hour; however, I highly doubt the patient's mother has the same goal. Maybe her goal is to hold her baby, but the nurse knows that's not currently possible because the baby is in the incubator due to temperature intolerance.

The nurse could compromise and tell the mother that she can do the next diaper change with the nurse's help or that she can hold the baby's foot or hand while the nurse changes the baby's diaper (if the mother is uncomfortable changing the diaper due to all the cords).

Be sure to ask what the patient's (or family's) goal is and make a list. Check off and review their goals on a continual basis, such as when you do hourly rounds. This is a great way to keep other caregivers in the loop of what has been discussed.

Hourly Rounds

Nurse continuity is a patient satisfier. Nurse-patient rounding that is purposeful and consistent is also a patient satisfier (Blakley, Kroth, & Gregson, 2011). It's a quite simple concept that nurses who round on patients with purpose and consistency are proactively caring for patients. In opposition, nurses who don't round on their patients consistently find the nurse call buttons used more frequently and at various times, for various reasons (Harrington et al., 2013). Some hospitals adopted a 4 Ps approach (pain, potty, position, presence) to purposeful rounding (Woodard, 2009). Specifically, every hour while the patient was awake, nurses would ask the following "purposeful" questions:

Pain   "How is your pain?"

Position   "Are you comfortable?"

Potty   "Do you need to use the bathroom?"

Presence   "Is there anything I can get you, such as the call light, phone, trash can, water, or over-bed table?"

Bedside Shift Reporting

Bedside shift reporting occurs when nurses conduct shift change reports at the patient's bedside. Patients have the ability to be more instrumental and engaged in their hospital care by ensuring accurate information is shared between all healthcare members. Patients can also elect a family member or close friend to participate. Bedside reporting is not limited to change of shift; it's also useful to introduce a replacement RN or care extender (medical assistants, licensed practical nurses, and so on) when primary nurses need to leave the floor for lunch breaks or to take other patients to various departments.

Bedside shift reports have many benefits including improved:

- Communication

- Participation in setting care goals

- Opportunity for patients to ask questions and share experiences

- Safe patient handoff and information-gathering opportunity

- Assessment of patient's surgical wounds, pressure ulcers, and so on

- Patient and caregiver trust, by confirming nurses are conveying information properly

- Team accountability, by encouraging a successful transition to practice environment for nurses

Here are some tips for effectively using bedside change-of-shift reports:

Phase 1

- Introduce staff, patient, and family members using AIDET.
- Ask for the patient's input (keep your stance in a triangle as to not exclude the patient when reporting).
- Ask patients about preference, such as to have family members and/or visitors leave room during report.
- Increase patient confidence by letting the patient know that a great nurse or provider is going to be taking care of them.

Phase 2

- Discuss clinical care issues and provide clinical updates (for example, patient information, laboratory results, wound care, medications).
- Discuss care goals for next shift.

Phase 3

- Facilitate two-way communication by answering patient/family member questions, addressing unresolved issues, and/or writing down questions or issues to be addressed later in the shift or hospitalization.
- Update communications on the whiteboard, such as the incoming nurse's and assistant's names, treatment goals, patient's goals, anticipated discharge date, and so on.

Discharge Phone Calls

Discharge phone calls are intended to maximize the patient experience and not necessarily provide medical advice. Nurses should spend a short time on the phone with the patient to ask follow-up questions to address the following:

- Does the patient understand all of the discharge instructions provided?

- Has the patient filled prescriptions?

- Does the patient have questions about medications?

- Does the patient have any pain related to the diagnosis?

- Has the patient made follow-up appointments?

- How does the patient feel about the care they received, and could anything have been done differently?

The information obtained from the call should be documented, and patients who have clinical questions, or are experiencing a medical problem, should be referred back to their physician or care provider as appropriate. The nurse should also loop back to the physician team to let them know the results of the phone call. Information about the patient's perception of care should also be forwarded to management as a learning opportunity and so that an action plan for remedy can be implemented.

Discharge phone calls are a great tool to reinforce and educate patients about their treatment plans as well as to ensure follow-up is executed. Because many patients are anxious to get home, they don't always take the time to fully understand the instructions given. Discharge phone calls give patients an added opportunity to double-check instructions, which possibly minimizes unnecessary calls to providers and visits to the emergency department. These phone calls also aid in service recovery.

Understanding the Nurse's Role in Patient Satisfaction Scores

Patient satisfaction scores are measurements used to determine how well healthcare providers meet patients' expectations, "how satisfied" patients are as a result of their visit/stay, and how well the outcomes they expected were delivered both clinically and experientially. It is assessed by how well healthcare providers performed as a team. The HCAHPS survey is the first national, standardized, publicly reported survey instrument of patients' perspectives of hospital care. HCAHPS provides the public comparisons of hospital performance on a local, regional, and national platform (HCAHPS Home page, n.d.).

With the HCAHPS survey, healthcare providers are now responsible for the quality of the hospital experience based on patients' perceptions. Patients answer questions about how well their nurses and physicians communicated with them, whether their needs were promptly addressed, and whether they were provided with medication information, to name a few of the many questions asked. The goal is for patients to give "Top Box," or the highest rating possible, for each item on the survey (Centers for Medicare & Medicaid Services, 2013).

The HCAHPS survey asks discharged patients questions about their recent hospital experiences. The survey contains core questions about various aspects of patients' hospital experiences, including communication with nurses and doctors, the responsiveness of hospital staff, the cleanliness and quietness of the hospital environment, pain management, communication about medicines, discharge information, overall rating of the hospital, and likelihood that the patients would recommend the hospital to someone (Centers for Medicare & Medicaid Services, 2013).

Administering the HCAHPS Survey

The HCAHPS survey is administered via random sampling of adult patients of varying medical conditions between 48 hours and 6 weeks after discharge. Hospitals may use an approved survey vendor, or the hospital may collect its own HCAHPS data (but only with approval by the Centers for Medicare & Medicaid Services). The HCAHPS survey can be executed in four different survey methods: mail, telephone, mail with telephone follow-up, or interactive voice response (IVR). Hospitals can use the HCAHPS survey alone or can include additional questions after the core HCAHPS items. Hospitals must survey patients throughout each month of the year. More specific information about the survey can be found on the official HCAHPS website at www.hcahpsonline.org.

In 2013, HCAHPS scores became 1 of 13 measures used by the Centers for Medicare & Medicaid Services (CMS) to calculate $850 million in payments from its new Hospital Value-Based Purchasing Program (VBP). Thirty percent of the VBP score will be based on HCAHPS, and 70% is based on clinical measures. Many hospitals and health systems are not only placing strategies on each of the core questions, but also on initiating strategies to improve the overall patient experience. Some strategies include comprehensive leadership training and employee satisfaction initiatives. These efforts are designed to concurrently improve scores on individual HCAHPS questions and protect their proposed CMS reimbursements (Centers for Medicare & Medicaid Services, 2013). This is especially critical as hospitals and healthcare systems are faced with many financial uncertainties (Hall, 2008).

time to reflect

How transparent ARE your hospital's HCAHPS? Use the acronym *ARE* to ensure your scores are transparent. Knowledge is power.

Accurate

Readily available

Easy to access

Patient communication represents the largest piece of the HCAHPS survey. Half of the core questions ask patients how they perceived interactions with their nurses, doctors, and other hospital staff. All nurses should become familiar with HCAHPS questions. When provided with scripting tools (for impromptu scripts), nurses can provide excellent patient care and excellent customer service while maintaining budget (Reynolds, 2013). By knowing what is asked of patients on the survey, nurses can better answer patient questions in real time as well as answer patients in a proactive approach based on forthcoming survey questions. Let's examine how some HCAHPS questions can be answered in real time and with an approach designed to achieve Top Box answers.

HCAHPS question	During this hospital stay, how often were you able to discuss your worries or concerns with nurses?
Scripting	"It sounds like you're worried/concerned about _____. Can you tell me more about how you're feeling?" Or, "I know you have received a lot of information today. Can you tell me what you understood?" Or, "I know you've discussed _____ with your physician. What worries or concerns do you have?"
HCAHPS questions	During this hospital stay, how often was your pain well controlled? Or, during this hospital stay, how often did the hospital staff do everything they could to help you with your pain?

Scripting	"I gave you [insert medication name] [insert hours ago]. Can you tell me about how your pain has been and where it is now?" Or, "Although you are not pain-free, we do want it as manageable as possible. It is important that we work toward your targeted pain score. You've put your acceptable rating as an [insert rating]. How do you feel now?" Or, "How are we doing at keeping your pain at your targeted level of [insert rating]?"
HCAHPS question	Before giving you any new medicine, how often did hospital staff describe possible side effects in a way you could understand?
Scripting	"We started you on [insert the name of the medication]. Can you tell me at what time you will take it each day and what it's for?" Or, "What side effects would tell you to call your doctor?"

Using SPIKES to Deliver Bad News

According to Buckman (2005) and Kaplan (2010), some healthcare professionals use the SPIKES acronym as a comprehensive approach to delivering bad news to cancer patients. This acronym assists clinicians in meeting the main objectives of delivering the information. This includes gathering information from the patient, transmitting the medical information, providing support to the patient, and obtaining the patient's collaboration in the treatment plan. Specifically, SPIKES includes the following components:

S   *Set up* the interview. When delivering bad news, it is important to make sure that patients have with them any family they want present and that you are meeting at a time when interruptions are limited.

P and **I**   *Perception* and *Invitation*. These both relate to how doctors determine what patients already know and how much they want to know versus how much they don't want to know. It is important to be open and understand that not everyone wants to know everything.

K   *Knowledge*. When delivering information, make sure to use layman's terms and words that the patient and family members can understand. For example, instead of using the word "metastasize" in cancer, use the word "spread."

E   *Empathetic*. Be more empathetic and pay attention to the patient's emotional reactions.

S   *Strategies*. Outline the next several steps of what the treatment plan is.

Ms. Anderson is a previously healthy 50-year-old accountant who initially presented with a seizure. A CT scan showed an enhancing mass, and she was referred to a neurosurgeon for a biopsy. Consider:

- How you would provide empathy?

- How do you help patients or families feel integrated into the patient's care?

Delivering bad news is never easy, but preparing for these conversations can make them more effective and less of a burden. Keep in mind these tips:

- Avoid reassuring phrases such as, "Don't worry."

- Bad news is not only about end-of-life, but also includes the patient's acceptance of their diagnosis, treatment plan, and transition of care.

- Breathe and observe your body language. Lower your shoulders and uncross your arms. If you notice anxious thoughts, breathe more deeply.

- Listen with respect and patience. Strive to understand, to appreciate what the patient is going through, and to find something to connect with for further discussion.

- Instead of trying to escape the patient's emotional experience, imagine the emotions are an ocean wave that will flow over you safely. The wave does not have to knock you over like a tsunami.

- Keep your tone of voice calm and avoid persuading, convincing, or arguing with patients and families.

- Be willing to acknowledge further steps such as stating, "This is a first step."

Using the aBEST Approach to Communicate With Patients

When nurses communicate with patients, incorporating the aBEST approach ensures authenticity. Implementing the aBEST approach helps to ensure key talking points are made and body language and emotions are considered. It is also important to recall the CAR framework for a more productive and comprehensive discussion.

C First *consider how you're asking these questions.* Are your emotions in check, or are you hastily asking the questions because something else is on your mind? Consider all the aspects of the 5 Rights to Communication Safety. Actively listen to patient concerns and reflectively respond to/address them accordingly without multitasking. Sitting with the patient rather than standing increases the perception of duration spent with the patient.

A Determine your *action or call to action.* This reminds you to be an active listener and follow through on answers received. Follow the QWQ formula to allow adequate time for the patient to formulate an answer. Use the whiteboard to document the patient's targeted pain score between nursing staff. Listen for medication effectiveness, interactions, and interventions that might be needed. Combining scripting and teach-back enables nurses to leverage how communication occurs at the bedside for achieving higher levels of therapeutic interaction and patient experience.

R The *return on investment (ROI)* is the level of time you're investing with the patient. Quality time rather than quantity of time is key. Review whether there is anything else you could be asking or doing for the patient. Make the ROI worth the investment by earning the trust of your patients and their families.

The largest part of the HCAHPS survey is based on communication. Because half of the core questions measure how patients perceive interactions with nurses, doctors, and other hospital staff, it is vital we become familiar with HCAHPS questions. I cannot emphasize enough that the goal of this awareness is to demonstrate just how doing the right things, like effectively communicating with patients, can impact the patient's outcome. Small acts of kindness, like taking time to build trusting relationships, has big rewards.

The Drive Home

Let's review the *driving it back home* pointers from this chapter:

- Patient perceptions are formed by ALL the experiences they had before, during, and after hospitalization.

- HCAHPS is a standardized survey that provides information about the patient's experience and quality of care. This information is publicly reported.

- Individual employees directly influence patient perceptions; therefore, each encounter is critical. It is not enough to satisfy patients some of the time. Healthcare providers have to be consistently satisfying patients at every interaction, by every employee.

- Communication tools have been shown to increase patient satisfaction. These tools include AIDET for patient greeting, whiteboards, hourly rounding, bedside shift change, discharge phone calls, understanding the nurse's role in patient satisfaction surveys; SPIKES for delivering difficult news; and incorporating the aBEST approach.

- Healthcare organizations that thrive and flourish in challenging times do so because they continue to do what is right for their patients.

- Patient-centered care is the right thing to do. Clarifying what patient-centered care means and how it works within the scope of the mission, vision, and values is only the first step. Laying the foundation means getting all nurses on board and leveraging resources so that your investment reflects your commitment to patient-centered care.

References

Alessandra, T. & O'Connor, M. J. (1996). The Platinum Rule. Retrieved from http://www.alessandra.com/dobusiness.htm

Baker, S. J. (2010). Bedside shift report improves patient safety and nurse accountability. *Journal of Emergency Nursing, 36*(4), 355–358.

Blakley, D., Kroth, M. & Gregson, J. (2011). The impact of nurse rounding on patient satisfaction in a medical-surgical hospital unit. *Medical-Surgical Nursing, 20*(6), 327–332.

Buckman, R. A., (2005) Breaking bad news: the S-P-I-K-E-S strategy. *Community Oncology, (2)*2, 138–142.

Centers for Medicare & Medicaid Services. (2013). HCAHPS. Baltimore, MD. Retrieved from http://www.hcahpsonline.org

Disney Institute (2001). *Be our guest: Perfecting the art of customer service.* New York: Disney Editions.

Driver, J. (2010). *You say more than you think: A 7-day plan for using the new body language to get what you want!* New York: Crown Publishers.

Hall, M. F., (2008). Looking to improve financial results? Start by listening to patients. *Healthcare Financial Management, 62*(10), 76–80.

Harrington, A., Bradley, S., Jeffers, L., Linedale, E., Kelman, S., & Killington, G. (2013). The implementation of intentional rounding using participatory action research. *International Journal of Nursing Practice, 19*(5), 523–529. doi: 10.1111/ijn.12101

HCAHPS Home Page. (n.d.). Autumn 2012 HCAHPS Executive Insight Letter. Retrieved from http://www.hcahpsonline.org/executive_insight/default.aspx

Hibbard, J. H., Greene, J., & Overton, V. (2013). Patients with lower activation associated with higher costs; Delivery systems should know their patients' "scores." *Health Affairs, 2*(32), 216–222.

Kaplan, M. (2010). SPIKES: A framework for breaking bad news to patients with cancer. *Clinical Journal of Oncology Nursing, 14*(4), 514–516. doi: 10.1188/10.CJON.514-516

Lindberg, L., & Kimberlain, J. (2008). Engage employees to improve staff and patient satisfaction. *Hospitals & Health Networks, 82*(1), 28–29.

Moran, D. K. (n.d.) Retrieved from http://izquotes.com/quote/130299

Niraj L., Sehgal, N. L., Green, A., Vidyarhi, A. R., Blegen, M. A., & Wachter, R. M. (2010). "Patient Whiteboards as a Communication Tool in the Hospital Setting: A Survey of Practices and Recommendations," *Society of Hospital Medicine (5)*, 234–239 doi10.1002/jhm.638

Reynolds, A. (2013). Setting yourself and your patients up for success: Utilizing scripting in the OB setting. *Journal of Obstetric, Gynecologic, & Neonatal Nursing, 42*(s1), 53. doi: 10.1111/1552-6909.12127

Rivers, P. A. & Glover, S. H. (2008). "Health Care Competition, Strategic Mission, and Patient Satisfaction: Research Model and Propositions," *Journal of Health Organization Management, 22*(6), 627-641.

Studer Group. (n.d.). AIDET: Acknowledge, introduce, duration, explanation and thank you. Retrieved from http://www.studergroup.com/aidet

Studer Group. (n.d.). Hourly rounding. Retrieved from http://www.mc.vanderbilt.edu/root/pdfs/nursing/hourly_rounding_supplement-studer_group.pdf

Studer, Q. (2004). *Hardwiring excellence: Purpose, worthwhile work, making a difference.* Gulf Breeze, FL: Fire Starter Publishing.

Stanford Hospital. (n.d.). Retrieved from http://medicalstaff.stanfordhospital.org/ms/medstaffupdate/articles/201304_hospital_rolls_out_discharge_phone_call_program.html

Woodard, J. L. (2009). Effects of rounding on patient satisfaction and patient safety on a medical-surgical unit. *Clinical Nurse Specialist: The Journal for Advanced Nursing Practice, (23)*4, 200–206.

> *"Going to work for a large company is like getting on a train. Are you going sixty miles an hour, or is the train going sixty miles an hour and you're just sitting still?"*
> –J. Paul Getty

Healthy Workplace Environments

A healthy work environment can be defined as a professional practice environment in which staff are proficient communicators and where all interactions are open, encouraging, and in alignment with all professional and ethical requirements (Kupperschmidt, Kientz, Ward, & Reinholz, 2010; Shirey & Fisher, 2008; Stichler, 2009). I would be remiss not to also include the World Health Organization's (2013) definition of a healthy workplace environment: "A state of complete physical, mental and social well-being, and not merely the absence of disease."

Clearly, definitions of a healthy workplace have momentously evolved over the years. From an almost exclusive focus on physical work environments, such as the jurisdiction of traditional occupational health and safety, the definition has now expanded to include health practice factors such as interpersonal and psychosocial factors as well as environmental issues, all of which can have a profound effect on employee health and workplace satisfaction (Cummings et al., 2010). Initiating, nourishing, and sustaining healthy work environments must be a priority in order to increase patient safety as well as staff retention and recruitment (Kramer & Schmalenberg, 2008; Tourangeau, Cummings, Cranley, Ferron, & Harvey, 2010).

As I was conducting my literature review for this chapter, I found the "ingredients" for a healthy workplace environment which seemed like common sense to me. These ingredients include (Ritter, 2011; Sherman & Pross, 2010; Spence Laschinger, Leiter, Day, & Gilin, 2009):

- Skilled communication

- Authentic collaboration

- Effective decision-making

- Appropriate staff matrix

- Meaningful recognition of others

- Transformational leaders

These ingredients seem to me like a no-brainer, but, as discussed in Chapter 1, common sense is not always so common. Also, those of us working in the trenches know we aren't always blessed with having all (or sometimes any) of these constituents. Case in point, in 2001, the Institute of Medicine (IOM, 1999) stated there were between 98,000 and 200,000 unnecessary, preventable patient deaths yearly. This was published in IOM's landmark report "To Err is Human." The release of this information brought to the forefront the urgent need to make improvements in healthcare. This work laid the foundation for healthcare organizations to take an in-depth look at the root causes of the issues contributing to this astonishing statistic. Another astonishing finding is that according to Borkowski (2009), 90% of the world's problems are due to ineffective or lack of communication.

The Driver's Seat: Getting Your Workplace Healthy

Get your workplace healthy. Let's start with the leaders in healthcare. But wait; I'm not pointing the finger at those who covet formal leadership titles. I'm looking in the mirror and asking you to do the same thing. Regardless of our titles, each of us is a leader and instrumental in leading change.

Before we discuss change, it is important to clarify the distinction between change management and change leadership. I often feel these terms are used interchangeably, although they shouldn't be. *Change management,* which is the term I often hear from students and colleagues when discussing change initiatives, refers to a set of basic tools or configurations intended to keep any change initiative under the control of someone or something. The goal of change management is often to decrease interruptions and effects of the change. Change leadership focuses on the strategic process that facilitates comprehensive transformations. *Change leadership* is a key part of patient satisfaction, employee satisfaction, and thus sustaining a healthy workplace environment. Changing behavior is one of the biggest obstacles for many healthcare organizations, yet according to McKinsley (2010), about 70% of all changes in all organizations fail. Let's review some common reasons why change is so hard.

Hurry Up to Wait

"Hurry up to wait" is the equivalent to rushing to be on time for your doctor appointment (because if you're 10 minutes late, they have to reschedule you) only to find out when you get there the doctor is running 20 minutes behind. So, although you hurried to get there, you end up waiting anyway. In essence, you had a false sense of urgency. In healthcare, we know formal leaders feel the pressure to implement improvements across their organization in an effort to keep up with their competition. Capturing larger portions of their market share, as well as sustaining current patient loyalty is very instrumental to the overall livelihood of the organization's existence. Formal leaders have that sense of urgency to implement changes that they feel will give their organization the competitive edge; however, they often fall victim to the hurry-up-to-wait fallacy. This happens because those who are on the front line to implement such changes either did not understand the emphasis on the change improvements or because there are no processes in place to support the change initiative.

For example, in an effort to increase emergency department (ED) visits, a hospital's leadership marketing team decides to advertise their ED patient wait times on their website so patients can know ahead of time how busy the ED is. This seems like a very attractive feature to incentivize patients to choose their ED, right? After all, through the marketing team's eyes, this idea had an impact analysis of high impact, low implementation. Well, in theory this may be true, but in reality, it wasn't. Since the marketing team didn't thoroughly investigate what the current wait times were (actual wait time) and what the future state should look like (preferred wait time), needless to say, this added feature did not increase visits. In some ED staff's minds, advertising poor ED wait times may have prevented patients from choosing their ED because the wait times were horrendous compared to what they benchmarked. The hurry-up-to-wait fallacy demonstrated here could have been improved by asking the ED team for assistance to see what improvements could be made. In essence, they hurried to advertise a potentially attractive feature for patients; however, they didn't invest the time to ensure the ED healthcare team had the needed resources to improve patient throughput. As mentioned in Chapter 1, leaders have the ready-fire strategy and often forget to aim.

Knowledge Deficit

There is often a deficit between what people know and what they actually do. Many leaders know what ingredients are needed to lead change effectively; however, there's a void between their knowledge and how they actually apply it. Leaders often think the foundational problem is a lack of knowledge when the real issue is how the knowledge is executed. For example, a nonclinical leader in charge of operations informs a nurse manager that the most recent report shows his unit's number of occupied beds is down; therefore, he needs to decrease staffing. The nurse manager explains that although the number of occupied beds is indeed down, the patient acuity is up. In fear of "getting into trouble" for arguing this point any further, the nurse manager starts canceling staff, and un-safe patient ratios are implemented. Another example: A staff nurse witnessed her friend and a colleague not wash their hands as they came out of a patient's room who was on isolation precautions because they feared they would come across as insulting or as "know it alls." We are all victims at one time or another of knowledge deficit. Learning how to communicate what we know into what we actually do is critical to establishing healthy workplace environments.

Lack of Skill and Practice

Just like in sports, when you practice, you get better. Unfortunately, practice is often missing from management and leadership education. For example, The Beatles played thousands of live shows before they made it big, and Bill Gates was writing software when he was just 13; after years and years of practice, both The Beatles and Bill Gates became massively successful. Unless you are born into old money or you hit the lottery (or have some other form of luck), the quality and quantity that you practice something often necessitates the level of your success.

I find many inexperienced managers who confuse knowledge with skill. They teach people change concepts, but they don't give people enough time to actu-ally practice their skills. This is similar to when you attend a training class and then your manager expects exceptional results as soon as you walk out of class. This type of expectation essentially sets one up to fail.

Silent Barriers That Impede Change

We often don't readily recognize traps that are resistant to change. Change is often inevitable by the time we realize we are acting like Albert Einstein's definition of insanity, which is "the state of doing the same thing over and over" while "expecting different results." For example, we all know we need to exercise and eat well, but do we? We may order fries or skip the gym, yet we repeatedly complain about weight gain.

The same thing happens in organizations. Healthcare organizations state that their number-one goal is to improve the patient experience (Pund & Sylar, 2012), but do they do everything they can to make this happen, such as improving staffing matrix, providing leadership training, implementing more recognition of staff, and coaching and mentoring for succession planning? Although research demonstrates that where leadership training has been effectively integrated into nursing it has a positive impact on nurse retention rates and patient outcomes (Cowden, Cummings, & Profetto-Mcgrath, 2011; Longo, 2009), there is strong evidence that leadership training is lacking (Sherman, Bishop, Eggenberger & Karden, 2007; Swearingen, 2009). Healthcare organizations need to continue to support leadership training, as well as promote leadership development in practice (Swearingen, 2009).

Culture Eats Change Strategy (For Lunch)

Although it is with good intention that formal leaders motivate staff to be accountable for their part of the change, they too need to look in the mirror and reflect on how active of a role they play. During one of my leadership presentations, a nurse manager told me she was warned early in her new job to never criticize her chief nursing officer's (CNO's) ideas, even if the CNO gave permission to do so. Fellow managers informed this new nurse manager that anyone who voiced a difference of opinion faced career suicide (meaning the person was fired or retaliated against in some way). So, it is crucial to know the formal and informal rules that support how change is accepted. The culture of an organization includes history and traditions, so no army of leaders will completely change an organization's culture. We can, however, change the climate of an organization. Changing the climate to a warm atmosphere will steer the organization into a positive light while still preserving its culture.

time to reflect

To improve your odds for a successful change initiative, consider the following:

- Are change goals realistic and SMART (Specific, Measurable, Attainable, Relevant, and Time-bound) (Meyer 2003)?

- Is there CNO, chief executive officer (CEO), or chief operating officer (COO) support?

- Do senior leaders walk the talk, not just talk the talk?

- Do middle managers and supervisors have a deep understanding for the need to implement change? Simply, do they really get it? Try using teach-back methods to ensure there are no miscommunications.

- Is the organization vested in the change initiative? They must be committed for the long haul.

Your Road Map: A Healthier Workplace Environment

A healthy work environment is one that supports and fosters excellence in employee satisfaction as well as patient satisfaction (Stichler, 2009). Nurse leaders who are strong advocates for developing a healthy work environment must be risk-takers. This means you must take risks to lead your organization in addressing the mental, physical, social, and economic welfare of your colleagues and patients. A shared responsibility for both formal and informal leadership lies in creating positive work environments where staff enjoys coming to work and where patients feel safe and valued. Geedey (2006) suggests the following tips to set the tone for a positive work environment:

- Foster an environment where humor is encouraged.

- Ensure unit values and expectations are well defined.

- Maintain a modest environment; one that flows seamlessly, is organized, and uncluttered.

- Recognize and promote volunteerism.

Although some major change initiatives need to start at the top in order to garner success, meaning there is commitment by the CNO, COO, and/or CEO, there are changes that can be made at the unit or any level. If you expand on some of the tips Geedey shared, you may be shocked at what you can do, regardless of your title.

Have you ever worked with a unit committee to accomplish goals for improving patient safety, fall reduction, or safe medication administration? As nurses, we are notorious for working on small projects with big impact. So, I challenge you to consider talking to your formal leaders about developing healthy workplace steering committees with your colleagues to improve your workplace environment. Open the committees to your nursing colleagues, those who work in social work, therapy, housekeeping, maintenance, materials management, human resources, or any other departments that you can think of.

Although the sky's the limit with the amount of innovative ideas these committees can suggest, some ideas that committees can focus on topics such as rewards and recognition, AIDET (see Appendix C), HCAHPS and scripting, hiring right, transformational rounding (see Appendix B), discharge follow-up call, welcome committee, leadership training and education, physician and staff engagement, and bright ideas (Studer, 2004). Valuable tools to weave into each of these committee's charge is the CAR framework and the aBEST approach. This ensures body language, emotional intelligence and competence, and easy-to-use language, such as acronyms, are embedded in order to develop buy-in from others.

After you've brainstormed some ideas that you can adopt, and assuming formal leaders are on board (even if it is just one committee to begin with), you need to obtain buy-in from your colleagues. In order to create buy-in, you need to motivate. By motivate, I am suggesting that you mandate everyone to sign up for a committee or shun them if they don't volunteer. You need to provide them with actual motivation and influence.

Motivation is about engaging others to behave in a way that achieves a specific and immediate goal (Brady & Cummings, 2010). A critical component to motivating others is to offer them something they want in return. I find using the "what's in it for me" approach is beneficial. To motivate others you need to consider framing the initiative to reflect how this is going to help the individual. I can almost guarantee that if you (or your CNO) sends out an email or holds a town hall meeting calling for volunteers to join committees to improve the workplace, the response won't be as grand as if the announcement includes specific benefits that answer the "what's in it for me" question for potential participants.

Motivating is equally important in caring for our patients. Using a motivational interviewing approach can be very effective to improving patient outcomes. For example, if your patient is not taking his medications properly, using a motivational interviewing approach can empower your patient to change her ineffective habits by exploring and resolving any ambivalence she may have. With successful motivation interviewing, the improvements made are intrinsic, or because the patient wants to, not because the nurse or doctor told them to (see Script 7.1). When patients have a better understanding of "what's in it for me," they are more opt to comply with their care regimen (Miller & Rollnick, 2013).

You can use the TELL acronym when preparing your motivational interviewing script:

T   *Tell* or *Talk* about what has been observed or the issue at hand.

E   *Explain.* Prior to going on about what's wrong in detail, ask about the positive aspects of the target behavior. You might be shocked to see that the patient has a pleasant reaction, and this is critical for understanding why they do what they do. After you summarize the positive aspects, ask them about what they see as the negative aspects. This is when you also need to find out the things in life that are of value to them.

L   *Lead* the receiver to what the desired outcome should look like, taking into account the person's ambivalence (as applicable) and their values. Restate their dilemma or ambivalence; then ask how they would like to proceed.

L   *Learn* the consequence. In other words, have the receiver teach back to you what the consequences will be if they change their behavior or they don't. Use SMART goals (Specific, Meaningful, Assessable, Realistic, Timed) when possible.

How to Motivate Others

Motivation is the art and talent of moving people to act in a way that achieves a change or desired outcome. The key to motivating others is offering them something they want in return. Motivation can be thought of as a transferable approach, meaning you can motivate others in various situations using similar tactics. It is about helping people see their own personal best. Witt (n.d.) provides few tips on how to motivate others:

- **Be specific.** Explain to others exactly what the goal is and openly discuss what their role would be. Don't be abstract, such as stating, "I want everyone to do their best." Instead use SMART goals and get feedback.

- **Be timely.** It's easier to ask people to commit to specific timeframes than to expect them to meet indefinitely. Set a start date and an end date.

- **Roll up your sleeves.** Thought leaders wouldn't ask someone to do something they wouldn't do themselves. In other words, do not instruct staff to work on a project and walk away from it. Share the load in some way so that the group doesn't feel neglected.

- **Look in the mirror.** People are motivated by positive emotions like excitement, honor, and joy. Don't expect others to be these things if you're not.

- **Inspire.** Give multiple and specific reasons why you are asking for participation, using a "what's in it for me" approach. This involves changing the way people think and feel.

Motivation is not a one-time effort. I see change fail not because people weren't good at motivating other people to join events, meetings, and so on; I see change fail because those trying to motivate others didn't sustain the momentum of motivation. Motivation must be constant and reenergized. Recognition of good work is a great motivator that is often overlooked because good work is expected. According to a 2006 Gallup survey, fewer than one in three American workers strongly agreed that they had received *any* praise from a supervisor in the past 7 days (Robinson, 2006). What is so concerning about this is that this survey also revealed employees who reported that they're not adequately recognized at work are three times more likely to say they'll resign in the next year.

time to reflect

Lack of positive reinforcement is also portrayed in patient care, as well. Take, for example, when we ask about the patient's smoking status, one of the meaningful-use questions required by The Centers for Medicare and Medicaid Services (CMS). When we ask if the patient smokes and they say no, we check "no" on the EMR. Do we take time to reinforce this good behavior, or do we just move on to the next question? What do you say if the patient says yes? This, of course, is a simple example, but take a minute and reflect on how many times you provide positive reinforcement to your patients (and/or staff). Is there room to improve?

Why Motivate Others

If you're not in a formal leadership role, you're probably reading this and think-ing, "Well, if I'm going to start motivating my colleagues to join committees to improve our workplace, then what's in it for me?" (I specified people who do not have formal leadership titles because it is obvious why those in formal leadership titles should be doing this—bonuses, staff retention, staff satisfaction scores, and so on.)

Why *you* should be motivating others is because of the effects of a certain chemi-cal in your body. This chemical could potentially harm or help your personal, professional, and social life. Increases of this chemical stimulates positive feelings and decreases frustration, depression, anger, and anxiety. The chemical is do-pamine, which is a neurotransmitter that is produced in your brain. Dopamine stimulates the parts of the brain that processes rewards and create positive emo-tions.

Positive emotions help us in making decisions. When you do the right thing or receive recognition, dopamine is released in the brain. When dopamine is released, we feel happy and pleased. Therefore, the antecedent is making good choices or being recognized for great work, the behavior is happiness, and the consequence is more dopamine will be released. This is why positive psychology and reinforcement is so effective—there is a synergistic effect.

The 5 Ps

As discussed in Chapter 1, many people have the ready-fire approach engrained and forget to aim, or fail to re-aim, prior to firing initiatives. Before you rush into your CNO's office to announce your big idea to create multiple committees to improve your workplace and blurt out how the effects will improve employee sat-isfaction, staff retention, patient satisfaction scores, and the bottom line, put on your brakes. Don't put on your brakes in terms of motivation and intention, but slow down and go easily through the "ready" stage. For example, before I start a project I always remember the 5 Ps of performance:

Proper Planning Prevents Poor Performance

In respect to the 5 Ps, you need to plan each of the committee's structure, possible barriers, and charge. When you form a committee with people at different levels of the organization and with varying personalities, chaos is likely. It is important to choose the right champions to lead individual committees. To make sure there is sound staff engagement, activate your "early adopters" who arc passionate about the idea so they will help influence others to become motivated.

Psychologist Bruce Tuckman (as cited in Wilson, 2010) introduced forming, storming, norming, and performing as a framework for teams to achieve high performance. Teams begin in the *forming* stage in which members are positive and polite. Some members are anxious because they don't know others or haven't worked out or determined their individual contribution to this committee. Tuckman explains that this is a brief stage and may even be as brief as an introductory meeting. During this stage, discussions may include team processes, which may frustrate the members who are more action oriented than process oriented (Smith, 2005).

Soon, reality sets in as emotions start percolating. Let the *storming* phase begin! As members learn their positions within the team, authority maybe challenged because some members will debate their position. The action plans are defined, and it's critical to discuss leader roles. Leader roles are important in keeping you informed of the committee's work, as well as handling those who are overwhelmed by how much there is to do or are uncomfortable with the approach being used. This stage is tricky because this is when many teams fail, so stay motivated and focused.

Next, the committee moves into a *norming* stage, where position titles within the committee are decided. Now that the team members are better acquainted, more socializing occurs, and they are able to ask for help and provide constructive criticism to each other. The committee builds cohesiveness and commitments to success.

Committee teams then reach the *performing* phase. This is where hard work creates a shared vision. The culture of the committee is established; therefore, if individual team members leave or new people join, the foundation of the committee's existence won't be significantly affected (Smith, 2005).

> Understand your role in coaching committee members through the forming, storming, and norming stages. Work with the committees on developing SMART goals. Remember forming, storming, and norming needs to happen before the committee starts performing. Communication, motivation, and leadership is your main role. Stay consistent in doing this.

Committee Charge

Now that you have examined how high-performing teams develop within themselves, it's time to review the existence and charge of the committees discussed earlier in this chapter. Those committees included rewards and recognition, AIDET (see Appendix C), HCAHPS and scripting, succession planning, hire right, transformational rounding (see Appendix B), discharge follow-up, welcome committee, leadership training and education, physician and staff engagement, and bright ideas.

As I describe each category I share some ideas and concepts for you to consider. The committees should be comprised of members of senior leadership, as well as a cross-sectional group of staff at every level. This will demonstrate upper management's commitment to the cause. A mix of leaders will also provide a reality check against a focus on "employee satisfiers," such as free coffee, cafeteria vouchers, and extra vacation time. I will not go too far into detail because many of the logistics, such as committee meeting times, occurrences, number of members (who and how members are picked), and tools are all specific to an individual organization's culture and policies.

Rewards and recognition committee. This type of committee can be looked to as a subcommittee if your organization already has a similar or more formal committee structure. In my vision, these committee members brainstorm reward and recognition ideas, survey staff periodically to determine what an ideal reward looks like, and determine what ways people would like to be recognized. The committee then disseminates the aggregate data (quarterly or biannually) to managers, supervisors, and anyone who wants to receive this information. This not only encourages and reminds formal leaders to recognize staff for doing good work, but it also gives them ideas on how to show it. This does the same for all staff, at all levels. Not only is rewarding others important, but it is also important to know when and how to administer rewards. After all, not everyone is an extrovert and likes to have his or her name announced across a busy cafeteria. Sharing aggregate data that reflects individual considerations brings awareness that one size doesn't fit all.

> Not every reward needs to have monetary value. You would be surprised how many people are just as happy with verbal or written recognition as they are with a $5.00 meal voucher. Try it.

This committee can also be responsible for implementing and monitoring recognition boxes placed throughout the hospital. Something as simple as "I caught [insert name] doing [insert act], and this should be recognized" cards can be developed. On a weekly or monthly basis (designate time), appointed committee members share these cards with formal leadership, who then informs the staff member that he or she has been recognized. Again, the committee can give ideas on how and when to do this, such as opening every staff meeting with someone who was recognized, or simply sending them a "kudos" email. The bottom line is that regardless of title, an informal rewards and recognition committee empowers others to speak up and do something when they see good work done, especially when formal leaders may not.

AIDET, HCAHPS, and scripting committee. This committee is responsible for developing impromptu scripting including AIDET (see Appendix C), HCAHPS, and any acronym for any common situation, which can be applicable to any department. It is important that this group encourages staff to use the scripts and acronyms as a guide so that staff is motivated to use them to their individual liking and not to memorize them, which can lead to robotic dialogue. This also gives departments flexibility in customizing scripts to their patient or staff population. Previous chapters discuss scripting for AIDET and HCAHPS, but other acronyms can be formulated for service excellence initiatives.

Moreover, some acronyms can be used for multiple purposes. For example, Chapter 6 describes how AIDET is a valuable tool in greeting others, but AIDET (Studer, 2004) can also be used in pain management. For example:

Acknowledge   Reminds nurses to acknowledge when they see patients in pain. "Mr. _____, you look very un-comfortable."

Introduce   Reminds nurses to introduce how important pain management is and that we care that the patient is at a level where their pain is tolerable.

Duration   Enables nurses to explain the duration of the medication and how the dosing is scheduled.

Explanation   Helps nurses remember the importance of ex-plaining to patients why pain management and assessment is important in their care. We can record their pain rating at this time. This is also a good time to discuss possible/existing side-effects.

Thank you   Reminds nurses to thank patients for trusting in them.

AIDET can be used for virtually any department that has members who interact with patients and staff. Similarly, as reviewed in Chapter 6, HCAHPS scripts can be further developed to include front desk staff, housekeeping, admissions, and all interdisciplinary departments. HCAHPS scripting doesn't need to be isolated to just the nursing department because this survey is a reflection of all staff who meet and greet patients.

Hire right committee. This committee is responsible for attending departmental interviews and educating others on how to conduct interviews. Typically, interviews are done in a silo approach, where departmental leaders only ask other members of the department to interview a candidate (if they ask anyone to help with the interview). Rarely do you see a lab associate sit in on a respiratory therapist candidate's interview, as an example. Why is it good to integrate departments? Well, it builds camaraderie among interdisciplinary departments and gives insight into the hiring process. The important piece to understand is that we shouldn't always hire based on clinical or technical skills only; we should also look for leadership and team-building skills, as well as many other soft skills, which is where an interdisciplinary approach to interviewing can be advantageous.

This committee will also become acquainted with behavioral-based interviewing (BBI) and help other hiring managers learn and apply this if they are unfamiliar. Briefly, BBI is built on the idea that your past performance is the best predictor of your future performance. When someone is asked BBI questions, they are asked to describe examples of specific events they experienced. Not only is the interviewer trying to learn what action steps the interviewee took in the example, but also what the final outcome or result was. This limits the ability of the interviewer to make stories up (Byham, 2004).

You can use a STAR approach for BBI interviews (Byham, 2004). STAR is an acronym (yes, another acronym) for guiding the interviewer to have the interviewee describe a prior work-related story or experience. The STAR model includes:

Situation   Describe events of the story (who, what, where, when, how).

Task   Explain the tasks that were implemented. Sometimes, the Situation and Task can be merged, depending on the question.

Action   Describe the actions taken that contributed to the outcome's success.

Result   Explain the result of the efforts. Try to solicit a quantifiable outcome if possible.

Here is an example of a BBI question and an appropriate response using a STAR framework:

Question: Tell me about a time when you had to handle a patient complaint. What was the complaint about, and how did you resolve it?

STAR-based answer:

Situation   Last week, I had a patient complain about the noise level on our unit. I apologized for this and offered him ear plugs. I thanked the patient for sharing this with me and told him I would start looking for more effective ways to reduce noise other than just ear plugs.

Task   I also told him I was going to speak with my manager
                about other ways we could remedy this. So, with man-
                agement approval, I started to research what other
                hospitals were doing to reduce noise levels, as this
                wasn't the first time a patient complained about this.

Action   I started the PinDrop Committee, and we worked on
                ways to reduce noise based on the literature and our
                own ideas.

Result   A few weeks after our first committee meeting, we
                were able to decrease overhead paging and move to
                more cell phone usage, as well as implement quiet
                hours in the afternoon in which staff had to whisper
                and dim lights in certain areas. Although this out-
                come didn't help the patient himself, he did share he
                was impressed with my idea and expressed gratitude
                that I cared.

Transformational rounding committee. The transformational rounding committee assists in developing and organizing content for various rounding questions for organization-wide and intra-/interdepartmental rounding, or check-
ins (Appendix C). Rounding for outcomes, as coined by Studer (2004), provides
a vehicle for asking questions that helps build relationships and connects with
teams for purpose and worthwhile work. Rounding provides a time not only to
build relationships, but also to be a role model or mentor, assess employee morale, harvest wins, and identify and remove barriers that prevent staff from doing their jobs. Rounding tools can be designed for executive leadership to round
on various departmental staff meetings, managers or supervisors to round on
individual staff members, nurse-to-patient rounding, and interdepartmental
manager to interdepartmental manager (e.g., housekeeping manager and nursing unit manager).

Discharge follow-up committee. Follow-up phone calls to discharged patient are most beneficial when made within 48 to 72 hours of the patient's discharge. The purpose of the call can be two-fold. First, it can be for clinical follow-up. Questions should be directed about the patient's condition, follow-up appointments, treatment plan, medications, and side effects. The second purpose for a follow-up call can be related to service excellence assessments. Questions should be directed to understanding the patient's perception of their hospital or outpatient experience, including identifying areas of improvement or if any caregivers should be recognized for doing great work, to name a few.

This committee works with individual departments to determine who will make these follow-up calls, helps departments in making scripts to guide callers in asking appropriate questions, and helps develop an algorithm to determine if another call from a clinician may be indicated. This committee is also responsible for tracking responses where patients identify any improvements for the organization. Committee members work with formal leadership and perhaps the performance-improvement department (or other appropriate departments) in making suggestions for action plans.

Welcome committee. The idea for this committee is similar to the transformational rounding concept; the welcome committee will round with newly hired staff on a consistent basis during the first year of employment. Committee members act as mentors and may choose to meet biweekly in the beginning and then at 30, 60, and 90 days, at 6 months of hire, and so on. This committee forms questions that will be asked during each rounding session to assess and help new staff with adjusting to the organization. Through such questions, the committee can ask new employees if they have suggestions to improve the orientation experience or ask if they need any further help in finding resources or support. The committee also evaluates the questions to ensure they are obtaining the most comprehensive information. This committee is very beneficial in helping to retain first-year employees, because first-year retention is typically difficult (Tourangeau et al., 2010; Studer, 2004).

Leadership training and education committee. The leadership training committee is responsible for the development of content that provides comprehensive knowledge, skills, and education to both aspiring and seasoned leaders. This committee plans and coordinates training, orientation, and leadership development for member leaders at all levels across the organization. In order for this committee to have the proper respect and credibility, initiatives to implement training and education must be approved and supported by senior leadership and human resources. If it is not approved, then the committee could still exist as a journal club in which published and evidence-based leadership research and outcomes are shared by committee members at various departmental staff meetings.

Physician and staff engagement committee. This concept could conceivably be two separate committees. First, a physician engagement committee or a physician advisory group or counsel introduces new programs and projects to the medical staff. This committee meets with senior leaders on a regular basis to discuss issues such as value-based purchasing, credentialing, onboarding, and other hot topics (which are developed by this group). This committee incorporates physician practice managers in medical staff meetings and establishes implementation teams composed of board, management, and physicians working on presence and voice in decision-making, leadership development, peer review, and so forth.

The staff engagement committee is charged with working closely with the rewards and recognition committee to ensure that the work of that committee is supported. Moreover, the staff engagement committee members review staff satisfaction surveys and look for commonalities and ways to make improvements on an organizational level. This committee is also responsible for creating employee engagement activities, such as celebrations or potluck meals, and assists in choosing employee annual gifts.

Bright ideas committee. This committee is instrumental in harvesting suggestions from staff for workplace improvements through bright idea boxes (tangible boxes or by electronic means, or both). This committee develops and launches special programs such as safety, cost reduction, or patient and staff satisfaction. This committee also implements safety huddles and encourages units to use briefings, debriefings, and other huddles to improve the interdepartmental communication highway. These methods and other tools in the TeamSTEPPS program can be used to create a culture of safety and transparency. TeamSTEPPS is an evidence-based teamwork system designed to optimize patient outcomes by improving communication and teamwork. It was developed for use in clinical practice (Agency for Healthcare Research and Quality [AHRQ], n.d.). Committee members often work as subcommittee members to organizations that have a project improvement department. This committee is responsible for having a process in place to evaluate and implement the ideas harvested. If dozens of suggestions are offered but not acted upon (either implemented or explained why they couldn't be implemented), suggestions will wither and die along with the attitudes and trust of staff.

ᵀᴴᴱREAL WORLD | LEADERSHIP STYLES VERSUS LEADERSHIP OUTCOMES

According to Casida and Parker (2011), transformational leadership training should be a foundational requirement of nursing managers. These researchers state it is a moral obligation of administrators to place competent transformational leaders into formal leadership roles.

The Journey of Leadership

"The development of leadership skills should be viewed as a journey" (Sherman & Pross, 2010, para. 11). Unfortunately, many people who hold formal leadership titles were designated for their roles due to their seniority need to fill the position, their proficient clinical skills, or technical abilities (Sherman, Bishop, Eggenberger, & Karden, 2007). Leadership training is a lifelong learning process, and it is every formal nurse leader's ethical and moral obligation to obtain training in an ongoing manner.

Leadership training can consist of formal leadership classes, courses, and lectures; online and CEU activities; and journal readings. For example, the American Organization of Nurse Executives, the Association of Perioperative Registered Nurses, and the American Association of Critical Care Nurses worked together to craft a model that would assist current and emerging nurse leaders in obtaining necessary leadership competencies. It is important for healthcare executives, or those in hiring roles, to understand that simply because a nurse has clinical expertise and acumen does not necessitate that they have leadership expertise, too. New leaders often battle with how to transfer their informal leadership ability into the formal role. Without mentorship and other means of participatory leadership training, many new nurse leaders become frustrated and fail (Sherman & Pross, 2010).

Transformational leadership is an optimal leadership style in which leaders create environments in which employees are motivated, supported, and encouraged to be creative and take risks. This leadership style is often seen in Magnet-designated hospitals (Ulrich, Buerhaus, Donelan, Norman, & Dittus, 2009). Characteristics of the positive environment associated with transformational leadership are (Salanova, Lorente, Chambel, & Martínez, 2011; Shirey, 2007):

- Shared goals, values, and missions

- Distributed power

- Education

- Behavior modeling

- Individualized guidance

- Open, effective communication

James McGregor Burns (1978) was the first author to contrast transforming and transactional leadership styles. Transactional leadership involves an exchange relationship, or a transaction between leaders and followers, such as when followers receive compensation for complying with a leader's request. In contrast, transformational leadership empowers employees to "go above and beyond" to achieve goals. Transformational leaders inspire employees to move beyond mediocrity and work toward the improvement of a process that helps to improve overall organizational excellence.

Bernard Bass (1985) identified subcomponents of transformational leadership, including charisma (which was later retitled as idealized influence), inspirational motivation, intellectual stimulation, and individualized consideration:

- **Idealized influence:** Transformational leaders hold themselves as role models to staff. They are respected, admired, and trusted by their followers because they are consistent in doing the right thing and display high moral and effortless ethical standards.

- **Inspirational motivation:** Leaders show enthusiasm and optimism as they create an atmosphere of commitment to goals and a shared vision.

- **Intellectual stimulation:** Transformational leaders encourage creativity and motivate followers to think about old problems in a new way.

- **Individualized consideration:** Individual desires and needs are respected and differences are accepted. Staff moves toward development of higher levels of potential, as they feel worthwhile and purposeful in the organization.

Accountability Versus Ownership

We need to encourage our colleagues to become "owners" of the organization, realizing that the success and future of our organization is directly related to the care we all provide our patients and colleagues. During my speaking engagements, I like to make a distinction between accountability and ownership. I simplify the two words by proposing the following scenario:

> Because I travel across the U.S. for speaking engagements, I stay at many nice hotels. When I arrive at my hotel room, I will occasionally open the window to get some fresh air. I have found that even some of the finest hotels have a little pollen collected in the window sill when I open it. This does not faze me. I accept it. After I open the window for some fresh air, I take a shower to freshen up. After showering, I place my used towels in the corner of the bathroom to indicate to the housekeeper they are dirty. I place my trash in the trashcans, and I make sure my used glasses are in the dishwasher and the counter is wiped up before I check out. I consider myself "accountable" for the way I left that hotel room.

> Now, when I return home, I like to freshen my house, so I open my windows. I find pollen in the sill. I don't accept this, of course; I clean it. After I clean the sills, I head for a shower to freshen up. After showering I don't place my used towels in the corner of my bathroom; I place them in my washing machine. I place my trash in trashcans and take the trash out, just like I run the dishwasher and put the items away when it's full. Finally, I not only wipe up my counters, but also I thoroughly clean them on a consistent basis. I consider myself as having "ownership" for the way I keep my home.

The next time you or a colleague speaks to accountability, ask yourself if you (or she) should instead be speaking to ownership.

It is essential to create and sustain organizational health. The key ingredient to this staff engagement. Engaged staff deliver higher quality of care than mediocre or disgruntled staff. Engaged staff will help their organization attract and retain patients and families. This includes the loyalty of staff, which is closely mirrored to the care delivered; loyalty of a patient and their family, in which they make your hospital their first choice; and loyalty of formal and informal leaders, in which to form trusting relationships.

The aBEST Approach

Healthy workplace environments should incorporate the aBEST approach for effective communication. Utilizing acronyms such as AIDET, TeamSTEPPS, SMART, and STAR with impromptu scripting can help hardwire conversations to be meaningful and purposeful. Understanding the roles of body language and emotions is key to improving intra- and interpersonal communications. It is important to recall the CAR framework as a guide to ensure your words match your body language and emotions:

C   *Consider* all the aspects of the 5 Rights to Communica-
     tion Safety. Actively listen to patient and staff concerns
     and reflectively respond/address them accordingly without
     multitasking.

A   Determine your *action or call to action*. This reminds us to
     be active listeners and follow through on answers received.
     Follow the QWQ formula to allow adequate time for the
     patient to formulate an answer.

R   The *return on investment (ROI)* is once again re-aiming your
     approach to customize it for improving the patient experi-
     ence. Review whether there is anything else you could be
     asking or doing for the patient. Make the ROI worth the
     investment you made by earning the trust of your patients
     and their families.

The Drive Home

Let's review the *driving it back home* pointers from this chapter:

- Initiating, nourishing, and sustaining healthy work environments must be a priority in order to increase patient safety, staff retention, and recruitment.

- Change leadership is a key part of the patient satisfaction strategy and of sustaining a healthy workplace environment.

- Changing behavior is one of the biggest challenges in organizations, but, according to McKinsley (2010), about 70% of all changes in all organizations fail.

- Healthcare providers must listen to patients to determine how best to meet their needs.

- Higher levels of patient satisfaction lead to better care outcomes and positive financial results.

- Sustaining healthy work environments must be a priority if healthcare organizations want to make meaningful contributions in the care of patients and patients' families.

- Patient safety is the top priority—*always.*

- To motivate others, we need to be specific, timely, participative, active, and inspiring.

- Recognition for doing good work releases dopamine in the brain, which creates feelings of pride and pleasure.

- All leaders, formal and informal, are responsible for keeping healthcare providers engaged in providing patient-centered care.

- Healthcare providers should involve patients in every decision about their care.

- Even though 70% of changes fail, you can succeed if you overcome cynicism and fear, lack of applied knowledge, and lack of practiced skills. Identify hidden conflicts that undermine your efforts and know the unwritten rules that work against change.

- Take a risk and start a committee to improve your workplace environment.

- Encourage your colleagues to become "owners" of the organization.

- Transformational leadership is an optimal leadership style in which leaders create environments in which employees are motivated, supported, and encouraged to be creative and take risks.

References

Agency for Healthcare Research and Quality. (n.d.). *TeamSTEPPS*. Retrieved from http://teamstepps.ahrq.gov

Bass, B. M. (1985). *Leadership and performance.* New York, NY: Free Press.

Borkowski, N. (2009). *Organizational behavior in health care.* Sudbury, MA: Jones & Bartlett.

Brady, G. P., & Cummings, G. G. (2010). The influence of nursing leadership on nurse performance: A systematic literature review. *Journal of Nursing Management, 18,* 425–439. doi: 10.1111/j.1365-2834.2010.01100.x

Burns, J. M. (1978). *Leadership.* New York, NY: Harper and Row.

Byham, W. C. (2004). "Development Dimensions International (DDI), Inc. Targeted Selection: A Behavioral Approach to Improved Hiring Decisions." Retrieved http://www.ddiworld.com/DDIWorld/media/white-papers/targetedselection_mg_ddi.pdf?ext=.pdf

Casida J., & Parker, J. (2011). Staff nurse perceptions of nurse manager leadership styles and outcomes. *Journal of Nursing Management, 19*(4), 478–486.

Cowden, T., Cummings, G, & Profetto-Mcgrath, J. (2011). Leadership practices and staff nurses' intent to stay: A systematic review. *Journal of Nursing Management, 19*(4), 461–477. doi: 10.1111/j.1365-2834.2011.01209.x

Cummings, G. G., MacGregor, T., Davey, M., Lee, H., Wong, C. A., Lo, E...Stafford, E. (2010). Leadership styles and outcome patterns for the nursing workforce and work environment: A systematic review. *International Journal of Nursing Studies, (47)*3, 363–385. doi:10.1016/j.ijnurstu.2009.08.006

Geedey, N. (2006). Create and sustain a healthy work environment. *Nursing Management, 37*(10), 17–18.

Getty, J. P. (n.d.). Retrieved from http://www.brainyquote.com/quotes/quotes/j/jpaulgett100752.html

Institute of Medicine. (1999). To err is human: Building a safer health system. Retrieved from http://www.iom.edu/~/media/Files/Report%20Files/1999/To-Err-is-Human/To%20Err%20is%20Human%201999%20%20report%20brief.pdf

Kramer, M., & Schmalenberg, C. (2008). Confirmation of a healthy work environment. *Critical Care Nurse, 28*(3), 56–63.

Kupperschmidt, B., Kientz, E., Ward, J., & Reinholz, B. (2010). A healthy work environment: It begins with you. *OJIN: The Online Journal of Issues in Nursing, 15*(1), Manuscript 3. doi 10.3912/OJIN.Vol15No01Man03

Longo, J. (2009). The relationship between manager and peer caring to registered nurses' job satisfaction and intent to stay. *International Journal of Human Caring, 13*(2), 27–34.

McKinsley Quarterly. (2010.) Helping employees embrace change. Retrieved from http://www.mckinsey.com/insights/organization/helping_employees_embrace_change

Meyer, P. J. (2003). *What would you do if you knew you couldn't fail? Creating S.M.A.R.T. Goals. Attitude Is Everything: If You Want to Succeed Above and Beyond.* Meyer Resource Group, Incorporated.

Miller, W. R., & Rollnick, S. (2013). Motivational interviewing: Helping people change. New York, NY: The Guilford Press.

Pund, L. E., & Sylar, P. (2012). Linking Quality Assurance to Human Resources: Improving patient satisfaction by improving employee satisfaction. Retrieved from http://www.iu.edu/~spea/pubs/undergrad-honors/volumn-6/Pund,%20Lindsey%20Linking%20Quality%20Assurance%20to%20Human%20Resources%20Improving%20Patient%20Satisfaction%20by%20Improving%20Employee%20Satisfaction%20%20Faculty%20Pam%20Sklar.pdf

Ritter, D. (2011). The relationship between healthy work environments and retention of nurses in a hospital setting. *Journal of Nursing Management, 19*(1), 27–32. doi: 10.1111/j.1365-2834.2010.01183.x

Robinson, J. (2006). In praise of praising your employees. Retrieved from http://businessjournal.gallup.com/content/25369/praise-praising-your-employees.aspx

Salanova, M., Lorente, L., Chambel, M. J., & Martínez, I. M. (2011). Linking transformational leadership to nurses' extra-role performance: The mediating role of self-efficacy and work engagement. *Journal of Advanced Nursing, 67*(10), 2256–2266. doi: 10.1111/j.1365-2648.2011.05652.x

Sherman, R., Bishop, M., Eggenberger, T., & Karden, R. (2007). Development of a leadership competency model from insights shared by nurse managers. *Journal of Nursing Administration, 37*(2), 85–94.

Sherman, R., & Pross, E. (2010). Growing future nurse leaders to build and sustain healthy work environments at the unit level. *OJIN: The Online Journal of Issues in Nursing, 15*(1). doi: 10.3912/OJIN.Vol15No01Man01

Shirey, M. R. (2007). Competencies and tips for effective leadership. *Journal of Nursing Administration, 37*(4), 167–170.

Shirey, M. R., & Fisher, M. L. (2008). Leadership agenda for change toward healthy work environments in acute and critical care. *Critical Care Nurse, 28*(5), 66–79.

Spence Laschinger, H. K., Leiter, M., Day, A., & Gilin, D. (2009). Workplace empowerment, incivility, and burnout: Impact on staff nurse recruitment and retention outcomes. *Journal of Nursing Management, 17*(3) 302–311. doi: 10.1111/j.1365-2834.2009.00999.x

Smith, M. K. (2005). Bruce W. Tuckman – forming, storming, norming and performing in groups. The Encyclopaedia of Informal Education. Retrieved from http://infed.org/mobi/bruce-w tuckman-forming-storming-norming-and-performing-in-groups/

Stichler, J. F. (2009). Creating a healthy, positive work environment: A leadership imperative. *Nursing for Women's Health, 13*(4), 341–346.

Studer, Q. (2004). *Hardwiring excellence: Purpose, worthwhile work, making a difference.* Gulf Breeze, FL: Fire Starter.

Swearingen, S. (2009). A journey to leadership: Designing a nursing leadership development program. *Journal of Continuing Education in Nursing, 40*(3) 107–114.

Tourangeau, A. E., Cummings, G., Cranley, L. A., Ferron, E. M., & Harvey, S. (2010). Determinants of hospital nurse intention to remain employed: Broadening our understanding. *Journal of Advanced Nursing, 66*(1), 22–32.

Ulrich, B., Buerhaus, P., Donelan, K., Norman, L., & Dittus, R. (2009). Magnet status and registered nurse views of the work environment and nursing as a career. *Journal of Nursing Administration, 39*(7/8), 54–62.

Wilson, C. (2010). Bruce Tuckman's forming, storming, norming & performing team development model. Retrieved from http://www.performancecoachtraining.com/resources/docs/pdfs2/BruceTuckman_Team_Development_Model.pdf

Witt, C. (n.d.) How to motivate and inspire your people in difficult times. Retrieved from http://www.reliableplant.com/Read/18525/how-to-motivate-inspire-your-people-in-difficult-times

World Health Organization. (2013). WHO definition of health. Retrieved from http://www.who.int/governance/eb/who_constitution_en.pdf

> *"We are what we repeatedly do."*
> –Aristotle

Organizational Culture and Behavior

Shelley Johnson (Chapter Contributor)

Most nurses seek a clear-cut methodology in decision-making and actions. The fear of failure can stifle our potentially courageous attempts at doing what we consider is correct, especially as it relates to organizational culture. The following vignette is an example of how an organization's culture can lure us into doing things the way they've always been done just to stay within the organization's norms (even though we know it's not the best choice).

> *A small rural hospital has a labor and delivery unit, postpartum unit, pediatric unit, and the newborn nursery, each with separate nurse managers within each area. Because the nurse managers were considered the clinical experts on their units, the normal procedure was for staff to always forward all problems to the*

respective nurse manager and let him or her resolve the issues. When the hospital decided to reorganize the nursing management structure among these departments, one nurse manager was appointed as a maternal-child director, and the other three nurse managers were placed into clinical coordinator roles. This organizational change made it increasingly difficult for the new director to know all the necessary facts of all the different units in order to make the best decisions.

The director was criticized by staff for the poor decisions she made due to her obvious lack of clinical expertise in the other three specialties. Although the director knew her weakness, she continued to try and independently resolve issues that arose because she feared that admitting her weakness to her staff would make her appear even weaker. Instead of allowing the clinical coordinators or front-line staff to help in the decision-making, the director continued to make independent decisions because historically, each unit leader resolved all the issues him- or herself.

A closer look at communication in the context of organizational culture and behavior is the focus of this chapter. More specifically, this chapter discusses how your role, as an effective communicator, contributes to the micro and mega of organizational culture and climate. As you read these thoughts regarding culture and behavior, I hope you will reflect on your environments, past and present, and consider how colleagues behave, as well as how you contributed to culture and climate creation through direct, intentional acts or through acts of omission as it relates to communication.

We need to move past a lexicon approach to understanding culture and cultural behaviors and move into a more respectful approach. I can't tell you how many times I have read textbooks on culture or sat in a classroom and heard lectures on culture that simplify culture to the point of stereotyping. Oftentimes, I found myself looking to the cultural categories that are meant to define me and found myself asking, "Who are these writers talking to or about?" Interestingly most nursing textbooks are written from the perspective of people attempting to shed light on beliefs, values, and practices of minority populations.

time to reflect

Try to reflect on your experiences, keeping in mind that organizational cultural and climate behaviors have visible figments and unseen values and assumptions shared by its stakeholders. Some visible figments may include symbols, customs, formalities, language, structures, clothing, technology, and history. Values and assumptions, although invisible, can be evidenced in beliefs, decision-making trends, support or nonsupport of administration, rules, procedures, and responses to change. Does your organization's culture affect how forthcoming you are in addressing issues with colleagues, patients, and/or administration? Why or why not?

The Driver's Seat: Defining Organizational Culture, Climate, and Cultural Behavior

Let's start by establishing shared definitions of culture, climate, and cultural behavior, because it's nearly impossible to separate these ideas. When we do, we oversimplify them.

Culture refers to characteristics shared historically by a group of people; therefore, the group is self-determined or defined by outsiders looking in. We can all agree that we belong to numerous cultures and subcultures. Some of the cultures that I am self-assigned to include, for example, nursing, science, academia, West Indian, and Christian. People are so complex and culturally integrated that attempts to neatly place individuals into distinct categories are impractical and ineffective when working toward organizational progress.

Organizational climate and *cultural behaviors* are made up of all the past and current experiences, values, strengths, and weaknesses of employees and organizations. Although leadership is very instrumental in defining organizational culture by way of their actions and decisions, every person in an organization contributes to it. Cultural behavior is one small aspect of social traditions used in shaping environmental and group values. I have worked in small and large organizations among racially and ethnically homogenous and heterogeneous groups. What I have gleaned from these experiences is that organizational

cultural and climate behavior has less to do with race and ethnicity than it does
with power and control.

Cultural and climate changes are slow, but fluid, in society and within
organizations. Learning new cultures is a requirement and frequent
occurrence as organizations grow and operate in the global economy.
When entering a new situation, take time to assess:

- Feeling in the atmosphere: Is there tension, calmness, chaos, high
  energy, or low energy?

- Treatment of people: How do people interact with each other and
  with you? Are they formal or casual? Do you ask open-ended questions, or do you assume?

- Team versus individual: Do the employees use team (we) or individual (I) language?

- Flexibility and tradition: Are traditions strictly maintained, or are
  innovations and change the way of life?

- Planning versus chaos: Are the workers willing to endure periods
  of disruption or must they adhere to strict arrangements during
  planning and implementation?

- Values: What do employees value in interactions, outcomes, and
  processes?

The amount of power and control exercised in an organization can greatly affect
the effectiveness of communication within the organization. Case in point: I
have worked in organizations that welcomed a shared-governance model and
found these organizations to have more effective communication, both horizontally and vertically within the hierarchy, than organizations that do not practice
this model. Shared governance is a culturally sensitive professional practice
model that emphasizes the principles of partnership, equity, accountability,
and ownership in order to promote accountability-based decisions. Shared
governance is also an interdisciplinary approach to providing excellent patient
care and provides front-line staff some power and control in decision-making
(Barden, Quinn Griffin, Donahue, & Fitzpatrick, 2011). When the power and

control of decision-making is not limited to administrators, the ability for staff to communicate problems or potential problems is more effective and efficient. See Script 8.1 for an example of a conversation you might have with your boss when you need to direct an issue to the attention of your manager's boss.

Your Road Map: Understanding Cultural and Climate Behaviors

Successful organizations have many commonalities in cultural and climate behaviors, such as:

- Providing employment security

- Engaging in selective hiring

- Utilizing self-managed teams

- Being decentralized

- Paying well

- Training employees

- Reducing status differences

- Embracing transparency

Intentional socialization to the cultural behaviors of an organization can assist in employee acclimation and evaluation of how personality fits in the organization. It can also serve to initiate needed change (Pfeffer & Veiga, 1999). For example, a previous CNO of mine attended every new nursing orientation to personally welcome new nurses to the organization. Although I have seen CNO presence at previous nursing orientations, what made me feel a "personal connection" to this particular organization's climate was when she asked each of us, as newbies, to challenge processes that "just don't make sense" and to personally share with her suggestions of things that we felt worked well in our other jobs that we noticed weren't implemented there. Her remarks granted us permission to communicate our thoughts and ideas.

Script 8.1 What to say when...
you feel you need to go above your nurse manager.

Tell

(After repeated conversations with your nurse manager on nurse–patient staff ratios)
To your nurse manager:

Jeff, I know we have exhausted the staffing issues on our unit. I feel the need to continue to pursue this issue.

Explain

Your response:

I feel like we are placing our patients in jeopardy of unsafe care. I appreciate you listening to my concerns in the past, yet my concerns still remain strong. I'd like to speak with Greg [Jeff's manager] to see if he has any other suggestions, and I welcome you in joining me in this meeting. How does that sound?

Lead by example

Your nurse manager is receptive:

Ok, I will schedule a meeting, but just so you know, I did already present this, and Greg didn't seem to think it was such an issue.

Your response:

I appreciate that you already addressed this, but I am eager to give my own personal angle on this. I think it's important that your manager sees from all of us just how important the issue is.

Your nurse manager is defensive:

There is no reason to beat a dead horse on this issue. I already spoke to Greg about this.

Your response:

I appreciate that you already addressed this, but I am eager to give my own personal angle on it. I think it's important that your manager sees from all of us just how important the issue is.

Your nurse manager is unreceptive:

Greg will be angry that you're wasting his time!

Your response:

Respectfully, I would still like to meet with him. It is important to me that I share this information firsthand.

Learn the consequence

Your nurse manager is receptive:

I'm anxious to hear if Greg tells you the same thing he told me.

Your response:

I will explain to Greg that you have been very receptive in listening to my concerns. And I will explain that I called this meeting because this issue is incredibly important to me and I really wanted to speak personally about this. I will start out by saying how grateful I am for your support in facilitating the meeting with me.
(This demonstrates a team approach.)

Socialization can occur through history sharing, through case study reviews that highlight expected behaviors, or by integrating into team situations where the long-term members model the organizational values.

The Importance of Cultural Behaviors

When are cultural behaviors important? ALWAYS!

- Forming and maintaining relationships with patients and with colleagues
- Interacting with patients and with colleagues
- Opposite gender interactions
- Like gender interactions
- Interactions within a generation and between different generations
- Interactions between races that are similar or different

The behaviors of those you work with can help you gain a better understanding of how well communication is embraced within an organization's culture, climate and cultural behaviors. The following list provides a few topics in which overarching workplace behaviors can demonstrate how effective interpersonal and interprofessional communications are acculturated within an organization:

- Power and control
- Adaptation or deception
- Etiquette
- Formality
- Time perceptions
- Hierarchy and gender
- Communication
- Cliques and work ethics

Let's take a look at each of these topics in more detail.

Power and Control

In the nursing world, power and control normally have negative connotations. Aversion to the outward display of desire for power occurs from cultural doctrinarian toward humility, self-sacrifice, and servant leadership. The result is passive aggression, a lack of transparency, and a culture of negative competition practices. Desperation fuels the need for control.

Think back to your own interactions with front-line staff, such as a receptionist who made you wait 5 to 10 minutes before acknowledging your presence. Recall the telephone operator who put you on hold for extended periods of time and then demanded that you explain exactly what you needed so that she could discuss it with the person that you are actually trying to talk to. The behaviors of these individuals position you as the victim to the cultural and climate behaviors that are practiced in their organization. This informs you who is holding the power base and how control is exercised.

The traditional culture of the organization may not have always tolerated poor performance, but the current climate does. In other words, the amount of power and control given to the receptionist or operator, as just described, is inappropriate. There is apparently too much power and control awarded to these employees, and it is being abused. In order to remedy this situation, customer service training is a must-have, as is a better management team to help coach these individuals. Do you see how culture withstands the test of time; however, the climate can change more readily, based on the tolerance of the leaders who allow certain behaviors from the employees?

Adaptation or Deception

Culture influences everything that we do. We all live in multiple cultures to the point where we move between cultural personas from one moment to another, based on our environments. As professionals, we like to think of ourselves as consistent because consistency has a positive connotation. Many of us thrive to be "consistent," which we equate with honesty, trust, transparency, and authenticity. Unfortunately, consistency is unnatural and is the opposite of honesty, transparency, and authenticity.

Consistency can even appear to be a form of dishonesty. Some time ago I worked in a small hospital where I was one of three nurse managers. The employees would take any chance they had to complain or make sarcastic comments about my upbeat and motivated partner. This manager was very professional, positive, and friendly—I wondered who could dislike that. The employees regarded her as dimwitted and flighty and as someone who had limited connections with reality because her personality was very different from theirs.

I can also remember attending a very suburban, fluent, Caucasian, fundamentalist Christian high school. I spent the majority of my days there and then returned to my home and church in an area populated with immigrants and other minority groups.

I learned that I had to become a chameleon and be able to adapt to different people if I wanted to successfully integrate into the varied settings in which I found myself. This is not to say that you should lose yourself, be a fraud, or pretend. Instead, you should take the time to learn about others and do your best to respect their culture while working to preserve your own identity.

I would be a liar if I didn't admit at times I felt like I was wearing different masks or even trying to manipulate others. Feelings of anger and resentment rose up in me occasionally out of the perceived mandate to conform and deny myself visibly due to fear of rejection. Acknowledging personal feelings of fear typically accompanies negative self-talk, doubt, and powerlessness, but if denied, these feelings cannot be recognized and adequately resolved.

I learned that *cultural balance* can emerge, and even new cultural norms can be formed as many cultures converge and unite internally and externally. Being culturally open can require that you temporarily put aside your values and norms to demonstrate acceptance through becoming active participants in other cultures and learning how to adapt in different climates.

Etiquette

Cultures and groups have varying reputations. For example, African and West Indian people are known for their excessive politeness and passivity. Constant smiles and nods can appear to be "saccharin" to those who are not used to it. As an immigrant from a West Indian country, I was very used to smiling and chatting with strangers, and then I was assimilated through fire. I learned quickly when riding on Philadelphia's SEPTA subway that smiles and uninvited conversation were similar to throwing a punch; the recipient would more than likely respond with surprise and aggression.

In business environments the culture of politeness can contribute to poor communication. Everyone smiling and nodding cannot necessarily be interpreted as agreement or support. In addition, disagreeing can be thought of as disrespectful to those in authority. It is vital to learn about others and their environment and not to take differences personally.

Formality

In my past employments, I have witnessed formality differences between two opposing healthcare settings. Healthcare setting A was a large multispecialty institution, internationally known for its research and nursing excellence awards, whereas healthcare setting B was a relatively unknown small rural hospital. In healthcare setting A, the majority of the nurses were experts in their fields. The nurses, doctors, and administrators referred to each other by first names.

Healthcare setting B often referred to patients as "consumers," and the nurses and administrators were always formal in their communications. Common practice dictated titles be used at all times, such as doctor, nurse, or professor. Patients were addressed as Miss, Mrs., or Mister.

Healthcare setting A appeared confident in their view of themselves and their ability. Healthcare setting B seemed to be working too hard to command respect and rigidly used hierarchy to divide the top people from the bottom, creating an "us versus them" mentality and practice. Healthcare setting B always appeared in a reactive state rather than a proactive state because the culture of inferiority persuaded front-line staff and even administrators not to speak up when they saw potential problems arising. Many staff adopted a submissive role, as this was viewed as respectful to the organization's culture.

Time Perceptions

In minority cultures, time perception and appreciation differs. To the business-minded person, time perception directly relates to productivity, efficiency, and finance. In the beginning of my career, I was hired to work for one of the first nurse-run health centers located in a Philadelphia housing development for underserved minorities. The center initially operated like most healthcare facilities with a set schedule (8:00 a.m. to 5:00 p.m., Monday through Friday).

Everyone, including me, complained bitterly that the population we were trying to serve rarely kept their appointments. The patients either came very late or didn't keep the appointment at all, and they also didn't provide notification calls that they were canceling. This issue is significant because the health issue would continue to worsen until the time the patient actually did show up for the appointment.

To fix the situation, we did what most people do when faced with issues—we complained more. We also took things personally and believed that we weren't appreciated. We assigned negative labels to the frequent offenders and carried on with other nonsense. Then one day we woke up and got our act together by reviewing our organizational culture. We looked at how we could change the climate to better reflect the culture we originally wanted to create. The problem we had unintentionally created was a climate of conflict; we expected our hosting culture to conform to our demands. Just imagine how the population we were trying to serve regarded us! We appeared pushy, condescending, sanctimonious, and egotistical. (Maybe their perceptions were not as bad as I imagined them to be, but my embarrassment taught me a lesson I will always carry with me.)

To remedy the situation, we decided to get rid of appointment times for 3 of the 5 workdays and institute flexible appointment times where patients would be double-booked. Patients were asked the reasons for missed appointments, which uncovered that many missed appointments were due to other pressing issues that the patients did not feel comfortable sharing. Willingness on the part of staff and healthcare providers to be more flexible helped increase trust and understanding, which in turn increased patient numbers into the facility.

Hierarchy and Gender

Some healthcare environments enforce a strict hierarchical structure because the leaders are very demanding to those of a lesser title and they have a strong desire to be reverenced like demigods. They feel they are untouchable and unreachable; they dictate commands without service-level input and portray dominance to the opposing gender. In these systems, you might hear statements such as, "I would never attempt to speak with the CNO directly," "Be willing to let your supervisors take credit for your work," or "You must be extra humble as sucking up is leading up." Giving respect is usually unidirectional, with the leaders commanding respect while having little regard for others. Submission is generally expected from the young and female.

THE REAL WORLD | AN EXAMPLE OF CULTURAL HIERARCHY

Mr. Solemn had an Ivy League graduate, doctoral-prepared research fellow working night and day on a laboratory research project. This paid research fellow was managing high-level research instruments. Many faculty and students would witness this fellow dashing to the side of Mr. Solemn. Excitement and contentment were evident on the fellow's face. He was willing to serve and approached every command and request with respect and urgency. A visitor at the facility was standing with Mr. Solemn when he raised his arm slightly and made a small gesture. The fellow broke into a sprint as if drawn by a powerful magnet to rescue Mr. Solemn. The visitor, attempting to be friendly and familiar, said loudly to the fellow, "There is no need for you to run." Mr. Solemn immediately turned to the visitor and said, "It is necessary, as I am his senior."

In many minority cultures men are viewed as the leaders and females as the servants. Gender-role beliefs heavily influence cultural behaviors within organizations. Having worked in healthcare and educational organizations for close to 20 years, I have observed that gender beliefs differ between races, ethnicities, and religions. In healthcare environments, males dominate administration. Women are rarely represented in upper executive management, whereas middle management is balanced between the genders. In nursing administration, women continue to be the controlling majority.

Communication

Elaborate and simple procedures are frequently enacted to demonstrate control and display power. Children of every culture have memories of being on the receiving end of "Mom eyes" or "The Look." Children and husbands stand corrected or frozen by the penetrating glare from a mother or wife who seems to deliver telepathic scolding. In organizations, supervisors can use body language to communicate with employees using the age-old skills used by parents to encourage or deter behaviors. As adults, we would like to believe that we are beyond basic conditioning, but tone, body positioning, grunts, and subtle eye movements can close mouths and bend heads in shame.

Control and power. The ability to communicate on any level exposes all people participating in the information exchange. Information is valuable. When you demonstrate having more information than your leaders, you are valuable only until you have no further information to share or you become viewed as the competition. Knowledge can be both a power and a threat.

The words we choose. Patients, for example, have been called consumers or customers. Scholarly literature has documented that information control is a well-known method used to intimidate, sabotage, and manipulate others. Words have a direct impact. Words are used to build or to completely decimate. Assimilation into the majority's culture is often more of a defense mechanism aimed to improve chances of survival than a tool to achieve acceptance or a true desire to integrate. For example, when we call a patient a consumer, it changes the context. This can be perceived as someone who is seeking care (patient) becoming someone who is buying care (consumer).

Cliques and Work Ethics

High school is often portrayed with social hierarchies in which there are nerds (the very diligent), sport players or jocks (respected for their physical look and abilities), and the cool group (known for their money, popularity, and self-centered, mean attitudes). Teen-targeted movies, especially in the late 1990s and early 2000s, glorified the cool slacker. In 2013, identities have changed slightly, but not by much.

Similar to high school cliques, office banter may sound like to this, "Look at Alicia. She is trying to be superwoman. We would include her, but she tries too hard. She must want to be liked. Why else would she pretend to be so motivated? This is just a job after all." Nothing about these comments displays collegiality; instead, the message oozes envy, malice, and bullying. Environments implode when small steps like these are ignored and become part of the culture. What drives people may be beyond social acceptance. Core motivators, such as spiritual beliefs or personal goals, can be the central driving force for many in the workforce.

I once read an article in which work was equated with happiness, but not because the work produced financial gain or recognition. Instead, workers felt personal gratification from a job well done. Healthy workplaces have been my axiom for some time, with an emphasis on the importance of work-life balance. I still believe this, but my perspective has now changed. Productive work is important. Employees must be invested in the work for the organization and for themselves. I prefer employees who truly enjoy what they do and seek to improve themselves and others. I have found that employees do not complain about work assignments or overload when they feel valued and competent to do the work assigned. Both supervisors and employees benefit emotionally and physically when expectations are clear and when choices are given. No one wants to feel like a slave to their job, yet feelings of self-worth, purpose, and dignity abound from a job well done.

Administrators help to create the work ethic and desired work-related behaviors. Handing down tasks or overdelegating does not reflect the characteristics of a good leader. Delegate tasks that fit an employee's job description or tasks that can facilitate professional growth. Be a role model who demonstrates continued productivity.

Organizational cultural and climate behaviors have a direct impact on employee work behaviors, their work ethic, and—ultimately—efficiency, patient outcomes, patient satisfaction, and the financial bottom line. Positive attitudes help to create a desirable milieu. Positive milieu begets affirmative outcomes, such as engagement, fair-mindedness, energy, team spirit, and inventiveness.

Using EMBRACE and ACCEPT to Improve Cultural and Climate Awareness

To improve your cultural and climate awareness, remember to EMBRACE and ACCEPT culture:

- EMBRACE

    Encourage openness and discussion

    Model standards of behavior

    Be still and observe

    Reflect, taking time to question assumptions and stereotypes

    Ask questions to seek clarification

    Consider how you reflect yourself

    Engage with others; become an active learning participant

- ACCEPT

    Acknowledge that differences exist

    Consider the opportunities

    Celebrate integration

    Empathize

    Perceive the environment

    Tolerate respect only

Your Role in Assessing and Improving Cultural and Climate Behaviors

As previously discussed, culture is an extension of the way people relate to one another, both internally and externally. We must take the lead and represent a strong and effective culture as it relates to social interactions, communication, shared interests, and responsibilities, collaboration, and friendships. The challenges we face are to consistently influence and energize others within the culture to follow a shared vision. We need to emulate and support the behaviors and actions that create a strong, positive organizational culture and climate that will thrive and forge ahead into the future. Formal leaders can influence organizational culture; they can shape and mold the values, basic assumptions, and beliefs shared by the members of the organization. Informal leaders also play essential roles in ensuring that their climate fosters strong relationships that empower one another (Tsai, 2011; Pachuta, 2014).

The element that is most essential to achieving the desired cultural and climate behaviors is respect (Tsai, 2011). Nurses can show respect for the cultural and ethnic backgrounds of all families and staff by not judging others and by being accessible. For example, inviting others to contact you shows your trust, availability, and willingness to focus on their concerns. You can also show respect to others by becoming aware of:

- Accepted behaviors such as language, customs, and habits that affiliates of the organization adhere to when they interact with one another

- Norms or standards that are accepted and practiced daily

- Values such as quality, diversity, inclusion, and collaboration that are supported by the organization

Evaluating Your Organizational Culture and Climate

To evaluate your organizational culture and climate, ask the employees within the organization to answer questions similar to these (Pachuta, 2014):

- What ideas and beliefs do the leaders of the organization hold as true and free from desecration?

- How do your coworkers feel about sharing their ideas among themselves and with formal leaders?

- How are nurses evaluated and promotions given?

- What is the organization's image in the community?

- How difficult is it to implement change?

The answers to these questions provide directions for analysis and improvement (Pachuta, 2014).

Your role in assessing and improving cultural and climate behaviors starts with an understanding and assessment of your perception of the organization's climate and cultural norms. Once you assess your own perceptions and acquire respect for the similarities and differences that exist, you can be successful as well as respectful in how you communicate to members within your organization. Your understanding and assessment should include a review of how communication affects the organizational dynamics, the level of enculturation and trust, and the amount of inspiration that exists within the organization. Let's examine these in a little more detail.

Organizational changes. There is always room for improvement within an organization because organizations are so dynamic in nature. In other words, organizations must change or shift in response to external (e.g., healthcare reform) and internal changes (e.g., staff and leader turnover). This forces organizations into a continual state of learning and developing. These perspectives provide the kind of holistic view that must be embraced and communicated by members of the organization (Watkins, n.d).

Enculturation. Enculturation is a socialization process where healthcare staff conform to the organizational culture of their new hospital, office, department, unit, etc. Some organizations implement new-hire orientations and mentorship programs to help enculturate all new hires. You can take an active role in becoming a mentor to new employees (see Chapter 7, "Healthy Workplace Environments").

Trust. The best way to promote positive enculturation is through providing a trusting work environment to your best abilities. The level of trust found in organizations is dependent on the level of transparency, respect, and authenticity derived from formal leadership, colleagues, patients and families. The integrity of the formal leadership of the organization is just as critical as the informal leaders. The organizational trust is unequivocally important to organizational health and viability. Trust is the prophecy to highly reliable organizations. According to Weick and Sutcliffe (2001), High Reliability Organizations (HRO) are mindful of what keeps them working safe, even when faced with unforeseen conditions. HROs are preoccupied with why things fail, resist simplified interpretations, are sensitive to processes, commit to resilience, and have reverence to expertise. Health care organizations that aspire to become highly reliable organizations need trust as their prerequisite. The quintessence of organizational trust includes inclusive and respectful structures and processes as well as individual accountability and cooperation that is cross-pollinated throughout the organization.

Inspire. Have you ever listened—really listened—to the stories that your colleagues share? Are they inspiring stories about the time the nurses and healthcare team worked hard and saved a patient? Or, are work stories more about complaining?

Share stories about the workplace that reinforce your desired work culture and tout the characteristics of you and your best colleagues. Present a picture of a work culture that you know will not undermine both your organization's success and your colleagues'. The tone and the content of your work stories are powerful forces in shaping and strengthening your work climate. The stories you share with colleagues and talk about frequently becomes imprinted on the organizational mind.

time to reflect

Take a moment and reflect on how you may have changed in your role or responsibilities because of the changes made within the organization. How have organizational changes been communicated externally versus internally? What would you suggest to improve internal and/or external organizational communications?

The Drive Home

Let's review the *driving it back home* pointers from this chapter:

- Culture refers to characteristics shared historically by a group of people; therefore, the group is self-determined or defined by outsiders looking in.

- Organizational climate and cultural behaviors can be defined by all of the life experiences, strengths, weaknesses, education, upbringing, and so forth of the employees.

- Cultural behavior is one small aspect of social traditions used in shaping environmental and group values.

- Socialization can occur through history sharing, through case study reviews that highlight expected behaviors, or by integrating into team situations where the long-term members model the organizational values.

- Understanding cultural and climate behaviors include power and control, adaptation or deception, etiquette, formality, time perceptions, hierarchy and gender, communication, cliques, and work ethics.

- Culture is a way people relate to one another.

- We must provide a strong and effective culture as it relates to social interactions, communication, shared interests and responsibilities, collaboration, and friendships (Tsai, 2011).

- Informal leaders play key roles in ensuring that their climate supports sound relationships that empower all (Tsai, 2011).

- We must show respect for the cultural and ethnic backgrounds of all families and staff by not judging others and by being accessible to them.

- In order to improve the culture and climate of an organization, it is vital to first understand how dynamic they are and how your perceptions of the organization affects the acculturation and trust that exists (Tsai, 2011).

- Organizational trust is unequivocally important for health care organizations to become highly reliable.

References

Aristotle. (n.d.). Retrieved from http://www.brainyquote.com/quotes/quotes/a/aristotle145967.html

Barden, A. M., Quinn Griffin, M. T., Donahue, M., & Fitzpatrick, J. J. (2011). Shared governance and empowerment in registered nurses working in a hospital setting. *Nursing Administration Quarterly, 35*(3), 212–218.

Pachuta, J. (2014). "A message about organizational culture." Retrieved from http://www.cultural-analysis.com/

Pfeffer, J., & Veiga, J. F. (1999). Putting people first for organizational success. *Academy of Management Executive, 13*(2), 37–48.

Tsai, Y. (2011). "Relationship Between Organizational Culture, Leadership Behavior and Job Satisfaction," BMC Health Services Research, (11), 98. doi:10.1186/1472-6963-11-98

Watkins, M. (n.d.). What is organizational culture? Retrieved from http://blogs.hbr.org/2013/05/what-is-organizational-culture/

Weick, K. E. & Sutcliffe, K. M. (2001). *Managing the unexpected- assuring high performance in an age of complexity.* San Francisco, CA: Jossey-Bass.

Conclusion

Everyone within an organization needs to be held accountable in articulating effective communications. Patients, nurses, nurse leaders and other leaders, and providers need to consistently practice clear, empathic, two-way communication that is respectful to the beliefs of others. Effective communication is the helm to providing safe, high-quality care.

Effective communication within a healthcare organization procures two benefits. First, it leads to patients being more informed and involved in decision-making. This creates an environment where patients are comfortable in asking questions, disclosing their perceptions, and becoming owners of their healthcare. Second, employees, at all levels in the organization, benefit from effective communication because they are more likely to be proactive in finding solutions to issues, resolve conflict timely and respectfully, and feel they have a worthwhile purpose for their existence in the organization. In other words, employees, regardless of title, feel their role and responsibilities are an essential part of the mission and vision of the organization. Effective communication connects people to people, and that is the antidote to practically any poisonous or draconian situation. Without effective communication, misinterpretations and assumptions are more likely to be made, which leads to poor outcomes for everyone.

Strategies to stimulate effective communication in nurse-patient interactions include service recovery readiness, purposeful patient hourly rounding, bedside shift reporting, conducting post-discharge phone calls, using open-ended questions, implementing scripts to safeguard all key talking points, actively listening, and using teach-back methods to ensure patients have the knowledge, skills, and abilities needed to implement new information. To promote interprofessional communications, strategies include implementing purposeful leader-staff rounding, use open-ended questions, and active listening.

There is one caveat to implementing these strategies: None of the aforementioned strategies is helpful if there isn't authenticity behind the words. For example, scripting should be implemented as a framework so that the scripting doesn't sound or feel so "scripted," or robotic. In other words, scripts do not need to be memorized, per se, but providing brief scripts in the form of acronyms can help staff remember how to frame conversations. Remember, using scripted phrases or acronyms isn't always enough because unless the words match the emotions and the body language of the speaker, the conversation will be ineffective. Hardwiring the aBEST approach will help you to remember to use acronyms when recalling key talking points (i.e., HEARD, SBAR), to be cognizant of body language gestures, to be aware of your emotional intelligence and emotional competence, and to use various scripting techniques within the acronyms (i.e., use 3WITH to recall how to ask an open-ended question).

Implementing effective interprofessional and patient conversations is simply the right thing to do. And doing the right thing has its benefits, such as keeping your job. I am not speaking to punitive measures where someone is fired because they didn't communicate well; I am speaking to fiscal stability of the organization at which you work. With the inception of value-based purchasing (VBP) programs regulated by the Centers for Medicare and Medicaid Services (CMS), a portion of Medicare payment on a hospital's performance is based on quality of care and patient satisfaction measures. CMS also began publishing patient satisfaction scores from the Hospital Consumer Assessment of Healthcare Providers and Systems (HCAHPS) survey on its HospitalCompare website so potential patients can see how satisfied other patients were in the care they received.

You may be thinking, what does this have to do with effective communication? Well, effective communication across an organization is reflected in those HCAHPS scores, which, again, are tied to hospital reimbursements—which are tied to whether your organization remains successful—and this may impact your employment status (e.g., hospital layoffs and cutbacks). Effective communication is the dogma in healthcare. For example, many studies have found compounding evidence of the correlation among patient satisfaction, communication, and HCAHPS scores. Boulding, Glickman, Manary, Schulman, and Staelin (2011) found that higher overall patient satisfaction scores were linked to higher patient satisfaction within the interactions they experienced with hospital staff. This research also associated overall patient satisfaction scores with the lower 30-day readmission rates. Hibbard, Greene, and Overton (2013) found better outcomes and lower costs with patients who were engaged with healthcare staff because patients had more knowledge and skills in making better decisions for their care. According to Press Ganey research of more than 3,000 hospitals, Nurse-Patient Communication scores are infectious to how the HCAHPS ratings would be on Responsiveness of Hospital Staff, Pain Management, Communication about Medication, and Overall Rating on HCAHPS (Press Ganey Associates, 2013). This means that when scores in the nurse-patient communication area rise, so do the scores in these other areas. Likewise, when the scores fall in nurse-patient communication, so do the other scores in the other areas, which has a profound effect on the overall survey score. Consider the following:

> Making investments that improve communications between nurses and patients does more than improve performance on the various accountability and payment programs. It is central to a hospital's ability to provide truly patient-centered care and positions the hospital to successfully meet the goals of CMS' Triple Aim and the National Quality Strategy. (Press Ganey, 2013, para. 10)

In summary, nurses need to be held accountable in embracing effective communication in both verbal and nonverbal ways. We are all responsible for consistently practicing clear, empathic, two-way communication that fosters emotional intelligence and body language gestures in a coalesce manner. We are one of the most instrumental participants in providing our patients with high-quality, safe care, and we interface with practically every hospital department on some level. Nurses, therefore, are uniquely positioned as the gestalt in communicating effectively with patients as well as with colleagues.

References

Boulding, W., Glickman, S. W., Manary, M. P., Schulman, K. A., & Staelin, R. (2011). Relationship between patient satisfaction with inpatient care and hospital readmission within 30 days. *American Journal of Managed Care, 17*(1), 41-48.

Hibbard, J. H., Greene, J., & Overton, V. (2013). Patients with lower activation associated with higher costs; Delivery systems should know their patients' scores. *Health Affairs, 32*(2), 216–222.

Press Ganey Associates. (2013). The rising tide measure: Communication with nurses [White Paper]. Retrieved from http://images.healthcare.pressganey.com/Web/PressGaneyAssociatesInc/Communication_With_Nurses_May2013.pdf

On Social Media

Social media is a method of communication that is changing the way people and organizations communicate and receive information. Social media, also known as *social networking,* engages us from a local level to as far as an international level via Internet sites and software. Social media provides us the ability to share and obtain professional, social, and personal information. Examples of popular social media sites include Facebook, Twitter, blogs, LinkedIn, and Meetup. Approximately 80% of Americans currently use the Internet, and between 70 and 80% of these users seek health information through this medium (PewResearch Internet Project, 2013).

Although we can't decipher body language and emotional intelligence in social networking as readily as we can with in-person conversations, we still seem to portray messages beyond typed words. For example, what message are you sending when you ignore a directed post from a friend on your Facebook wall or Twitter stream? What message is sent when a person does not follow you back or accept your friend request? These questions are the same rhetorical questions others ponder (and I'm sure you have, too). Nonetheless, it can send the wrong message, even if the oversight was an innocent case of forgetfulness.

Consider how reactive and emotional individuals are when their posts go unnoticed. Think about it: If you didn't comment on a posting from a friend who shared they were sick today, how should you be viewed? What if you post that you were sick and no one commented on your post with something as simple as, "Feel better"? Are you quick to judge others for not posting?

Social media can make it easier or harder, depending on the context, to decipher information. Oftentimes, I typically answer email, text, and posts with a smiley face at the end of messages to ensure the receiver feels a tone to the written response. There is no body language in written responses, so the smiley face brings interpreting communication to a whole new level ☺.

Like many things in life, there are pros and cons to social media.

The Pros of Social Media

Social media has brought many benefits to the healthcare arena. More educational content is shared that helps inform patients about health-related issues, and it has provided the ability for people to connect online for personal and professional reasons. Social media is a prevailing tool for nurses to communicate, influence, and educate more rapidly and efficiently. Here are a few other benefits of social media:

- **We're learning a new language.** Terms such as *LOL* (laugh out loud) and *BTW* (by the way) have evolved, to name a couple of the hundreds of terms that are part of texting and social media communication.

- **We're reaching broader audiences.** Before the Internet, most people simply wrote letters to communicate with one other person. Now we reach hundreds or thousands of people in seconds with just a single post.

- **We're sharing more and at faster speeds.** People post personal issues to their Facebook accounts that normally would have never reached the same number of people by making individual phone calls.

- **We're more succinct.** Certain social media sites, such as Twitter, limit the number of characters you can use, so you have to get your point across in a faster way. Blogging is another social media tool where efficacious bloggers know they have only a few seconds to draw a reader in before that reader clicks away to another site.

- **We're learning to multitask.** (Like we haven't already mastered this.) It is becoming more and more difficult to hold a live conversation, meeting, or conference without people checking their smartphones.

But just as there are many advantages to social media, there are also some disadvantages.

The Cons of Social Media

The cons of social media are often found with the inappropriate use of postings. The significance of the consequence will depend, mostly, on the nature of the person's conduct. The laws charting the basis for punitive action by a board of nursing (BON) can vary between jurisdictions. According to the National Council of State Boards of Nursing (2011a), the BON may investigate reports of inappropriate postings on social media on the grounds of any of the following:

- Unprofessional or unethical conduct

- Maladministration of patient records

- Revealing a privileged communication

- Breach of confidentiality

Some inappropriate postings are considered patient abuse, a Health Insurance Portability and Accountability Act (HIPAA) violation, or exploitation. "HIPAA regulations are intended to protect patient privacy and confidentiality by defining individually identifiable information and establishing how this information may be used, by whom and under what circumstances. The definition of individually identifiable information includes any information that relates to the past, present or future physical or mental health of an individual, or provides enough information that leads someone to believe the information could be used to identify an individual" (NCSBN, 2011c, p. 7).

If a nurse is found guilty of inappropriate conduct, the BON may impose fines or loss of his or her registered nurse license. Nurses who improperly use social media are at high risk of violating state and federal laws. These laws were initiated to protect patient privacy and confidentiality. Misuse of social media has significant consequences including civil and criminal retribution. Nurses may also face personal liability, which means they may be individually sued for defamation, invasion of privacy, or harassment.

> A 2010 survey of BONs conducted by NCSBN indicated an overwhelming majority of responding BONs (33 of the 46 respondents) reported receiving complaints of nurses who have violated patient privacy by posting photos or information about patients on social networking sites. The majority (26 of the 33) of BONs reported taking disciplinary actions based on these complaints. Actions taken by the BONs included censure of the nurse, issuing a letter of concern, placing conditions on the nurse's license or suspension of the nurse's license. (NCSBN, 2011a, para. 13)

Due Diligence, Social Media 2.0, and Nurses

It is a nurse's due diligence to be aware of and adhere to legal, regulatory, educational institution, and/or employer guidelines and policies. The following recommendations, although not all-inclusive, provide guidance for appropriately using social media (ANA, 2011; NCSBN, 2011a; NCSBN, 2011b; NCSBN, 2011c; Spector & Kappel, 2012; Stryker McGinnis, 2011):

- Ensure patient privacy and confidentiality—always!

- Do not take photographs or videos of patients or distribute any electronic media of any patient-related information unless it is for professional reasons, used on professional, encrypted media and consent is granted.

- Do not accept patients as social network "friends." A "friend request" does not sanction the nurse to have a personal relationship with a patient.

- Do not discuss work-related issues online, including complaints about other nurses, patients, or organizations.

- Do not criticize or admonish your place of employment or educational institution or name specific professors, colleagues, administrators, etc.

- Be cognizant that everything you post online is public and can be copied and redistributed (regardless of your privacy setting).

- Report inappropriate material and take action if you are the subject of complaints or abuse via social media.

- Separate your personal and professional lives. Create different accounts for professional and personal activities.

- Understand that you send messages beyond words even in the social media world, such as when you reply and don't reply to others' postings.

- Understand some postings can be considered patient abuse, a HIPAA violation, or exploitation.

As social media continues to grow, so will the potential for both benefit and harm. In other words, although nurses should make the most of social media's prosperity, nurses also need to know how to avoid potential pitfalls. Nurses need to be mindful of their ethical and legal obligations to patients and understand the delineation of the professional boundaries that are warranted whenever social media is used.

References

American Nurses Association. (2011). American nurses association social networking principles toolkit. Retrieved from www.nursingworld.org/socialnetworkingtoolkit.aspx

National Council of State Boards of Nursing (NCSBN). (2011a). White paper: A nurse's guide to the use of social media. Retrieved from www.ncsbn.org/Social_Media.pdf

NCSBN. (2011b). ANA and NCSBN unite to provide guidelines on social media and networking for nurses. Retrieved from https://www.ncsbn.org/2927.htm

NCSBN. (2011c). Social media guidelines for nurses. Retrieved from https://www.ncsbn.org/NCSBN_SocialMedia.pdf

PewResearch Internet Project. (2013). Health fact sheet. Retrieved from http://www.pewinternet.org/fact-sheets/health-fact-sheet/

Spector, N., & Kappel, D. (2012). Guidelines for using electronic and social media: The regulatory perspective. *OJIN: The Online Journal of Issues in Nursing, (17)*3. doi: 10.3912/OJIN.Vol17No03Man01

Stryker McGinnis, M. (2011). Using Facebook as your professional social media presence. *Imprint, 58*(4), 36–39.

Sample Rounding Reports

Sample Transformational Rounding Report

The purpose of this report is to provide you with a comprehensive tool for rounding with staff or other direct reports. If you have fewer than 30 direct reports, it is advised you meet monthly. Bimonthly or even quarterly rounding is recommended if you have more than 30 direct reports.

Sample Transformational Rounding Report

Leader name: _____ Date: _____

Direct report name: _____ Department: _____

Sample Impromptu Scripting for AIDET (Role Model) (Studer, 2004)

Acknowledge
"I appreciate the time you are taking out of your busy schedule to meet with me."

Introduce
"As you may know, my role in the organization is to ensure we have a healthy workplace environment." (Introduce your name and role if this is the first meeting.)

Duration
"Our one-on-one will take approximately 15 minutes to 1 hour depending on the acuity of our responses. Every month, I will ask you approximately 9 questions that will help me gain a better understanding of how things are going and will also give you the opportunity to share any concerns or feedback with me."

Explanation
"The purpose of our meetings is to provide shared transparency. We will discuss career planning, rewards, and recognition, as well as how we can improve current systems and processes. Please feel free to be up front with me. Your opinion matters."

Thank you
"Thank you for taking time to talk with me. Your feedback is recognized and appreciated."

Questions to Build Individual Trust and Succession Planning

1. "Tell me what you feel is working well. This can include initiatives on our unit, within the organization, or even at home." (Make personal connection.)

   Notes: _____
   _____
   _____

   a. If positive, notes made are to follow up in future meetings.

   b. If negative, ask what solutions the employee may have to help the situation. Notes are made to follow up in the next meeting. If personal, offer Employee Assistance Program information (if applicable).

2. Tell me about where you would like to see your career in 5 years?
    10 years? At retirement? (This question doesn't have to be asked
    at every meeting, but should be incorporated in question 2
    as a talking point and depending on the answer, questions 2a
    through 2d can be interwoven in the conversation.)

    Notes: _____
    _____
    _____

    a. "Based on your career goal, have you taken any steps (e.g.,
        reading, education, committees, etc.) to achieve this goal?"

        _____
        _____

    b. "Is there anything pertinent you have heard or learned
        of that you would like to share at the next staff meeting?"
        (This question is great to incorporate if the nurse is in
        school or has recently attended a conference, etc.)

        _____
        _____

    c. "Have you implemented any actions to achieve your
        career goal?"

        _____
        _____

    d. "Is there anything I can do now to help you achieve your
        short-term/long-term goals?"

        _____
        _____

Questions to Ensure a Healthy Workplace Environment

3. "Are there any systems or processes that do not meet your expectations?" (Circle.) In other words, have you ever asked yourself why something is so complex when you feel it could have been done so much easier?

    a. No—all systems and processes meet my expectations.

    b. Yes—please provide solutions on how to meet your expectations.

        _____

        _____

4. "Are there any systems or processes that exceed your expectations?" (Circle.) In other words, what have you seen or done in our unit or organization that you said, "Wow! That was great!"

    a. No—all systems and processes meet my expectations.

    b. Yes—please provide your rationale for why this exceeds your expectations.

        _____

        _____

Questions to Ascertain Staff Rewards and Recognition

5. "Do you feel any of your coworkers have gone 'above and beyond' their role?"

    a. Name _____

    b. Situation (Describe the event.) _____

        _____

    c. Action (What specifically did the coworker do?)

        _____

    d. Response (What was the specific outcome?)

        _____

6. "Do you feel any providers (physicians or mid-level providers) have gone 'above and beyond' their role?"

    a. Name _____

    b. Situation _____

    c. Action _____

    d. Response _____

7. "Do you feel any other departments have gone 'above and be-yond' their role?"

    a. Name _____

    b. Situation _____

    c. Action _____

    d. Response _____

8. "Do you feel any staff member(s) in other departments gone 'above and beyond' their role?"

    a. Name _____

    b. Situation _____

    c. Action _____

    d. Response _____

Coaching Questions

9. "We all experience difficult situations at different times. Have you experienced any since our last meeting?"

    a. No issues at this time to be addressed.

    b. Situation _____

    c. Action _____

    d. Response _____

e.   Use the TELL acronym to address tough issues or difficult conversations that you need to address

Tell or talk about the behavior:

_____

Explain why there is an issue: _____

Lead what is expected: _____

Learn the consequence: _____

Thank You.

"Thank you for meeting with me. Is there anything I can help you with right now? I have made time available to help you."

Notes: _____

_____

_____

Action Plan to Sustain Strengths

Specific   _____

Measurable   _____

Attainable   _____

Realistic   _____

Timely   _____

Action Plan to Improve Weaknesses

Specific   _____

Measurable   _____

Attainable   _____

Realistic   _____

Timely   _____

Topics to Discuss at Next One-on-One Meeting

Topic: _____ Level of difficulty_____

> First Floor (Easy to implement)
>
> Second Floor (Moderately difficult to implement)
>
> Third Floor (Hard to implement)

Impact: _____ Follow-up _____

> Immediate Response Necessary (before next 1:1)
>
> Moderate Response (at next 1:1)
>
> Latent Response (within 6 weeks)

Sample Rounding on Internal Departments

The purpose of this report is to provide a comprehensive tool for rounding with managers or directors of internal departments that support our department (i.e., housekeeping, maintenance, human resources, lab, radiology). This tool will help you identify interdepartmental wins and opportunities. Monthly rounding with various departmental managers or directors helps to build rapport in a proactive manner.

Sample Rounding on Internal Departments

Develop the Rounding Plan for Key Internal Customers

(Determine who in the department you will round with and the frequency; i.e., monthly or bimonthly.)

Leader name: _____ Date: _____

Direct report name: _____ Department: _____

Sample Impromptu Scripting for AIDET (Role Model) (Studer, 2004)

> Acknowledge   "I want you to know I appreciate the time you are taking out of your busy schedule to meet with me."

Introduce   "As you may know, my role in the organization is to ensure we have a healthy workplace environment." (Introduce your name and role if this is the first meeting)

Duration   "Our one-to one-meeting will take approximately 15 minutes to 1 hour depending on the acuity of the responses. I will ask you approximately 7 questions that will help identify wins and opportunities between our departments."

Explanation   "The purpose of our meetings is to provide shared transparency. We will discuss rewards and recognition, as well as how we can improve current systems and processes. Please feel free to be up front with me. Your opinion matters."

Thank you   "Thank you for taking time to talk with me. Your feedback is appreciated."

Questions to Ensure a Healthy Workplace Environment

1. "Are there any systems or processes that do not meet your expectations?" (Circle.)

   a. No—all systems and processes meet my expectations.

   b. Yes—please provide solutions on how to meet your expectations.

   Notes: _____

   _____

2. "Are there any systems or processes that exceed your expectations?"

   a. No—all systems and processes meet my expectations.

   b. Yes—please provide your rationale for why this exceeds your expectations.

   Notes: _____

   _____

Questions to Ascertain Staff Rewards and Recognition

3. "Have any of my staff gone 'above and beyond' in their role?"

   a. Name _____

   b. Situation _____

   c. Action _____

   d. Response _____

4. "Have any providers in my department gone 'above and beyond' their role?"

   a. Name _____

   b. Situation _____

   c. Action _____

   d. Response _____

5. "Have you seen any other department go 'above and ' beyond' their role?"

   a. Name _____

   b. Situation _____

   c. Action _____

   d. Response _____

6. "Have any staff member(s) in other departments gone 'above and beyond' their role?"

   a. Name _____

   b. Situation _____

   c. Action _____

   d. Response _____

Coaching Questions

7.　"We all experience difficult situations at different times. Do you have any at this time that I can address?"

　　a.　No issues at this time to be addressed.

　　b.　Situation _____

　　c.　Action _____

　　d.　Response _____

　　e.　Use the TELL acronym to address tough issues that you need to address with the department manager or director about their staff, department, etc. (Studer, 2004)

　　　　Tell or talk about the behavior:
　　　　_____

　　　　Explain why there is an issue: _____

　　　　Lead what is expected: _____

　　　　Learn the consequence: _____

Thank You.

"Thank you for meeting with me. Is there anything I can help you with right now? I have made time available to help you."

Notes: _____

_____

_____

Action Plan to Sustain Strengths

Specific _____

Measurable _____

Attainable _____

Realistic _____

Timely   _____

Action Plan to Improve Weaknesses

Specific   _____

Measurable   _____

Attainable   _____

Realistic   _____

Timely   _____

Topics to Discuss at Next 1:1

Topic: _____ Level of difficulty_____

        First Floor (Easy to implement)

        Second Floor (Moderately difficult to implement)

        Third Floor (Hard to implement)

Impact: _____ Follow-up _____

        Immediate Response Necessary (before next 1:1)

        Moderate Response (at next 1:1)

        Latent Response (within 6 weeks)

References

Studer, Q. (2004). *Hardwiring excellence: Purpose, worthwhile work, making a difference.* Gulf Breeze, FL: Fire Starter.

Develop Your Own AIDET Worksheet

A (Acknowledge) (Studer, 2004)

Examples

- Make patients/customers feel you are happy to see them (smile).

- Make patients and families feel comfortable (assess your body language).

- Ask permission to enter a room (show manners).

I (Introduce)

Examples

- How can you introduce yourself?

  Name/title:

  Years of experience or years of employment:

  Special training:

- How can you introduce others?

  Name/title:

  Years of experience or years of employment:

  Special training:

D (Duration)

Examples

- How long the process, test, procedure, etc. will take

- When results will be back or when medications are due

- When the provider or nurse gets here

- How long the referral process takes

- How long before a physical assessment can be completed

E (Explanation)

Examples

- Explain the procedure or process and how the patient will obtain the results.

- Explain what will be taking place in terms the patient and family can understand.

- Explain who is involved in providing the patient's care.

- Explain whether the process will cause pain or discomfort.

- Explain what will happen after the procedure is completed, or if any post procedure instructions are necessary. Offer to answer any questions, respond to concerns, or resolve any complaints.

- Equipment: Explain the noise (if any).

- Explain why you move patients (to prevent pressure ulcers).

- Explain why patients have food restrictions.

- Explain why you are closing the curtain or door (to ensure privacy).

T (Thank You)

Examples

- Let patients/customers know you appreciate them/enjoyed working with them.

- Thank the family for entrusting you with the care of their loved one.

- Ask if the patient or family has any final questions or concerns.

Index

T–U–V

W–X–Y–Z

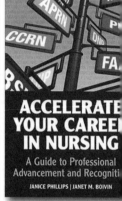
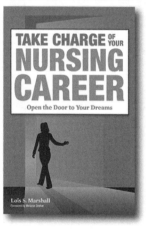
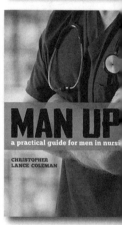